Stand and Be Counted

MAKING MUSIC, MAKING HISTORY

*The Dramatic Story of
the Artists and Events That
Changed America*

David Crosby
and David Bender

HarperSanFrancisco
A Division of HarperCollins*Publishers*

Grateful acknowledgment is given to the following individuals and organizations for the photographs that appear in this book. First photo insert: Joan Baez: Everett Collection; Phil Ochs: courtesy of Graham Nash; Bob Dylan: Danny Lyon/Magnum; Harry Belafonte, et al., Charles Moore/Black Star; Washington Mall: Fred Ward/Black Star; Civil Rights marchers: Dan Budnik/Woodfin Camp; Mahalia Jackson: Bob Henriques/Magnum Photos; John Sinclair poster: © 1999 by Poster Planet; Bob Dylan: courtesy of Graham Nash; Joan Baez, et al.: Corbis/Bettmann; James Taylor, et al.: Everett Collection; Bruce Sprinsteen [top] and Pete Townshend, et al. [bottom]: Everett Collection; Bonnie Raitt [top] and Stevie Wonder, et al. [bottom]: Lisa Law (2). Second photo insert: USA for Africa group: Everett Collection; Mick Jagger and Tina Turner: Everett Collection (2); Crosby, Stills and Nash: Jacques Chenet/Woodfin Camp; Bono: Lehr/SIPA; Live Aid group: J.Langevin/SYGMA; Bob Geldof, et al.: Bob Taggart/Reuters/Archive; Willie Nelson: Morgan Renard/SYGMA; John Mellencamp: Tom Reusche/RETNA; Farm Aid shirt: Debra Trebitz/Liaison; Bridge School benefit group: John O'Hara/San Francisco Chronicle; Bruce Springsteen and Neil Young: Corbis/Neal Preston; Peter Gabriel, et al.: Henry Diltz; Amnesty International concert: Martin Thomas/Liaison; Sean Lennon: Chester Simpson/SIPA; Adam Yauch: Patrick McMullan/Liaison; David Crosby and Sean Lennon: Otto Kitsinger. *Toronto Star* article reprinted with permission of the *Toronto Star Syndicate.*

HarperCollins books may be purchased for educational, business, or sales promotional use. For information please write: Special Markets Department, HarperCollins Publishers, Inc., 10 East 53rd Street, New York, NY 10022.

HarperCollins Web site: http://www.harpercollins.com
HarperCollins®, ➍®, and HarperSanFrancisco™ are trademarks of
HarperCollins Publishers, Inc.

FIRST EDITION
Designed by Joseph Rutt

Library of Congress Cataloging-in-Publication Data
Crosby, David.
Stand and be counted: making music, making history: the dramatic story of the artists and events that changed America / David Crosby and David Bender. Includes index.
ISBN 0-06-251574-8 (cloth)
ISBN 0-06-251575-6 (pbk.)
1. Popular music—History and criticism. 2. Social movements—United States—History—20th century. 3. Musicians—Political activity. I. Bender, David.
ML3477 .C76 2000
781.5'92'0973 21—dc21   99-045179
00 01 02 03 04 ❖/RRD 10 9 8 7 6 5 4 3 2 1

To find out how you can Stand and Be Counted, go to our website at
www.standandbecounted.com

WE ARE TREMENDOUSLY GRATEFUL to everyone whose belief in *Stand and Be Counted*—and its authors—has sustained us on the long road to completion. Foremost among these are the more than fifty artists and activists who graciously agreed to be interviewed for this book and the companion documentary for television. This is their story. We are honored to have the privilege of telling it.

Literally hundreds of others helped in so many ways, large and small, that to mention all of them would require a second volume devoted solely to that purpose.

However, there are a few people without whose kindness, support and friendship this book would not have been possible. When it counted, you stood with us . . . thank you. tom Campbell, John Cossette, Dan Davis, Mike Delich, B.G. Dilworth, Roy Furman, Todd Gelfand, The Hart family, Mac Holbert, Micheal Hong, Michael Jensen, Larry Johnson, Tom Leonardis, Gary McGroarty, Debbie Meister, Craig Moody, Graham Nash, Greg Odom, Charlotte Patton, David Permut, Hart Perry, Dan Polin, Elliott Roberts, Jeff Rosen, Kathy Schenker, Tim Sexton, Rachel Sheff, The Sofen family, Conrad Stanley, Ron Stone, Caroline Thompson, Tim Tobin, Norm Waitt, and Alicia Winfield.

Special thanks to our friend and agent, Al Lowman, whose passion has blessed *Stand and Be Counted* from its inception, and to everyone at HarperSanFrancisco, past and present, for their enormous efforts in guiding this book safely into port: Laura Beers, Margery Buchanan, Clayton Carlson, Mark Chimsky, Diane Gedymin, Ken Fund, Stephen Hanselman, David Hennessy, Meg Lenihan, Terri Leonard, Liz Perle, and Susan Raythons.

CONTENTS

PREFACE   vii

ACKNOWLEDGMENTS   xii

CHAPTER 1 **The Civil Rights Movement**
           "We Shall Overcome"   1

CHAPTER 2 **The Antiwar Movement**
           "And It's One, Two, Three . . .
           What Are We Fighting For?"   25

CHAPTER 3 **The Birth of the Benefit**
           "With a Little Help from My Friends"   48

CHAPTER 4 **Political Activism**
           "Power to the People"   97

CHAPTER 5 **The Antinuclear Crusade**
           "We Almost Lost Detroit"   118

CHAPTER 6 **Global Activism**
           "We Are the World"   141

CHAPTER 7 **Lending a Hand**
           "That's What Friends Are For"   178

CHAPTER 8 **Human Rights**
           "Keep On Rockin' in the Free World"   212

CONCLUSION   234

INDEX   235

PREFACE

Before you turn the page and begin reading, let me say two things right up front. The first is that *Stand and Be Counted* is not about me. Although these stories of activism are told from my perspective, that fact is not meant to imply anything more than the truth—which is that I've been privileged to witness some amazing, even pivotal, musical events. I played at some of them myself; the rest I've done my best to describe based on the accounts of artists and others who were there.

The second thing I need to say is that this book does not pretend to be a history text. It would be impossible to recount fully the whole scope of artist activism in this country, let alone the world. Whether it's Jackson Browne's annual benefit concerts for the Verde Valley School to fund scholarships for Native American students, or Mimi Farina's Bread & Roses events that support her organization's work with shut-ins, the disabled, and prisoners, or Paul Simon's Children's Health Fund that provides mobile health services to impoverished kids, or Billy Joel's work on behalf of the Long Island fishermen, or Pete Seeger's sloop, the *Clearwater*, which sails the Hudson River as a floating classroom on environmental protection, the list of artists and their commitments is as long as you want to make it. Because of the constraints of space, I must apologize in advance for having to leave out many important efforts. Rather than attempting to list every event and every concert, I've included stories that are meant to give a sense of the wide range of activism in which artists are involved. Sometimes well-chosen stories can provide more insight into a subject than a perfectly detailed chronology. And speaking of chronology, the narrative of *Stand and Be Counted* will occasionally jump around in time because I felt it was more important to follow the people and the story than the calendar.

The purpose of *Stand and Be Counted* is to convey an ethic. It is my hope that the stories of these great events—the marches, the rallies, the benefit concerts—will offer a glimpse of where that ethic of activism came from, how it's grown over the years, what it's accomplished, and how it's been transmitted down the line. And I want to show how it affects the lives of those who try to live by it.

A final note: while *Stand and Be Counted* has been written in my voice, that voice is actually a composite of two people, myself and my friend and coauthor, David Bender. From volunteering as a twelve-year-old to work on Robert Kennedy's presidential campaign, to marching in the moratoriums against the war, to producing many benefit events himself, David has been a dedicated activist for over thirty years. As much as mine, his insights and experiences inform the narrative of this book.

. . . .

All of my life I've been thrilled by people being courageous. That's always been a thing that really excited me. When I became conscious of the fact that people were standing up against the system, standing up against injustice, that there were people who would fight for what they believed in, it aroused in me a great need to know.

I wanted to know why they did it. I understood the emotional desire to be courageous. I felt that. But I wanted to know how they got to there. Did someone teach them? Is it a thing that just occurs? Is it spontaneous combustion? What puts a person in the path of oncoming evil, standing there courageously saying, "No, I will not submit." What does that? I asked a lot of my friends, which is what I do. I asked my friend David Bender and he and I started to think about writing a book.

Taking a stand shows a depth of character and a generosity of spirit. It shows the quality in human beings that makes me proud to be one. And that's really what we're after here.

We'll follow people. We'll witness tales of tragedy and tales of courage. And we'll try to give you a feeling for how this all came about. When you get done reading this you'll know that Pete Seeger is a national treasure, and that every single musician in this entire country was affected by him, all of us, every single one.

You'll also realize that if we had any smarts at all, we would have run Harry Belafonte for president years ago, just because he's brilliant and lucid and he's a walking history book. And he has more dignity than any human being I've ever met. Hopefully you'll also get a glimpse into something else. There isn't an instruction booklet for any of this. There isn't a manual of how to become an activist. We learn it by watching people we admire stand up for what they believe in.

Musicians rightfully are entertainers. Our main job is to make you feel good, make you feel something, make you *feel*. That's really what we do. But there's another, older part of our job that comes from the tradition of the troubadours. We're sort of the town criers, the "twelve o'clock and all is well" kind of guys. Or maybe it's 11:30 and things aren't so damn good.

We've been carrying those messages for hundreds of years. It's a very tricky balance. First of all you have to be very careful. You have to have your information right. And you can't preach. It just won't work. But you *can* focus people's attention on issues and ideas; and we've learned that you can use music to gather people together for a cause.

Now here's a major magic: I forget who it was, one of the musicians who was active in the civil rights movement, maybe Peter Yarrow, maybe Joan Baez. They sat together in the basement of a church with a few hundred black people whose lives were being threatened simply for wanting to go out and register to vote, a constitutional right in this country, a right that they were being systematically denied.

And they had good reason to be afraid for their lives. They'd been attacked with dogs, with guns, shot, killed, dragged behind tractors, buried alive, hung from trees, hosed down with fire hoses and they were frightened. Courageous and frightened. And in their fear, they would sing. They would sing great spirituals that would make them feel better. There's a magic there.

Somewhere along the line some of us realized—and it was probably Pete Seeger first—that it could go further than people singing in a church, and it could go further than religious music, that it could be people gathering together in a larger cause, as he and Woody Guthrie did in the union movement. They had songs like *Joe Hill*. That was sort of the inception, when artists realized they had the power to bring people to a cause with the power of music.

This was long before any of us realized that we could also use these events to raise money and then apply that money as a force for good. And it was before anybody realized that we could use music to achieve media focus, that trickiest of all demons to dance with. It was still a fairly pure thing. They knew that they could simply gather together and sing a song and that there would be unity of purpose and a unity of spirit, and that they would feel stronger, and this was a good thing.

You'll see in these stories that activism, although it started very small, began with one person standing up and saying, "No, I won't be quiet." Then it got very big. It got to hundreds of thousands of citizens marching on Washington to demand their civil rights. It got to an entire generation saying "We don't believe in this war." It got to millions of people saying "We don't think it's right that there are people starving in a world where there is plenty of spare food." The events got big; they got very powerful, very emotional. And I think they scared the power structure too. I hope they did.

To me the real heroes of this thing are not the artists, even the people that I think are national treasures, like Pete Seeger. The true heroes are the people that you've never heard of. They're people who got up one morning and said, "I cannot sit idly by. I'm going to take my time, my effort, and I'm gonna work for change." People who volunteer their time. People who in the regular course of their lives say, "I'm going to count, I'm going to make a difference. I have a choice, I'm making that choice and I *will* stick up for what I believe in." You see *us*. You don't see them. We're the face, they're the muscle, the heart, the blood. Those people to me are the heroes. They are the reason it works, and I love them for it.

The main reason we felt compelled to write *Stand and Be Counted* is that no one else has told this story. Here's one of the major social forces in the latter half of this century, one of the reasons that positive things happened and important changes came about, one of the birthplaces of great ideas and some of the most inspirational behavior we've seen out of human beings in this last half century, and we didn't see any history. There wasn't any chronicle. It's a phenomenon. Nobody mandated, "There shall be benefits." These events grew up out of the cracks. Whenever they were really needed, somehow they managed to happen. But how? The truth is that no two events are alike and there are fascinating stories behind all of them. How did they happen? We couldn't resist trying to follow the thread of each one, just to see where they'd lead.

I think you'll see how human beings can be elevated by their commitment, by their courage, by their valor, by the hero in them. They can rise to levels of behavior that are inspirational. I don't think any of these artists saw themselves as great heroes. I'm sure they felt like they were ordinary people just sticking up for what they believed in. But they did it with such courage and such poetry in their souls that they made a whole generation of us want to stand next to them.

Stand and Be Counted

There was a piece of a song I heard the other day
Some words that I heard this singer say
Something in me loved the way it sounded
When he sang how he wanted to stand and be counted

Sometimes I talk to myself in the early dawn
Before all the fragments of the dreams are gone
Pieces of things you don't know why your mind held on to
Or else sometimes you know more than you want to

I wonder who that kid was standing brave and trim
And I hear myself breathe and I know that I was him
Defender of the poor and those who cannot speak
Thought I would be the one standing by the dam
     trying to stop the leak

Fiercely concerned with matters of the heart
Knowing the millennium was just about to start
And thinking some how we'd make it all different

I want to stand alone in front of the world and that
     oncoming tank
Like that Chinese boy we all have to thank
He showed us in a picture I have mounted
Exactly what it means to stand and be counted

Stand and be counted
Stand on the truth
Stand on your honor
Stand and be
Counted

Music by James Raymond
Words by David Crosby

CHAPTER 1

The Civil Rights Movement:

"We Shall Overcome"

Wherever I go in the world and I look for forces that

are struggling against injustice, I always seem to

find somebody with a guitar and a voice and they're

always singing to something that inspires the

community, no matter how ravaged that

community may be.

Harry Belafonte

Even in the fifties, the Pat Boone era that I grew up in, anybody who listened to folk music was usually turned on at the same time to black folk music—it was just part of it—because the folk music scene was as antiracist as it could be. Blacks were still kept separate from "mainstream" music, but the fact was a black performer like Nat

King Cole could still be a star because he was so good. He was just too good to ignore. Same with Satchmo—Louis Armstrong. You couldn't say, Oh, he can't really play the trumpet as well as Harry James. Because he could. He was doing it and he was better. That's the wonderful thing about music. It levels the playing field. There's a quote that just floors me from, of all people, Bill Haley. He actually said, "Rock and Roll *does* help combat discrimination. We perform to mixed groups all over the country, and we've watched the kids sit side by side, enjoy the music while being entertained by white and Negro performers sharing the same stage." Now Bill Haley was certainly no activist (the last show he ever played was to an all-white audience in South Africa), but what he said was completely true. Guys like the Big Bopper would have a black act on right after them, and kids would find out that they didn't really have any natural antipathy for one another. They learned an essential truth that we now take for granted, which is that racism has to be taught—that if you took a hundred kids of every stripe and color in the country and let them raise themselves on an island, they'd grow up not even knowing they're any different.

I have a vivid and powerful memory of the first time I ever talked about racism, when I was only about ten years old. First, you have to understand that we always had music in our house. We had the first ten-inch LP player when it was just a box with a spindle sticking out of it. My mother would bring home records by people like Harry Belafonte, Josh White, or the Weavers . . . who knows why she liked them, but she did, and we all listened to them together as a family.

There was this one song where the lyrics didn't make any sense to me. It was on a Josh White record (he was the legendary black singer who people still call the Father of American Folk Music) and the title was "Strange Fruit."

Southern trees bear strange fruit,
Blood on the leaves and blood at the root,
Black bodies swinging in the southern breeze,
Strange fruit hanging from the poplar trees.

I listened to those lyrics and asked my mother, "Mom, what's he talking about?" She got this look on her face and started crying. I didn't understand why. She turned to my father and said, "I have to tell him, Floyd," but he told her that I was too young to understand. She insisted. She sat me down, her eyes still red from crying, and she said, "The strange fruit are people being hung in trees by other people who don't like them." And I was shocked. I remember how it felt. My little brain just went "tilt," and a couple of things got fried in there, because it just didn't compute. I didn't know that anybody would do that—*could* do that—to another human being. I couldn't even picture it. I couldn't wrap my mind around that image.

In the course of writing this book, I had the privilege of meeting Harry Belafonte for the first time. Realize this is a man who's been a hero to me my entire life; it's no exaggeration to say that he was one of the main reasons I became a musician. When I was standing there waiting for him to notice me in the lobby of his apartment building in New York, I felt just like a fifteen-year-old kid.

I'm in awe of very few people, but Harry Belafonte is one of them. Shortly after that I ran into his daughter, Shari, at an event and I told her how deeply I felt about him. I said, "You know, I'm pretty good with words, but I don't know how to tell him how much he means to me." "Don't feel bad, David," she told me sympathetically. "None of the rest of us do either. Trust me, he affects all of us that way."

During our interview I told Belafonte the story of how the words to "Strange Fruit" hit me hard as a kid, and in that rich, hoarse whisper of a voice that makes you lean in close to hear him, he said, "You know, I was born in Harlem and I was born into poverty and born into a whole lot of racism, and from my earliest of years all I can ever remember was constantly doing combat with the residuals of that poverty and residuals of racism and constantly looking for where I could go and fearful of where I was told I could not go."

"It was different then, it was a different world," says my friend Whoopi Goldberg. "And when you think about it and you think of the three little girls who were burned up in the church, and you start to remember the visuals of those pictures on television . . . you know, Walter Cronkite sort of pointing you in the direction of watching these dogs bite people and hosing people. That's when it finally changed. Once we had the medium of television directly in our houses, our consciousness changed and our innocence disappeared. Because it's one thing to commit genocide in the dark, you know? It's another thing when somebody turns the lights on it, and then you can't say you didn't know anymore."

She's absolutely right. That's exactly how it worked for me. After I saw how Rosa Parks refused to go to the back of that bus, I started paying attention. We all did. We saw things that were ugly and brutal and we were never the same.

The bus boycott in 1955 is the first place where I have any conscious memory of activism. I was a teenager, still living at home in Santa Barbara, California, when I saw something on TV about how this minister named Martin Luther King had organized people into walking, instead of riding the buses, in Montgomery, Alabama. I remember standing in our kitchen and asking my mother, "Why are they doing that? What's wrong?" And she explained it all to me. She described to me what life was still like in the South for "Negroes" at that time.

Pete Seeger told me that he "was reading the *New York Times* in December 1955, and I read about a bus boycott being started in the city of Montgomery, Alabama, and it's led by a young preacher named Martin Luther King and they have new songs they made up, so—I've done this all my life—I wrote a letter saying 'Could you send me copies of some of the songs you're singing?' I got a nice letter in reply from E. D. Nixon, secretary of the Montgomery Improvement Association. 'Dear Mr. Seeger, thank you for your contribution. Here's a copy of our song sheet.' And there it was . . . "

We are moving on to victory,
We are moving on to victory,
We are moving on to victory.
We know the time ain't long.
We know love is the watch word,

Love is the watch word,
Love is the watch word,
For peace and dignity.

Whoopi, who would later portray a Rosa Parks-like character on the screen, says that when she was growing up in New York in the sixties, all this seemed very far away: "It never occurred to me that I couldn't go to the bathroom where I wanted to and drink from a fountain. My mother had to say, 'You know, not everybody has these privileges.' I had no clue. I had no idea that women in Montgomery, Alabama, shut down the bus system just by walking."

Harry Belafonte was born into poverty in Harlem in 1927, the son of Jamaican immigrants. He served two years in the navy in World War II and came out at the age of nineteen "looking around for where to go and what to do with my life." I asked him if there was a particular event that inspired him to become an activist at such an early age, and he said, "It was a time in America when everyone was very heavy with a sense of the future. The AF of L and the CIO had spent the years before the Second World War trying to organize and get the labor movement going in this country. We had just come out of a huge experience in the struggle against fascism, the fight with Hitler, and we'd come back to America filled with expectation. And those expectations were not being met when we found no honor in the nation for those of us who were of color and who had made our commitment to the nation's agenda. I had to begin to hunt for ways to change how business was being done. This led me to an association with the labor movement, which seemed to have the best handle on all of it. And it was in that period where I met Woody Guthrie and Pete Seeger and Josh White and all the men and women who made up the voice of American democracy."

By the time of the Alabama bus boycott, Harry Belafonte was already a huge star, the first solo artist—of any color—to sell more than a million copies of a single record. So it made perfect sense that Dr. King would quickly try to enlist him in his emerging crusade: "When he called and asked that we meet, he really didn't have that much convincing to do about the righteousness of the cause. What I found quite unusual, however, was his methodology, because my beliefs were firmly grounded in the fact that only acts of aggression, only acts of violence, would be the instruments with which to meet the enemy. The idea that we meet the enemy with love and with a moral force that was so powerful that it could force the gun to be silent was to me a hugely curious thought."

Other artists were also deeply affected by King, some while they were still very young. Joan Baez was raised as a Quaker, which meant that she got the whole ethic of nonviolence at an early age. We both grew up in California at around the same time, but while I was still running around getting high and getting laid, she was reading Gandhi. She told me that "when I was fifteen, I heard Dr. King speak at a high school gathering at Asilomar, California, where they brought kids in from all over the country. And they always had a major speaker. That year it was King. He was twenty-five. I was fifteen. He talked about the beginnings of the bus boycott in the South and I was just in tears. That didn't change my life; it solidified what I had already felt from learning about Gandhi. Hearing about the boycotts—hearing this man speak and knowing he was a part of it— brought the actuality of [nonviolence] into my life for the first time."

Carly Simon's experience of meeting Dr. King was very different from Joan's, but it also had a lasting impact on her life. Because her family (her father was the founder of Simon and Schuster) was extremely close to Jackie Robinson, the man who broke the color barrier in baseball, they all were active in the civil rights effort right from the beginning. While Carly was still a young girl, the Simons held civil rights benefits at their Stamford, Connecticut, home: "When I say we had Martin Luther King on our lawn, that's true. My mother gave a benefit for him, and who was the entertainment? It was all of the Simon sisters. The three of us, Joey, Lucy, and myself. Ever since I was very small we were always singing for the benefit of some cause. Sometimes it had to do with Hungarian pianists and sometimes it was for children's rights, but basically it was for the cause of integration. I never actually attended a civil rights march in Washington, the way a lot of my other friends did. But I attended civil rights marches on our front lawn, many of them."

My partner and friend Stephen Stills grew up in the South, first in Texas, then in Florida. He says, "I was drawn to the civil rights movement and when it really started getting organized, I was just coming of age. I was fourteen and I jumped in, I was right in it. And then Judy Collins and Joan Baez inspired me with their work with Martin."

Joan Baez. God, was she beautiful. She still is. And her voice: she has this incredibly pure bell of a voice that gives you shivers the first time you hear it. I had a crush on her for a long time. She was very easy to have a crush on.

I met Joan for the first time at a party in Santa Barbara; I think it was in about 1959 or 1960. I know she was already this big star and I wasn't, so it had to be around that time. The Byrds didn't happen until a lot later, so she had no idea who I was. But I went right up and talked to her. My friends couldn't believe I had the balls, but I just did it. And she was amazing. Over the years we've become good friends and she's raised my consciousness on so many issues, particularly about human rights abuses both in this country and all around the world.

I never got a call from Dr. King and for good reason: I wasn't big enough yet. In the early sixties, I was just a kid with a guitar case over his shoulder showing up at hootenannies and trying to get by month to month. Now if Baez had pulled up to the curb in front of me and said, "Here, get in," believe me I would have been in that car next to her in a hot second.

The first time I actually saw segregation for myself was in 1962. I'd already been living in Greenwich Village for a while, playing in small clubs and generally doing nothing worth writing home about (unless it was for money). People started telling me that I could get work down in Florida, in Coconut Grove. They said there were two or three coffeehouses where I could make good money if I could get myself down there. So my friend Kevin Ryan and I put all our stuff in cardboard boxes, got on a bus, and headed for Florida. It was just after the Interstate Commerce Commission had ordered the word *Colored* removed from all public facilities. When we got south of the Mason-Dixon line, we'd stop at these dingy, fly-specked bus stations and on the bathroom wall there'd be a brand-new painted square, and underneath it you could clearly see that it said COLORED. They hadn't used good paint on purpose.

The night we got down there I went into a market and saw that there really *were* separate drinking fountains for white people and colored people. I couldn't believe it. I asked my friend, "Is that real?" And he said, "Yeah, it's real, shut the fuck up before someone hears you." Of course, that's all it took for me to drink out of the colored one.

In the early sixties there were still only a few white musicians who had the guts to go south and try to do what they could to help by singing at rallies or marching for voter registration. Pete Seeger was there first, then Baez and Peter, Paul & Mary and, for a few years, Bob Dylan. That was about it. I noticed what they did and I remembered it. And it definitely shaped my own involvement later on.

Joan says she was stunned at what she saw when she went down there for the first time in 1961: "It was in the contract that there were no blacks allowed and I didn't know that. So the next year, when I came back, I said that it had to be an integrated audience. And it was very humorous, because the blacks didn't know me. I mean, after I'd made such a big deal out of having an integrated audience, it would have been very embarrassing if no blacks actually wanted to see me. So we had to get people from the NAACP and the Southern Christian Leadership Conference to come and sit in the house. The third year—it was 1963, but before the March on Washington—I went down and sang in black colleges. And that's how I learned what those colleges were. They were nothing. They had no money. They had a bathroom with curtains in this one little place. And white people came onto the campus. They'd never been there before. So in that way we did our own integration. It was very, very dangerous—way more dangerous than I knew. And when I would leave, all sorts of bad things could happen and sometimes they actually did happen. But it was still an enormous thing to have white people and black people sitting together in places like Mississippi and Alabama. It was probably my biggest contribution to the civil rights movement."

I remember I was playing at the Bitter End in the Village when Peter, Paul & Mary first started happening. "If I Had a Hammer" was all over the radio. I didn't know much about them at first, even though I would see them everywhere.

You have to remember that Peter, Paul & Mary were people who had actual recording contracts, which meant that they were one step above the general riffraff. That didn't mean they didn't have to hit the street the same as everybody else; that's the great common denominator in New York: everybody from the mayor on down has to hit the street. But even though I really didn't get to know them until later, I admired them tremendously for being so willing to put their success on the line for what they believed in.

Peter Yarrow, who has remained a committed activist throughout his life, explains how they got involved in the civil rights cause: "Number one, you believe in something that is an ethic. You believe that it's wrong to have a two-tiered system of justice in America, one for whites and one for blacks. You also believe that your country is good. You believe in the goodness of your elected officials. There *was* danger. But you know something? We believed. We believed that there was something else that was so powerful that we almost felt a shield. It was partly courage. It was partly determination. It was partly the audacity of our youth. But mostly I would say it was the extraordinary steamroller effect of the commitment itself. We could see the effect it was having on the country as a whole."

Mary Travers knows that it also affected their careers: "We had a southern tour scheduled that was canceled after we joined the march with Dr. King from Selma to Montgomery. And we used to do a lot of Junior Chamber of Commerce concerts and they sent us a letter saying that we'd never work for the Jaycees again, *anywhere* in the country. Our record sales took a nosedive in the South and never really picked up again. We were never, never as big there as we were every place else."

Then there was Dylan. When I first encountered him, he was singing at Gerdie's Folk City in New York and I didn't like him. I didn't like the way he sang because I was always a very melodic singer and he wasn't. What he was was a tale teller. He had learned from Woody Guthrie, where I had learned from Odetta. (Years later, after we became friends, he told me that even before Guthrie, his first influence was also Odetta.) If truth be told, I was actually jealous of him. Because the words were *so* good. He has, at certain moments in his writing career, crystallized stuff so well that it will last for a thousand years of human history. If we don't destroy ourselves by then, in the year 3000 someone somewhere will be singing "He Not Busy Being Born, Is Busy Dying." That's significant. That's really making a contribution to your art.

I get along with him pretty well now because I've managed to keep him from knowing that I'm impressed (at least, until he reads this). The minute you let him know you're completely impressed with him, he starts to mess with you. He'll stir your brain like a spoon.

With Bob it was always the songs. "Blowin' in the Wind," "The Times They Are a Changin'," "Chimes of Freedom"—I mean, *c'mon*. We knew how good his songs were, even if they hadn't been huge hits when he did them. It was no coincidence that the Byrds' breakthrough was "Tambourine Man." That's really when I got to know Bob and we became friends.

At first, back in those early days with Baez, Bob was willing to go to places like Greenwood, Mississippi, in 1963 and play at a rally after Medgar Evers, the civil rights leader, had been shot down in his own driveway in front of his wife and children. Dylan's lyrics (which would later become much more cryptic) were powerful and direct in the song he wrote about Evers's murder. It was called "Only a Pawn in Their Game" and he performed it for the first time at that rally:

A bullet from the back of a bush took Medgar Evers' blood.
A finger fired the trigger to his name.

. . . .
His epitaph plain:
Only a pawn in their game.

Dylan's life as an activist—at least as someone willing to talk about it—was brief. He hated being described as a "protest singer," and by 1964, the year after the Greenwood rally, Dylan had just stopped showing up at political events entirely.

The nail in the coffin for Bob came at a New York banquet in December of '63 where an old-line civil rights group gave him an award for his activism. Here's what he told the *New Yorker*'s Nat Hentoff about that experience: "As soon as I got there, I felt uptight. First of all, the people with me couldn't get in. They looked even funkier than I did, I guess. They weren't dressed right, or something. Inside the ballroom, I really got uptight. I began to drink. I looked down from the platform and saw a bunch of people who had nothing to do with my kind of politics. I looked down and I got scared. They were supposed to be on my side, but I didn't feel any connection with them. Here were these people who'd been all involved with the left in the thirties, and now they were supporting civil rights drives. That's groovy, but they also had minks and jewels, and it was like they were giving the money out of guilt."

When Bob feels cornered, he gets extremely uncomfortable and he's likely to do something outrageous—which is exactly what happened that night. "I got up to leave and they followed me and caught me," he told Hentoff. "They told me I had to accept the award. When I got up to make my speech, I couldn't say anything by that time but what was passing through my mind. They'd been talking about Kennedy being killed, and Bill Moore and Medgar Evers and the Buddhist monks in Vietnam being killed. I had to say something about Lee Oswald. I told them I'd read a lot of his feelings in the papers and I knew he was uptight. Said I'd been uptight too, so I'd got a lot of his feelings. I saw a lot of myself in Oswald, I said, and I saw in him a lot of the times we're all living in. And, you know, they started booing. They looked at me like I was an animal. They actually thought I was saying it was a good thing Kennedy had been killed. That's how far out they are. I was talking about *Oswald.*

"And then I started talking about some friends of mine in Harlem—some of them junkies, all of them poor. And I said they need freedom as much as anybody else, and what's anybody doing for *them?* The chairman was kicking my leg under the table."

One of the best things I've ever heard Bob say about himself was in somebody else's words. He was quoting Henry Miller, who explains Dylan's whole life in this one sentence: "The role of an artist is to inoculate the world with disillusionment."

I'm not sure who said it first, but I always *say* it was me: "If you can remember the sixties, you weren't there." It's a clever line and like every good joke, there's some truth to it. But an easy line just doesn't cut it when you're talking about 1963. There are two events from that year that I still remember as clearly as if they'd happened only last week.

Everybody who was over the age of five in '63 knows that one of the things I'm talking about happened on a November day in Dallas when nothing—no music, no words, *nothing*—could have inoculated us against the pain of our disillusionment.

I was on the road, touring with my brother Ethan (we were playing together for a while) and a bunch of other young musicians—one of them was Cass Elliot—and we were in Baltimore. Just as I was walking out the front door of the hotel, someone shouted, "The president's been shot!" I ran off to find my brother, who was in this little restaurant a couple of doors down the street. Somebody had a radio turned up and everybody in the place was just stone still, listening. I remember I was crying. I couldn't believe they could *do* that—shoot the president, the symbol of the country.

It seems incredible to me now, but the owner of the club we were booked into still wanted us to play that night. We just refused. We said, "In honor of the passing of our president, we're *not* playing tonight. Keep your money." Cass was totally devastated. She couldn't stop sobbing. She was smarter and more politically aware than the rest of us, and she understood better than we did what it meant to lose that man.

I think he scared them. I think the establishment was terrified that he was going to cave in and give the country away to the *niggers*. These were bigots and bad guys, but they weren't stupid. They saw what King was doing and that Kennedy was basically on his side. And both of them were dead within five years. Accident? Crazy lone gunmen? Yeah, *right*. Why were they dead? Because they were dangerous to the power structure of the country, King in particular. King patterned himself after Gandhi, a single man who nonviolently ended British rule in India. King and Kennedy were dangerous men because they believed what *we* believed, that you could stand on principle and effect change for the better. They weren't saints. We know that now and it doesn't matter. What matters is that they were right.

A few years later, Roger McGuinn wrote a song for the Byrds about President Kennedy called "He Was a Friend of Mine." I loved when we played it onstage because it always gave me an opening to tell the crowd exactly what I thought about Kennedy's murder. I'd start yelling, "The Warren Report is a lie. John Kennedy was shot by conspirators. The Warren Report is a lie, don't be taken in by it, it's all bullshit." Roger used to get really pissed off whenever I'd do it, and we got into it a bunch of times. Of course, this only guaranteed that I would do it even more.

The other unforgettable event of 1963 happened only a few months before the Kennedy assassination, on August 28. Led by Dr. King, it was the great March on Washington for civil rights, the largest single gathering of people that Washington, D.C., had ever seen.

A quarter of a million people (at least fifty thousand of them white) marched first to the Washington Monument and then on to the Lincoln Memorial, where Dr. King delivered what everyone agrees was the greatest speech of his life: "I Have a Dream." What most people *don't* know is that he hadn't planned on using those words in it. King's original speech didn't contain the phrase *I have a dream*. It was an *artist*—one of America's greatest singers—who inspired him to say it.

But I'm getting ahead of the story.

It's important to understand that from the earliest days of the civil rights movement, when Pete Seeger first went down to Birmingham to support the bus boycott, Martin Luther King had a keen appreciation of the power of artists to command attention—and he used it any way he could.

Jesse Jackson told me that King was constantly working to recruit major Hollywood celebrities to participate in the movement. Then—and without any preparation on his part—Jackson told me something so eloquent and powerful that I have to repeat it here word for word, exactly as he said it: "The Bible teaches us that since the days of David, the athlete and musician who slew Goliath, since then people who have extraordinary gifts or the gift of charisma also have obligations to save nations, not just to glorify themselves. There is a tradition of artists in our country, whether it is Paul Robeson or Harry Belafonte or whether it is Stevie Wonder, there's a generation of artists who have stood for racial reconciliation rather than racial polarization. And they've used their platforms, their stages, to break down ancient barriers. They operated outside the political box and they made politics better. They bring oxygen to our politics. We are all indebted to artists who have the capacity to write and the courage to project their convictions. When there is no music there is no power. When there is no power there is no progress."

Dr. King made a major push to get both actors and musicians to come to Washington for the march, enlisting Harry Belafonte to organize them. He remembers that "my colleagues not only listened but they were ready for it. Some didn't even need the instruction. All they needed was somebody to say, 'Where do we go?' They just needed someone to point and since I'm always pointing anyway, Dr. King made me the pointer."

Their efforts paid off. A special plane from Hollywood came in carrying some of the biggest white stars of the day: Marlon Brando, Burt Lancaster, James Garner, and even the once-liberal Charlton Heston (who still says he's proud he was there). Black performers like Lena Horne, Sammy Davis Jr., Ossie Davis and Ruby Dee, and

Dick Gregory also lent their enormous stature to the march. Even the legendary singer from the twenties Josephine Baker, flew in from Paris wearing her Free French uniform,

The Student Nonviolent Coordinating Committee or "Snick," as it was popularly called, played a major role in bringing young black people into the civil rights movement, as well as to the march. One of them was a young woman from Georgia with a terrific voice named Bernice Reagon who, along with her husband, Cordell, organized a group called the SNCC Freedom Singers. (Years later, she formed the wonderful all-woman group Sweet Honey in the Rock, which is how I met her.) She once told a reporter that "My transformation was the civil rights movement. There's a taste that I got from singing what I felt. I got the taste of fighting against oppression; at the same time it was like affirming myself."

At the time of the march, the Freedom Singers had just returned from a nationwide tour of northern cities, playing at college campuses and even YWCA gatherings. With songs like "We Shall Not Be Moved" and "Ain't Gonna Let Nobody Turn Me Around," they'd taken their message of the black struggle for justice in the South directly to young white people, many of whom were hearing about it for the first time. Joan Baez says of them, "By that time the SNCC Freedom Singers had really emerged and they really represented the South in a black way and wrote songs for it."

Joan was the first person to perform at the march, stepping up to a single microphone in front of the Washington Monument at 10:00 A.M., while thousands of people were still disembarking from the buses and trains that had been steadily arriving since the night before. Her choice of songs—the Odetta classic "Oh Freedom"— couldn't have been a better one. She remembers being blown away by the sheer mass of humanity in front of her: "By early in the morning we all knew this was going to be an enormous moment in history. My knees were shaking. I'd never seen that many people before in my life. Dr. King had moved me for so long and I got to *be* there. And by the time—with my somewhat quavering voice—that I started singing 'We Shall Overcome,' I was very nearly overwhelmed."

On a day that would be a constant visual reminder of the long tradition of black and white folk artists playing each other's music, it was only fitting that Odetta herself came out right after Joan and sang the classic gospel tune "I'm on My Way." One of my boyhood heroes, Josh White, then joined her, and he in turn invited Baez and Peter, Paul & Mary to sing with both of them. Peter, Paul & Mary then crowded around one microphone to sing "If I Had a Hammer" and their popular cover of Dylan's "Blowin' in the Wind," only to have Bob amble up behind them and sing the last few choruses. Dylan followed with a solo performance of "Only a Pawn in Their Game," and then Joan returned to sing with him on "When the Ship Comes In," after which both of them sang backup while the great black folksinger Len Chandler did a stunning version of the old Negro spiritual "Keep Your Eyes on the Prize."

Looking back at it now, Yarrow believes that "the March on Washington was a pivotal and critical day because it was so filled with an energy—a positive energy of decency and goodness and belief in ourselves and one another—that you could just scoop it up."

As the hot August sun bore down on the crowd, the program shifted in the afternoon from the Washington Monument to the Lincoln Memorial. This was also the moment when all three television networks decided to go live in order to show this historic event to the whole country.

Two people were asked to perform one song each before Dr. King's closing remarks: the brilliant opera singer Marian Anderson, who did "He's Got the Whole World in His Hands," and Mahalia Jackson, the glorious gospel legend, who came out wearing a grand, flower-covered hat and sang this soaring a cappella version of the old slave spiritual "I Been 'Buked and I Been Scorned" (a song Dylan and I both knew because it was on Odetta's first album, a record each of us had learned by heart as soon as it was released).

The tired crowd was roused by the sheer power of her voice, and Jackson was called back for an encore. This time she got them clapping and singing along with her on the classic gospel number "How

I Got Over." Years later, a friend told me that Jackson's performance so moved Dr. King that, on the spot, he said, "Haley, when I die I want you to sing at my funeral," and she agreed. Less than five years later, she was obliged to keep her promise.

One more speaker followed Mahalia's performance, then Dr. King came to the podium to deliver the last but most anticipated speech of the day. Every speaker had been held to an absolute maximum of seven minutes and even King was to be no exception. His prepared text ran just under seven minutes, and that was the speech he intended to give. Until he got to the microphone. Shouts of *Martin* filled the air, and an ocean of black and white faces stretched out in front of him as far as he could see. As he neared the end of his written speech, King began to improvise. His words took on the cadence he used from the pulpit, urging this huge congregation not to "wallow in the valley of despair." Then, as he searched for some way to bring it all to a close, he heard Mahalia Jackson's powerful voice booming out from behind him. Because she'd performed at so many rallies with King, she'd already heard him speak many times before. And she knew exactly what he hadn't yet told the crowd. As if she *was* in church, she shouted out: "Tell them about the *dream,* Martin!" And he did.

> I have a dream that one day on the red hills of Georgia, the sons of former slaves and the sons of former slave owners will be able to sit down together at the table of brotherhood. . . .
>
> I have a dream my four little children will one day live in a nation where they will not be judged by the color of their skin, but by the content of their character. I have a dream today!
>
> When we allow freedom to ring, when we let it ring from every village and every hamlet, from every state and every city, we will be able to speed up that day when all of God's children—black men and white men, Jews and Gentiles, Protestants and Catholics—will be able to join in the words of the old Negro spiritual, "Free at last, free at last, thank God Almighty, we are free at last."

The speech lasted seventeen minutes, but no one noticed. Finally, the massive crowd began to disperse and, as they did, they all sang together one last time for the world to hear, "We Shall Overcome."

We couldn't know it then, but the March on Washington was like a great flare that briefly lit up the night sky, then slowly faded, forcing things back into the shadows. Less than three months later Kennedy was dead and, for a long time, the incredibly hopeful spirit of that day seemed to be dead and gone as well.

Ironically, it took another bullet—and another death—to bring that spirit back to life. In February of 1965, Jimmie Lee Jackson, a young black civil rights activist from Selma, Alabama, tried to stop a state trooper from attacking his mother and his grandfather, who were lying on the ground, bleeding. For his efforts, he was beaten and shot in the stomach, dying a few hours later. His death sparked outrage across the South and around America. At his funeral, a protest march from Selma to the state capital of Montgomery was planned for Sunday, March 7. Six hundred marchers began the march that afternoon, but when they attempted to cross the Edmund Pettus Bridge just outside Selma, they were ambushed by state troopers who beat them with bullwhips and billy clubs and sprayed them with tear gas. More than one hundred were injured, some of them seriously. John Lewis, the head of SNCC (and now a member of Congress from Georgia), was taken to the hospital with a fractured skull. The *New York Times* described the scene this way: "The first 10 or 20 Negroes were swept to the ground, screaming, arms and legs flying, and packs and bags went skittering across the grassy divider strip and onto the pavement on both sides."

Peter Yarrow was in New York and remembers reading that newspaper story: "As the marchers proceeded, they were beset by dogs, by hoses. And yet, the spirit of the marchers emanated from the Gandhian tradition. It was a nonviolent march, and therefore they were not going to let their adversaries set the terrain. They were not going to respond with violence. They really believed in the truth of what King was saying—that it was the only way to be successful."

Two weeks after "Bloody Sunday" the marchers began again, this time led by Dr. King, and now more than three thousand strong. In a principled act that surprised many of us, LBJ sent down federal troops to protect them on the three-day, fifty-mile march.

Numerous artists and celebrities flew in to lend their stature. Belafonte, of course, was already there. Yarrow recalls that "We got a call from Harry Belafonte. I know Peter, Paul & Mary were on tour and he said, 'You've got to get down here.' We loved Harry. The dignity and authority with which his voice was heard, by us and others, was unquestioned. So, of course we agreed."

Musicians who joined them along the way included Sammy Davis Jr., Pete Seeger, Tony Bennett, Leonard Bernstein, Joan Baez, Nina Simone, Odetta, John Stewart, Leon Bibb, Oscar Brown, Billy Eckstine, and the Chad Mitchell Trio. Other performers like Anthony Perkins, Shelley Winters, Gary Merrill, Mike Nichols and Elaine May, and Alan King also flew in to show their support.

There's no question that all those people put their lives on the line by going down there. Protesting segregation in the South could get you badly beaten or even killed, and it didn't matter whether you were famous or not. Mary Travers remembers the FBI agents who were there to "protect" them telling her that the most they could guarantee would be a thorough investigation *after* something happened to her.

Oddly enough, when you ask the people who were there about the danger, they usually shrug and try to change the subject. They never give themselves much credit for doing what they did.

"Very early on I understood that it was life threatening," says Belafonte now, "that there certainly had been a willingness of the enemy to use violence in response to us and to take life, almost with a sense of omnipotence. When the injustice was so legislated and so organized, we had no place to turn, there were no voices to appeal to. We had no choice."

Joan Baez was twenty-four when she went down to join the Selma marchers, and she didn't fully understand what she was getting herself into: "People who had lived in relatively secure situations as

I had didn't know how dangerous it was. Oftentimes I found myself in situations where I should have been a lot more nervous. After the Selma to Montgomery march ended, everyone disappeared very quickly. It was getting dark and it hadn't occurred to me to be nervous or frightened. I was in an open car with James Baldwin and some other people, I think a couple of blacks and some whites. All of a sudden James just became terrified and rightfully so. Somebody *was* shot on the highway to the airport that night, but I didn't understand it. But they knew, because they lived in that fear."

On March 24, the night before they arrived in Montgomery, the marchers—who now numbered more than ten thousand—gathered together in a muddy church playground for a concert designed to cheer them on for the last leg of their journey. A makeshift stage had been built from pine coffins stacked on top of one another, with a sheet of plywood laid over them. Belafonte, Sammy Davis Jr., and Peter, Paul & Mary were among those who performed that night. Many described it as having the exuberant feeling of an old-style revival meeting.

Peter Yarrow remembers the need for ingenuity: "It was raining and there was a field filled with mud and there were thousands of people who'd been waiting there for hours and hours, because the sound system had, for some reason, gone on to New Orleans. At that point, we rightfully had a kind of paranoia that there were people trying to stop all this from happening. You never knew why something went wrong and you always presumed that there was a sinister reason. I remember running around backstage. There were army trucks and jeeps, it looked like a war zone. So we took these little horns from the jeeps and we hooked them up—a whole bunch of them—and that's how we made a sound system."

Dick Gregory, the black writer and comedian who had become a major civil rights activist, was one of the speakers that night. He says: "The last night of the march, before we went into Montgomery, was like getting ready to do battle. If it were a movie, it would be like the Christians moving up for the final battle. Many of the entertainers were scared; it was the first time many of them had ever been in the South and if they had been killed, it wouldn't have surprised them. The army was there and the world press was there. And people came. They came up on that hill—just like ants—bringing their chairs before the show. You had the sense something big was going to happen and we all knew it was the next day. Tomorrow it could be death but right now it was love, and black folks that had been scared all these nights were not scared that night. If there could be a prepa- ration for heaven, it would have to take a backseat to that night. It was joy and happiness. Most of these black folks had never heard of Peter, Paul & Mary. But I knew when they got up on that stage, the songs they did were so close to the black spirituals . . . that's why they were always a big hit. Their music had the rhythm that we had in the Baptist church. They were one of the few folk groups that black folks could understand."

It remains one of the most vivid images of Yarrow's life: "These were the poorest people I'd ever seen. I went out to be with them while the other people were making their presentations from the stage, and I'd never seen such poverty. I'd never seen people in such threads. By the time we got onstage there was only one microphone, and all three of us gathered around [it]. Instead of singing "Blowing in the Wind" the way we did on the record, we sang it slowly, in the rhythm of that weariness, of that long march. And I remember feel- ing that our lives made sense."

"The music made them strong," says Dick Gregory, "but more than that, it was the fact that the entertainers were who they were. They were from out of town; they were big-time celebrities; they were people you could never touch under normal circumstances. All at once, they're here. It gave them strength and it gave them power. It said that what we're doing is right."

Sammy Davis Jr., who had closed his entire Broadway show, *Golden Boy,* for one night in order to fly down there, called that moment "the biggest thrill of my life."

The next day a crowd of more than thirty thousand people gath- ered in front of the Alabama State Capitol. Governor George Wallace refused to meet with them, but he was watching with binoculars from his office window. Harry Belafonte, Joan Baez, Peter, Paul & Mary, Leon Bibb, Oscar Brown, Len Franklin, and the SNCC Freedom Singers all performed.

When he spoke, Dr. King made direct reference to one of the songs they'd just heard, "Ain't Gonna Let Nobody Turn Me Around": "We are not about to turn around. We are on the move now. Yes, we are on the move and no wave of racism can stop us."

It was through the civil rights movement that we first saw injustice so glaringly. Remember, this was at a time in our country when people were gathering together knowing they could be killed at any time just by standing up for their basic rights as citizens. The right to vote. The right to assemble. They were called communists or anarchists to justify it, but men, women, and even children were still being shot down like rabid dogs. In America. But they didn't quit fighting, because they knew it was their only chance.

And no matter how bad it would get, the music always sustained them. Belafonte, Seeger, Baez, Yarrow—all of them told me that at one point each saw a scene almost identical to this: a church basement full of black faces, terrified, sweating, afraid they could die at any moment, even afraid that their babies could be murdered. Then somebody in the corner would start singing "Ain't Gonna Let Nobody Turn Me Around" or some other spiritual. It was like a lightning bolt to the soul. People went from being so terrified that they were literally huddled in a corner, tears streaming down their faces—to where they could put that child on their shoulders, walk up those stairs, walk right out the front door of that church, and confront a line of policemen with police dogs and water cannons. They could look them right in the eye and still be singing "Ain't gonna let nobody turn me 'round, / God is standing at my shoulder, / God is watching what we do here."

Everyone who witnessed something like that told me the same thing—it was the most powerful musical moment of their lives. Not playing to 200,000 people at some great concert, not playing at some glitzy affair at the Hollywood Bowl, not being given a Grammy or an Oscar or any other award. All of them said that watching other human beings draw that kind of courage from a song—courage that allowed them to stand up to impossible odds, risk their lives and even the lives of their children—was one of the greatest experiences they've ever had.

Nobody comes close to describing that experience more eloquently than Harry Belafonte: "Many of us in the civil rights movement learned very early on that what you have to come to grips with is the fear of death. And if you're trying to answer that bigger question about death, forget it. Nobody knows. But I think the *fear* of it was very central to our ability to get on with the work that we had to do. Even Dr. King had to go through a process, through a metamorphosis, to find his own relationship to the issue of death and his fear of it. We discussed it a great deal. And one of the mechanisms that works best when you're facing a life-threatening moment is a song. It is a remarkable encounter. When we were incarcerated in the white prisons of the South run by racist sheriffs who had no qualm about snuffing out a black life—and things seemed to be the most desperate—someone would break into song. Not only did it take our spirits to places we never dreamed of, but what it did to the enemy was also a remarkable thing to behold. I watched men of power become impotent, I watched men of ruthlessness become tamed, I watched them become hypnotized."

I was hypnotized just listening to Belafonte, who finished by telling me a story I'll never forget: "We did a concert with Dr. King at the University of Maryland in their big field house and thousands of people showed up. Dr. King was delivering his speech and there was a redneck sheriff who was part of the state police force there. And when I walked into the holding area for the artists, I saw him watching us with a scathing look on his face, I saw how unyielding he was. And then at the end of the event, after Dr. King's speech and Mahalia Jackson's magnificent singing, I went back to the holding pen and there was that same sheriff. And he stood, and tears came into his eyes and he started to make a remark and couldn't. He just turned and walked away. The next morning, as we were leaving to go on to our next stop, the attendant at the desk gave me an envelope.

And in this envelope, which felt very heavy, there was a note and with the note were six bullets. That same trooper—I still have the letter—wrote this: 'I give you the bullets from my weapon because I know they will never be used. I have found a force far greater than any I have ever imagined. What you all did with song and what Dr. King did with words showed me that the gun is not the way and I will resign from such a role and find something to do with my life that will make a difference.' And it proved the wisdom of what Dr. King had always said, 'Judge not your enemy even though he may do deeds of evil, for somewhere in him there may be something redemptive. It is up to you to find that redemptive place and bring him to your cause.'"

Amen.

C H A P T E R 2

The Antiwar Movement:

"And It's One, Two, Three . . .
What Are We Fighting For?"

When you talk about people making a leap from

music to activism, you first have to believe that

people can change, that the times can change, and

that you can have a part of that. That's why I

became a folksinger, because I believed that. And

once you make that connection, it's a natural

evolution to say, 'I will go and march, even though

my life is in jeopardy.'

Peter Yarrow

In early 1965, while the march from Selma to Montgomery was being organized in Alabama, I was across the country in a California recording studio with the Byrds, the group I'd formed only a few months before with Roger McGuinn, Chris Hillman, and Gene Clark. We'd recorded Dylan's "Tambourine Man" as our first single and it was an immediate hit, unbelievably big. I remember all of us driving down Sunset Boulevard in the '56 Ford station wagon we'd bought from Odetta for six hundred dollars when we heard it on the radio for the first time and they played it not once, but *twice*. We were so freaked out, we had to pull over and stop the car. It was like a huge tidal wave had washed over us and just knocked us flat. We couldn't even begin to deal with it.

I mean less than two months later we were out on tour with the Rolling Stones. Everything felt like it was happening at the speed of light and in slow motion at the same time.

And we started getting this incredible amount of publicity. All of a sudden I wasn't just some kid with a guitar; I was in a hit group and people were paying attention to what I had to say. We all tried hard to work it out between us so that we could use that media spotlight to have some significance. The problem was that Roger and I could never agree on how we should do it or even what there *was* to do.

It's not because I didn't have strong opinions—remember, I'm the guy who once wrote the lyric "Anything you want to know, just ask me. / I'm the world's most opinionated man." It's just that the opinions I had on sex and drugs and politics made a lot of people very uncomfortable, especially my band mates.

At that time I really believed that LSD was the answer to all of society's problems. Something you could use to clean out all the cobwebs and get free from the kind of rigid thinking that kept people uptight and angry, the kind of thinking that led to racism and war and all those other things we were rejecting from the fifties. A sort of spiritual enema. Advocating it became my political statement. I'd do things like getting up at a gig and yelling out, "McCartney takes acid, why don't you?" Not very subtle, but to the point.

The music was changing just as rapidly as we were. The Beatles had arrived the year before, spearheading a "British invasion" of American pop music, and nothing was ever the same again.

The folk musicians of the early sixties—Pete Seeger, Joan Baez, Peter, Paul & Mary—were giving way to a new breed of rock 'n' rollers who had taken their music and plugged it in. In addition to "Tambourine Man," the Byrds did Dylan's "Chimes of Freedom" and "All I Really Want to Do," and we had our second big hit when we covered Seeger's "Turn, Turn, Turn." Although Pete loved our version of it (Roger still has the note he sent us), he took it very hard when Dylan, the man he'd championed as the next generation's Woody Guthrie, decided that he, too, would "go electric." The famous story is that when Dylan first picked up an electric guitar at the Newport Folk Festival in '65, Pete tried to find an ax to cut the cables, then wept as his former folk protégé donned a black leather jacket and rocked the house. After Bob's set, Peter Yarrow had to calm down the stunned and angry crowd that felt personally betrayed by what they'd just heard.

In addition to electric music, psychedelic drugs were a significant barrier separating us from the older generation of folk musicians. Because the Pete Seegers and Harry Belafontes didn't drop acid or smoke pot, we didn't feel connected to them. Although we still appreciated them musically, they seemed more like our parents than our peers. We were stoners and we were high and we had an attitude and a secret language. We had our own secret world.

As I look back at it now, it's something I really regret. If I'd been smart enough to have been studying at Pete Seeger's elbow back then, I would have been a much more effective activist later on when, for a time, Crosby, Stills, Nash & Young were the biggest group in America.

At that point, in 1965, the Beatles were the biggest group on the *planet.* They'd been a pop group; that's all they were conceived as. Then they turned out to be far more talented at it than anybody ever expected. They had a raunchy, wonderful, happy, joyous, rockin'-out kind of approach to it that was better than anything we'd ever even imagined possible.

But even then the Beatles were starting to break out of the pop music mold. They were way too smart for it. There was that infamous moment when John said that the Beatles were "bigger than Jesus Christ." The American press crucified him for it, but they still couldn't shut him up. I think I felt a particular connection with John. He would almost always be sarcastic, or at least kind of dry, which I loved. And he approached things obliquely. He wasn't the kind of person who would just speak his mind about a subject, but if you talked to him for a while, he'd let you know exactly how he felt.

I was at the press conference in Los Angeles when the Beatles were asked directly about the Vietnam War and John replied, "We think of it every day, we don't like it, we don't agree with it, we think it's wrong, but there's not much we can do about it. All we can say is we don't like it." Then someone asked them, "What's your opinion of Americans who go to Canada to avoid the draft?" John's answer was a classic truth-said-in-jest Lennonism: "We're not allowed opinions." It was McCartney who actually answered the question: "Anyone who feels that fighting is wrong has the right not to go in the army." Jackson Browne remembers being deeply impressed as a teenager that "John Lennon opposed the war in Vietnam and he used his stature to do it."

After a couple of years of U.S. involvement in Vietnam, it started to smell very wrong. We began asking ourselves, Why are we there? When I interviewed him for this book, my friend Phil Lesh of the Grateful Dead could have been speaking for any of us when he said, "I thought it was a civil war between two parts of the same country and I didn't believe we had any business being there. I thought that we should pull out and let them fight it out. I certainly didn't believe in the famous domino theory, which held that if one country goes communist, then their neighbor country will go communist, and pretty soon we're going to have communists all over the world. I mean in the hindsight of history it all seems so ludicrous now. After all, communism failed miserably."

And the casualty numbers the military was feeding us in the daily press briefings from Saigon (we called them the five o'clock funnies)—*two Americans wounded, ten thousand North Vietnamese killed*—just didn't add up. Then, slowly, reports of the actual number of American casualties began filtering out from the front lines. Some very dedicated journalists started to report what they were really seeing, not what the government was *telling* them to see. It was a fucking meat-grinder and it was only getting worse. From the day Kennedy was killed to the middle of '65, Johnson had increased the number of our troops there *sevenfold*—from 25,000 to 175,000.

Jimmy Buffett told me how he found out what was really going on over there: "My information about the war was something that came from a really unique source. I was going to school at a college in Mississippi at the time. Not a hotbed of activism by any stretch of the imagination. I worked in a bar that was frequented by the 82nd Airborne, and I was playing guitar because they'd fired the piano player. And from those soldiers I heard stories that were absolutely astounding to me, because they contradicted everything that I had been taught about what we did when we went to war. That experience fueled my first amount of activism because it was obvious to me, and to a lot of other people, that we were not being told the truth. That infuriated me, and that was why I first got active in the Vietnam War movement, playing at antiwar rallies."

Peter Yarrow sums it up with his usual eloquence: "That was the beginning of the end of our innocence. We were being lied to. What, before, was the presumption of a decent America and a good America, now had become the presumption of lies."

Characteristically, Joan Baez was out front very early in opposing the war, way ahead of the rest of us: "About that time we were really heading into the Vietnam War—the 'nonwar' war. I was just deeply offended by it. It was getting very personal for me. And I knew that if I made a statement, it would probably be heard." Joan's statement was as powerful as it was courageous. She made the decision not to pay the percentage of her income tax that supported the war effort. "It was one of those protests that was made because it was something I had to do and I did the research of how much of our budget was being spent on the military. And it was something like 60 percent. So I said, 'I'm not going to pay that part of my income tax.' I remember the man that was working with me on taxes was just mortified and stunned and afraid I'd go to jail."

She did go to jail, but not for tax evasion. Twice in '65, Joan was arrested for protesting the war in front of the Alameda County (California) Induction Center in Oakland. "There were demonstrations planned in which we knew we would be arrested. We went down to the induction center at five o'clock in the morning, sat in the doorway, and asked these young men on the way in, 'What are you doing here at five o'clock in the morning? Have you really thought about it? Is this really what you want to do with your life?' And if they questioned it at all, I said, 'There's draft counseling over there.'"

Just as she'd done in Alabama and Mississippi, Joan ignored any risk to her personal safety: "Some of them wanted to trample us—but most of them were scared stiff. They were very young and they were frightened and they were doing it because they'd been told to do it. And then we were arrested. I spent fifteen days in the Santa Rita Rehabilitation Center but I didn't get rehabilitated," she says, laughing, "so I went out and did the demonstration again. And I was arrested a second time and this time I did a three-month sentence, with forty-five days suspended. It's true what's been said about jail. If you go in as a criminal, you learn more about criminology. If you go in as a pacifist, you come out a stronger pacifist."

Helping to keep up the spirits of the protesters at those induction center protests was a young navy veteran turned musician who called himself Country Joe McDonald. Although he hadn't gone to Vietnam, McDonald strongly believed the war was morally wrong. His parents were communists and Joe was a so-called Red diaper baby. After he got out of the navy, Joe moved to Berkeley and began putting out an independent leftist magazine called *Rag Baby*. In 1965, after the free speech movement had already dominated the political scene in Berkeley for almost a year, Joe had the idea of putting out a "talking edition" of *Rag Baby*. This took the form of a record that included two songs written by Joe. One, about Lyndon Johnson, was called "Superbird"; the other was a jug band tune that would last a lot longer than Joe's magazine. He called it the "I Feel Like I'm Fixin' to Die Rag."

Now come on all of you big strong men
Uncle Sam needs your help again
Got himself in a terrible jam
Way down yonder in Vietnam
Put down your books and pick up a gun
We're gonna have a whole lot of fun
And it's one, two, three
What are we fightin' for?
Don't ask me
I don't give a damn
Next stop is Vietnam
And it's five, six, seven
Open up the Pearly Gates
Well, there ain't no time
To wonder why
Whoopee! We're all gonna die.

It became an immediate anthem for the emerging antiwar move-ment. No less an expert in anthem writing than Pete Seeger says, "In my opinion, the best song about the war was written by Country Joe McDonald. And it would have been number one by 1970 if our country had been as free as it would like to be. It was on the lips of every young person in the country."

(I was standing on the side of the stage when Joe led the crowd at Woodstock in the famous F.U.C.K. cheer that always preceded the "Rag." I've got to say that half a million people yelling *fuck!* at the top of their lungs is one hell of a powerful political statement.)

McDonald, who now works actively with Vietnam-era veterans, believes his song was "the beginning of a brand-new attitude, the generation's attitude. Because the attitude militarily speaking before this was do-or-die. It was set down in poetry by Tennyson in 'The Charge of the Light Brigade,' when soldiers were expected to just follow orders and die if they had to—and never question anything. This was a brand-new point of view that we're still liv-ing with."

By 1966, the attitude that Country Joe was expressing in song had spread from the barricades in Berkeley to the streets of Los Angeles. Ironically, the issue wasn't politics, it was music. New music clubs like Gazzari's and the Whiskey a Go Go had sprung up along the Sunset Strip in Hollywood and were attracting thousands of kids from all over southern California who wanted to hear new bands like the Buffalo Springfield, the Jefferson Airplane, the Doors, and us. The Los Angeles police and sheriff's departments were not happy about the scene and were looking for any excuse to hassle the kids. It all reached a boiling point one night in December. Angered by the abrupt closure of a popular club (a coffeehouse with the appropriate name of Pandora's Box), hundreds of kids started marching up Sunset Boulevard in protest, only to be met by baton-wielding cops in a scene that was eerily reminiscent of the confrontation on the Edmund Pettus Bridge a year earlier. I don't mean to suggest that the issues were of equal importance; shutting down a coffeehouse is not the same as denying an entire race its constitutional rights. What *was* the same was the outrage that comes when authorities who are supposed to be protecting us from harm are the ones inflicting it. I remember that night very well. I was there with my friend, the actor Brandon De Wilde, and we saw it all go down. The cops and sheriffs came at the kids from both directions on Sunset, cutting off any escape. Someone got pushed through a plate-glass window and then all hell broke loose. The cops waded into the crowd, beating, macing, and handcuffing people, then throwing them into police buses. A couple of hundred kids were arrested and dozens were injured.

At his house later that night, Stephen Stills sat down with a guitar on his lap and tried to process the brutality we'd both witnessed. The result was "For What It's Worth," a song so haunting and powerful that you only need to hear it once and it will stay with you forever:

There's somethin' happening here,
What it is ain't exactly clear.

There's a man with a gun over there,
Tellin' me I got to beware.
I think it's time we stop,
Hey, what's that sound,
Everybody look what's going down.
There's battle lines bein' drawn
Nobody's right if everybody's wrong
Young people speakin' their minds
Gettin' so much resistance from behind
I think it's time we stop,
Hey, what's that sound,
Everybody look what's going down.
What a field day for the heat
A thousand people in the street
Singin' songs, and carryin' signs
Mostly say "Hooray for our side"
I think it's time we
Stop! Children, what's that sound?
Everybody look what's goin' down
Paranoia strikes deep
Into your life it will creep
It starts when you're always afraid
Step out of line, the man come and take you away
I think it's time we stop,
Hey, what's that sound,
Everybody look what's going down.

"What had been rolling around in my mind was that I wanted to write something that had to do with the guys in the field in Vietnam," says Stephen now, "and how they had very little to do with the policy that put them in harm's way in the first place. And then I ran into this ridiculous situation on Sunset Boulevard and the two things just came together and I wrote the song in about fifteen minutes. All at once, blam. As to the historical importance of it, I didn't intend for it to be an anthem or anything like that. It was not browbeating. The whole tone of it was very general and more in keeping with some of the most effective pieces of music that have created an atmosphere for people . . . for a change of mind. But the intention was never to preach."

The Byrds' manager, Jim Dickson, organized a political group called Community Action for Artistic Facts and Freedom (CAFF) to support the kids and help pay their legal expenses. A few months after the Sunset Strip riot, he put on one of the very first benefit concerts in rock 'n' roll. He brought together an amazing combination of acts, most of whom had never done a benefit before—and never would again: the Byrds, the Buffalo Springfield, and the Doors.

Somehow (and don't ask me how), Peter, Paul & Mary were also on the bill that night. Although I'd like to tell you that all of us sat down together in a circle and listened while they told us stories about the great tradition of artist activism—about Woody Guthrie and Pete Seeger and the labor movement—the truth is we didn't. The only torch passed that night was a joint.

Ray Manzarek of the Doors has a very clear recollection of the CAFF concert: "Everybody had something to say about the brutality of the police on the Sunset Strip, things like, 'The whole point of this concert is for peace and love and to allow us to do what we want to do without harming anyone else. The police have no right to crack down on us for just peacefully assembling.' It was like a revival meeting. Anytime somebody would say anything about the police— the word *pig* was used a lot—the audience went *Yeah!* And we played a classic Doors set: 'Light My Fire,' 'Break On Through,' 'When the Music's Over,' 'The End,' 'Back Door Man'—it was a great set. The audience was right there and we were there and everybody was stoned, so we just played the hell out of it." Manzarek agrees that there was a lack of "chemistry" between the folk musicians and the rock 'n' rollers: "All those older activists, they were not potheads. Then along came the psychedelic warriors of the Byrds and the Springfield and the Doors. Although we were all on the same side of the political equation, there was still a giant generation gap and I can't say for sure, but I don't think that Peter, Paul & Mary much cared for the kind of music we played."

There was a larger point about activism that Manzarek wanted to make too: "That may have been the only benefit we ever played, but I always felt that just the *existence* of the Doors was anathema to the establishment. It was something about Jim Morrison—son of the admiral, college graduate—who, had he not gone into rock 'n' roll, could easily have gone into the diplomatic corps. This man could have gone all the way to become president of the United States. Instead, he chose to become a shaman. The existence of the Doors was such a profound political act that every gig we played was a political statement of us-against-them."

As we'll see many times in this book, benefit concerts often have unintended and sometimes life-changing consequences for the people who do them. For me, the CAFF concert led directly to an experience that got me kicked out of the Byrds.

The man whom Jim Dickson asked to produce the CAFF concert, Alan Pariser, used the success of that show to begin planning an even larger one—not a benefit, but a festival of rock 'n' roll. His plan was to use the CAFF model on a larger scale and bring together some of the biggest new bands around: the Mamas & the Papas, the Jefferson Airplane, Big Brother & the Holding Company (who had this ballsy, bluesy, fucking-incredible singer from Texas, a girl named Janis), and a guy who played the guitar better than anyone I've ever seen before or since—Jimi Hendrix. The event was eventually called the Monterey International Pop Festival, and both the Byrds and the Buffalo Springfield were invited to play it. Neil Young had just left the Springfield, and I wasn't getting along well at the time with the other Byrds. So when Stills asked me to play with the Springfield during their set, I said sure, even though I knew it would piss off the rest of my band. It did. A few months later Roger and Chris drove up to my house, walked in, and said, "We think we'll do better without you." Uh-huh. So it's fair to say that without the CAFF benefit, there wouldn't have been a Monterey Pop Festival, and without Monterey Pop, Crosby, Stills, Nash & Young might never have happened. As I said before, benefit concerts can have some entirely unpredictable . . . *benefits* of their own.

On April 4, 1967, exactly a year to the day before he was assassinated, Martin Luther King publicly declared his opposition to the war in Vietnam, stating, "There can be no peace without justice, nor justice without peace." Peter Yarrow remembers that King was "greatly criticized for opposing our involvement in the Vietnam War, and the expansion of it."

Two weeks after Dr. King's dramatic statement, the Mobilization Committee Against the War held the largest antiwar rallies to date, drawing more than 300,000 people in New York City and 60,000 in San Francisco. King and Belafonte were marching together again, this time for an end to the war.

When we first started having big demonstrations against the war, we thought we'd stop it pretty quickly. But we greatly underestimated this thing called societal inertia. Society has inertia just like a falling body. And it took us ten years instead of the two or three we initially thought it would take. I believe in my heart that at some point, some farmer in Iowa finally turned around and said, *I don't want my boy to go.* Then other fathers and mothers in every part of the country stood up and said the same thing. That's what did it. And I think that Joan Baez and Country Joe and Pete Seeger and a hundred others who played at those rallies and marches really *did* make a difference in helping to change people's minds about the war.

One of the best singer-songwriters around today, Melissa Etheridge, remembers growing up "in the sixties and seventies—those were my childhood and my teenage years. I was twelve years old when the Vietnam War finally ended. And I was just starting to listen to music when they were protesting. There were songs on the radio, protest music. Bob Dylan, Crosby, Stills & Nash, and Joan Baez were singing and putting their hearts and spirits into it. Those were the years of playing for meaning."

Someone who unquestionably put his whole heart and spirit into his music was Phil Ochs, a folksinger who arrived in Greenwich Village a few years after I did. Early on, he was considered to be as gifted a writer as Dylan, with whom he quickly became friends. But in the mid-sixties, as Bob turned away from direct political activism (he wrote Ochs a bitter letter calling all politics "bullshit"), Ochs became completely consumed by it. Their friendship ended abruptly one night in New York when they were sharing a cab ride uptown from the Village. Ochs criticized one of Dylan's new songs and Bob got the cab driver to pull over, forcing Ochs to get out and walk.

I didn't know Ochs well, but he was impossible to ignore. Right from the very beginning he was one of the most outspoken critics of the Vietnam War, playing almost nonstop at benefits and rallies to generate opposition to it. His songs like "There but for Fortune" (which Baez covered and made into a hit), "I Ain't Marching Anymore," "Draft Dodger Rag," and "Love Me, I'm a Liberal" were highly political, so much so that they were kept off the radio most of the time. The father of folk activism, Pete Seeger, was an early fan of Ochs. Talking about all protest songs, he says, "Now, somebody will ask me, Pete, how can you prove these songs really make a difference? And I have to confess I can't prove a darn thing, except that the people in power must think they do something, because they keep the songs off the air. But this has been true throughout history. Somewhere in Plato's *Republic*, he says it's very dangerous for the wrong kind of music to be allowed in the republic."

Being censored only made Ochs more defiant. He'd do things like release an album with poems by Mao Tse-tung printed on the jacket and the question "Is this really the enemy?" scrawled underneath. Although he was becoming increasingly radicalized by the late sixties, Phil Ochs considered himself a great patriot. He still believed in the political system and was one of the few musicians who actively supported the antiwar presidential campaign of Eugene McCarthy in 1968. After Robert Kennedy entered the race, Ochs was torn because he'd been close to Kennedy, even flying down to Washington the year before to see him deliver his first speech in the Senate opposing the war. He stayed loyal to McCarthy for most of the campaign but was on the verge of switching over to

Kennedy after the California primary on June 4. He never got the chance.

The night they shot Bobby Kennedy, Ochs was devastated, crying uncontrollably for hours. I stayed up that whole night, waiting to see if he'd live or die. As the sun was coming up, it was obvious to everyone he wasn't going to make it. That's when I wrote this:

It's been a long time coming
It's gonna be a long time gone
And it appears to be a long
Appears to be a long
Appears to be a long time
Yes, a long, long, long, long time before the dawn
Turn, turn any corner
Hear, you must hear what the people say
You know there's something that's going on around here
That surely, surely, surely won't stand the light of day
And it appears to be a long time
Appears to be a long
Appears to be a long time
Such a long, long, long, long time before the dawn
Speak out, you got to speak out against the madness
You got to speak your mind if you dare
But don't try to get yourself elected
If you do you had better cut your hair
'Cause it appears to be a long time
Appears to be a long
Appears to be a long time
Before the dawn
It's been a long time coming
It's gonna be a long time gone
But you know the darkest hour
Is always, always just before the dawn
And it appears to be a long time
Appears to be a long

Appears to be a long time
Such a long, long, long, long time before the dawn

"Long Time Gone" wasn't just about losing Bobby. It was about losing him *and* his brother *and* Dr. King. Three of them in a row. One is an accident, two is kind of weird, and three is on purpose. You can't take it any other way. I was really angry at ballot by bullet. I remember the feeling of *They can't do this to us, they can't take away our right to elect and believe in who we want to simply by shooting them. We can't let them do this.* And if I'd known the guy to blame, I'd have probably taken a gun and put a few bullets through his window. But I didn't know. All I knew was that I had a pen and a guitar, so I wrote what was probably one of the most impassioned songs I've ever written.

My friend and coauthor, David Bender, was a twelve-year-old volunteer on Bobby Kennedy's campaign and he was there the night Kennedy was shot: "I met the singer Rosemary Clooney there at the Ambassador Hotel. She'd been a strong Kennedy supporter and had performed at rallies and victory parties like the one we were having that night, for the California primary. Probably because I was around the age of her own kids (who were with her), she took a shine to me and kept me with her the whole time. When the senator was shot, I remember Rosemary dropping to her knees and clutching her children to her, while people were screaming all around us. That was the last time I ever saw her." David had a hard time dealing with Kennedy's death, as did Rosemary Clooney. "I read later that she suffered a nervous breakdown after the assassination and spent time in a hospital. I went back to school (I'd dropped out of the seventh grade to work on the campaign) and it took me quite a while to understand and process my own feelings about the assassination. Completely by chance, the first album I ever owned had a song on it called 'Long Time Gone,' which I played many, many times. That song helped me make it through the worst days, because it let me know that I wasn't alone."

It was very cathartic for a lot of people. In concert, we'd play a song and get a huge amount of applause and then we'd play another song and get more applause and then we'd start "Long Time Gone" and the entire place would come unglued. I mean un-fucking-glued. Usually you're writing songs and sending them out there. It's like folding up paper gliders with messages on them and throwing them out the window. You hardly know where they land. But sometimes you just nail what people are thinking and you can give voice to the zeitgeist. And if you do, you've tapped into some stuff that's bigger than you are, and you have to be very careful with it.

After Bobby was killed, we had a strong feeling that traditional politics had been taken out of our hands. So we thought, *Oh, I get it, the only way we can actually participate in this system is to disempower it. We won't be a part of it, we will drop out.* Some very bright people didn't agree with that view. They believed (accurately, as it turned out) that the war would never be stopped by all of us just withdrawing from the world. They thought it was no different from the self-deluded denial of the hawks—the supporters of the war—who refused to believe that a growing number of Americans were morally and passionately opposed to our involvement in Vietnam.

So people like Joan Baez and Peter Yarrow and Country Joe McDonald started urging more artists to take a stand against the war. They gently (and sometimes impatiently) said to us, "We know you've dropped out, but can't you still come join us when we link hands around the Pentagon for peace? Or, can't you drop back in again for just a few minutes and come to the moratorium in Golden Gate Park?" And they found ways to bring us in as participants in the political arena anyway, even though many of us still felt disenfranchised by the whole system.

The years 1968 and 1969 were when Crosby, Stills, Nash (and eventually Young) really started to happen. Most people seem to remember our second live gig, a little gathering in upstate New York called Woodstock Music & Arts Fair. I'm asked about Woodstock so often, I usually feign only a dim recollection of it. But the truth is my memory of it is very good. I loved it. I thought it was a very heartfelt, wonderful, accidentally great thing where a lot of incredible music got played. There was a genuine feeling of brotherhood among the people who were there. Nobody killed anybody, nobody raped anybody, nobody shot anybody. In the history of humankind, I think it's probably the only group of people that size that didn't do any of that. Anytime you get half a million people together, even at a religious gathering, somebody beats somebody up. The most aggressive moment I can remember was when Pete Townshend kicked Abbie Hoffman off the stage for trying to use the Who's microphone to promote the Yippies and get people to go to the upcoming trial of the Chicago Eight.

Woodstock was definitely not a political event in the traditional sense of that word, but because it was so *huge*, it had a significant political impact just the same. Joan Baez (who was six months pregnant at the time) remembers it as "an extraordinary weekend at a certain time in history where the atmosphere was charged with politics and with meaning. People there had a spirit and instead of choosing to act like idiots for three days, even the police decided to act like *human beings* for three days."

My friend Paul Kantner, who was there with the Jefferson Airplane, takes a somewhat more cynical view, as he usually does: "Woodstock was the last great burst of innocence in the face of the oncoming seventies and war and hard drugs and Nixon and disco."

Even though Abbie Hoffman didn't succeed in recruiting many new supporters at Woodstock, a good number of people turned up in Chicago for the so-called Days of Rage, timed to coincide with the show trial of the Chicago Eight, all of whom had been arrested a year earlier for attempting to disrupt the Democratic National Convention. I didn't agree with the guerrilla theater tactics of the Yippies. Although I know that as a manipulation of the media it works, getting out in the street and trying to force a confrontation just wasn't the way I wanted to go about it. And the most militant wing of the antiwar movement, a spin-off from the SDS called the Weathermen (they took their name from a Dylan lyric, "You don't need a weatherman to know which way the wind blows"), was blowing up buildings in the name of "peace." Brilliant.

Still, as much as I didn't agree with people like Abbie Hoffman and Jerry Rubin, it was hard not to get outraged watching their trial. When the Black Panther leader Bobby Seale was literally chained to his chair in the courtroom—with a gag in his mouth—it made me wonder what America I was living in. During the trial, Graham Nash got a call from our old friend Wavy Gravy, asking if Crosby, Stills, Nash & Young would fly into Chicago and do a benefit to help pay the legal expenses of the Chicago Eight. An Englishman who'd adopted America as his new country because of his deep love for democracy, Graham was even more angered by the trial than I was. He immediately told Wavy he'd play and then he called me. I told him, "Count me in. I'm there." Then he tried Stephen and Neil. For whatever reason, they couldn't go; none of us remembers why anymore. And so the benefit never happened. But out of Graham's failed pleas to Stephen and Neil came a song that somehow manages to be both angry and hopeful at the same time:

> Though your brother's bound and gagged
> And they've chained him to a chair
> Won't you please come to Chicago
> Just to sing
> In a land that's known as freedom
> How can such a thing be fair?
> Won't you please come to Chicago
> For the help that we can bring
> We can change the world
> Rearrange the world
> It's dyin'
> If you believe in justice
> Dyin'
> If you believe in freedom
> Dyin'
> Let a man live his own life
> Dyin'
> Rules and regulations

Who needs them?
Open up the door
Politicians sit yourselves down
There's nothing for you here
Won't you please come to Chicago
For a ride
Don't ask Jack to help you
'Cause he'll turn the other ear
Won't you please come to Chicago
Or else join the other side
Somehow people must be free
I hope the day comes soon
Won't you please come to Chicago
Show your face
From the bottom of the ocean
To the mountains of the moon
Won't you please come to Chicago
No one else can take your place
We can change the world
Rearrange the world
It's dyin'
If you believe in justice
Dyin'
If you believe in freedom
Dyin'
Let a man live his own life
Dyin'
Rules and regulations
Who needs them?
Open up the door

Nash says, "The first time we played that song live was actually *in* Chicago, and the crowd went nuts. Years later, Dan Fogelberg told me he was in the audience—he was like twelve or something—and that was the night he decided to become a musician."

On October 15, 1969, the Vietnam Moratorium Committee held the first of what they pledged would be monthly Moratorium Day rallies to bring about an end to the war. Fifty thousand people gathered in Washington, D.C., led by Martin Luther King's widow, Coretta, and there were similar events in dozens of cities around the country. The next day, the *New York Times* reported that "It was the largest public protest of the many that have been held against the Vietnam war. Historians in the Library of Congress said that as a nationally coordinated antiwar demonstration it was unique. There was no way to estimate immediately the total numbers involved, but counting the demonstrators, the children who stayed out of school, the workers who did not report for their jobs, those who did and wore armbands and those who prayed in homes and churches, possibly millions were involved."

A month later, on November 15, major marches were again held on both coasts. This time more than 500,000 people congregated in Washington (as many people as there were at Woodstock) to hear speeches and performances from a wide variety of musical acts. Peter Yarrow had gone from being only a participant to becoming a principal organizer of the entire event, an enormous undertaking that he met with his characteristic energy and enthusiasm. "I got married between the moratorium rally in October and the March on Washington in November," recalls Peter, "and I remember saying to my wife, 'We can't have a honeymoon.' I became very involved in organizing the artists who took part in the march. It not only brought people together to say *We cannot continue to fight this war*, but it also challenged the entire notion of the way in which we were leading our lives. In a political way, it was the counterpoint to Woodstock. It was a celebration of life, and we had John Denver (who sang 'Last Night I Had the Strangest Dream'), Earl Scruggs, the cast of *Hair*, Pete Seeger, and Mitch Miller—all different kinds of music so that we could demonstrate the breadth of national opposition to the war. Even the Cleveland Symphony Orchestra had all agreed to come down together, but when Vice President Agnew said there would be a bloodbath at the march, a lot of people got frightened. So we wound up with only a string quartet."

I was in San Francisco, playing a series of dates at the Fillmore with CSNY. The rally in Golden Gate Park was scheduled for the afternoon of the third night of our four-night stand. Joan Baez and Phil Ochs had already committed to perform. We were asked to play and agreed immediately. What I remember most about that day is the satisfaction of being able to stick up for what we believed in, and in such a spectacular manner. It's nice when two or three of your neighbors are out there in the street with you picketing for a cause. But when you see the Polo Field in Golden Gate Park full all the way up to the rim—I mean people were hanging off the trees, it was that jammed—it's just an unbelievably satisfying feeling. And I thought that if we could get enough crowds of that size in enough different places, it would severely affect the course of the war.

Yarrow is convinced that we had a substantial impact, much more than we knew at the time: "We now know that the White House was very frightened by the power of these gatherings of ordinary folks, and that the entire premise of the way the war was being fought— even the decisions about whether to continue the bombings—was affected by what we did."

My friend John Lennon had come a long way since the days when we were hanging out together in L.A. By late 1969, the Beatles were all but officially broken up, and he and Yoko had become dedicated peace activists. Even though we hadn't seen much of each other in the intervening years, I still thought of us as friends, at least until the night I went to visit him at a recording studio in New York. We were sitting around talking and every time I'd start to say something to him, Yoko would answer. This just kept happening and it irritated me no end, until I finally called him on it. I said, "Look, can you and I go out in the hall and talk? Because every time I try to say something to you, Yoko's answering me, and I don't have anything against you or anything against Yoko, but I wanted to talk to *you*." And John said, "Where I go, Yoko goes." And I understood that—I feel the same way about my own wife. So either by design or simply because she didn't know any better, Yoko drove a serious wedge between me and John. And it took me a long time to forgive her for that.

Despite my personal feelings, I still admired much of what John & Yoko were doing to promote peace. In December they'd spent hundreds of thousands of dollars putting up billboards in eleven cities around the world, declaring WAR IS OVER! IF YOU WANT IT. HAPPY CHRISTMAS FROM JOHN & YOKO. I thought that was a great idea, very cool. At about the same time, John and George Harrison reunited at a benefit concert in London for UNICEF, the first time they'd shared a stage together in more than three years. It was one of those magical moments that only happen at a benefit, where the cause is bigger than the people.

In the spring of 1970, Richard Nixon launched a full-scale attack on Cambodia, suddenly and arrogantly increasing U.S. involvement in Southeast Asia. Campuses across the country exploded. On May 4, students at Kent State University in Ohio rallied in angry opposition to Nixon's action. The governor called in the National Guard, and at noon the students gathered to protest its presence on campus. They were ordered to disperse but refused. The Guard then released tear gas into the crowd, causing a temporary retreat. The kids threw the tear gas back at the Guardsmen, along with rocks and whatever else they could find. But none of them was armed. Then one of the Guardsmen thought he heard sniper fire and panicked. He started shooting, which led to a burst of troop fire that left four people dead and a dozen wounded. All the Guardsmen denied firing their weapons (including a sergeant who was later pictured with a gun in his hand and the slide racked back as it ejected the spent shell). Not one of them has ever been convicted of any crime, but they murdered four innocent people just for exercising their constitutional rights—the right of free speech, the right to assemble, the right to their own beliefs.

I was in Butano Canyon in northern California with Neil when we saw the famous picture in *Life* magazine of the girl kneeling over the kid on the ground in a puddle of blood with that "Why?" look on her face. I handed Neil the magazine, and I watched it hit his face and hit his brain. Then I handed him the guitar and he set the picture down in front of him and wrote "Ohio." And I watched him do it, sang with him as he wrote it, and then I called Nash and said, "Nash, Neil's written a song and we have to record it now. Right *now.*" He got us a studio, got Stephen. We went in, I think it was the next night. We gave it right to Ahmet Ertegun, the head of Atlantic Records, who was headed to New York on a red-eye flight that night. At the time we had "Teach Your Children" halfway up the charts as a hit and Nash said to pull it and release "Ohio" instead. And they did. It was immediate, it was direct; it was, "Nixon, this is you. We're pointing the finger at *you*, asshole."

Tin soldiers and Nixon's coming
We're finally on our own
This summer I hear the drumming
Four dead in Ohio
Gotta get down to it
Soldiers are gunning us down
Should've been done long ago
What if you knew her and found her dead on the ground
How can you run when you know
Tin soldiers and Nixon's coming
We're finally on our own
This summer I hear the drumming
Four dead in Ohio

Later on, Neil said, "It's still hard to believe I had to write this song [about] probably the biggest lesson ever learned at an American place of learning." Don Henley remembers hearing it on the radio for the first time: "It made the hair on the back of my neck stand up. It had what I would describe as a terrible beauty to it."

"Ohio" got a huge amount of airplay. Even today, people still connect to it deeply. In the best tradition of troubadours, we put the truth out there and it worked. It remains one of the proudest moments of my life.

The Birth of the Benefit:

"With a Little Help from My Friends"

And because of the nature of bringing people together,

there's just something about music that heals.

Bonnie Raitt

People like to remember the sixties as a time when the music was always free and still uncorrupted by the soon-to-be pervasive influence of corporate greed. It sounds real good, but it's not true. Remember, even Woodstock started out as a paid concert. The only reason it didn't end up that way was that the promoters, who had no idea what they were biting off, just totally underestimated how many people would show up. When a quarter of a million of them ignored the fence that had been put up around old Max Yasgur's farm, Woodstock suddenly became a "free" concert.

I'm not saying that corporate money didn't change rock 'n' roll. Of course it did. When the suits started to realize just how many millions of dollars they could squeeze out of those tie-dyed, flower-haired kids, they did the only thing they know how to do: they exploited them. But tie-dye boutiques and flower-power florists were just the small-time stuff. Music was where the big bucks could be made.

We were very ambivalent about the money. On the one hand, it was great to be in our twenties and own a Porsche (or two), to be able to buy the coolest clothes, the biggest houses, and, of course, the best drugs on the planet. But we didn't trust it either. It represented the values we thought had screwed up our parents, and the new world we were inventing wasn't going to be based on anything as fucked up as material possessions.

It didn't quite work out that way. Paul Kantner, Stephen Stills, and I wrote a song called "Wooden Ships," the basic idea of which was that we could all just sail away from a broken world into a better, more ideal life that wasn't based on war or greed. Although we wrote it to describe the aftermath of a nuclear apocalypse, it quickly became a metaphor for escaping all of society's evils. Jackson Browne gently rebuffed our well-intentioned but naive premise with his own song "For Everyman" when he wrote: "Make it on your own if you think you can / Somewhere later on you'll have to take a stand / Then you're going to need a hand."

The problem, as Jackson pointed out and even I had to admit, was that most people didn't have their own ships to sail away in, and no matter how high we were or how far we went, the human problems of the world—war, poverty, disease—would travel with us. This meant that ultimately we still had to deal with them on society's terms, not our own. And like it or not, those terms usually required money.

Until the seventies, most musician activism was used to raise awareness, not money. The sea change came around 1970 when a number of major rock concerts were organized with their primary purpose being to raise cash for the cause. Not surprisingly, many of these early fund-raising events were organized by the indefatigable Peter Yarrow. Peter's credibility as an activist was long established, so when he began approaching some of the young rock 'n' roll artists to get involved—particularly against the war—we listened to him.

Peter's energy was hard to resist, especially since he never took no for an answer. "It may or may not be a Jewish thing," he says now, "but it's a premise underscored by Jewish tradition. You really must act on your beliefs or you haven't made the commitment. You can't merely believe and not do something about it."

Yarrow's first big fund-raising concert was a benefit at Madison Square Garden for the Vietnam Moratorium Committee, the same people with whom he'd organized the 1969 marches on Washington. Billed as the Winter Festival for Peace, it was a marathon event that began at 8:30 P.M. on January 28, 1970, and ended at about 4:00 A.M. the next morning. On the bill were Peter, Paul & Mary, Harry Belafonte, Judy Collins, the Rascals, Blood, Sweat & Tears, Richie Havens, Dave Brubeck, and the cast of *Hair*. The Rascals and Blood, Sweat & Tears drew standing ovations from the capacity crowd of twenty-one thousand, but most were eagerly anticipating the arrival of the man who was scheduled to close the show, Jimi Hendrix.

It was only the second benefit concert Hendrix had ever done. The first had been several months earlier for a block association in Harlem when he'd told the audience, "People say, 'He plays white rock for white people. What's he doing up here?' I wanted to show them that music is universal—that there is no white rock or black rock." Jimi didn't play on his blackness. He was part of the hippie milieu. He played on being a psychedelic warrior, and he was. He was equally comfortable with black and white people of all stripes. For me that was one of the proudest parts of being a citizen of the Woodstock "nation." We just didn't do that . . . see colors. We weren't into separating blacks and whites.

The Winter Peace Festival concert was Hendrix's first and only public appearance against the war in Vietnam, and it marked a major turnaround for him. Jimi's decision to oppose U.S. involvement in Vietnam was very significant. First, he was the premier musician of our times, and second, he came to being a musician after serving for three years as a paratrooper in the 101st Airborne. In 1967, Hendrix made a few public comments in support of the war, primarily because he believed it was an important place to take a strong stand against the threat of world communist domination. His view changed after somebody pointed out to him that although only 10 percent of the U.S. population was black, somehow blacks accounted for almost twice that percentage of our troops in Vietnam. That didn't fly with him—or with any of us, for that matter.

Although the symbolism of Hendrix's appearing at the Winter Festival for Peace was very important to the antiwar movement, his performance there was one of the saddest public displays of his career. The story is that before Jimi went on, a fan gave him a hit of very bad acid. Although a lot of people now find it hard to believe, in those days we often just took whatever drugs people gave us, no questions asked. By the time Hendrix and his Band of Gypsies finally took the stage at 3:00 A.M., he was in no condition to play. He stumbled his way through two songs and then, halfway through the third, he sat down in the middle of the stage for about five minutes. Eventually one of the guys in the band had to say, "We're just not getting it together," and they helped him off. It was left to poor Peter Yarrow to placate a monumentally disappointed crowd of Hendrix fans who had waited seven hours for almost nothing. Peter says he told them how committed to the cause Jimi obviously was for trying to play even though he had the "flu." Only nine months later that "flu"—otherwise known as the disease of drug addiction—would do more than just ruin a show. It would kill Jimi at the age of twenty-seven.

Despite Hendrix's aborted performance, the show accomplished its main purpose, raising almost $100,000 and wiping out the Moratorium Committee's entire debt. At the time, it was the largest gate for a nonsporting event in the history of Madison Square Garden.

Encouraged by the financial success of the Winter Festival for Peace, Yarrow conceived an even bolder plan: two huge antiwar concerts in Shea Stadium in New York and JFK Stadium in Philadelphia, to be held that summer. Although he again managed to line up an impressive array of musicians to perform (the Shea Stadium concert included Credence Clearwater Revival, Paul Simon,

Steppenwolf, the Butterfield Blues Band, and John Sebastian), the political climate in 1970 made it extremely difficult to obtain the necessary city permits to actually *hold* a big antiwar concert. New York's liberal Republican mayor, John Lindsay, cooperated to the extent that the Shea Stadium show was able to go forward, but Frank Rizzo, the right-wing police chief-turned-mayor of Philadelphia, flatly refused to rent JFK Stadium to Yarrow's group, Peace Inc. Although they went to court and successfully sued the city, it was essentially a meaningless victory. Rizzo was permitted to drastically limit the running time of the concert, and the city was still able to charge more than ten times the normal stadium rental, making even a sellout show a guaranteed money loser. Says Yarrow, the decision not to hold the Philadelphia show ultimately came down to one of safety for the fans: "Rizzo said that if even one girl took off her top, there would be blood on the seats."

The Shea Stadium Peace Festival show was held on August 6, 1970, to coincide with the twenty-fifth anniversary of the bombing of Hiroshima. Even though *Rolling Stone* described it as "as good a line-up as New York has seen in ages," the show was a huge disappointment to its planners, drawing only twenty thousand people—a third of Shea Stadium's capacity—and barely breaking even.

Musically, however, there were a couple of memorable moments. John Fogerty recalls that he gave what was described as a "blistering version" of his powerful antiwar song "Fortunate Son." Fogerty says that when he went offstage somebody said to him, "John, that was a really angry version," and he replied: "I meant every word of it." Although the New York City police were out in force to keep the crowd in their seats and off the field, "Fortunate Son" had people up and dancing in the aisles.

It was the surprise appearance of the completely apolitical Janis Joplin, though, that makes the Shea Stadium Festival for Peace a truly important event in the history of rock 'n' roll benefits. She originally hadn't planned on showing up but changed her mind at the last minute.

Until that point, Janis Joplin had never done a political event of any kind. Basically, she was a funky, tough, dusty little Texas girl

Joan Baez during a rally on the U.C. Berkeley campus in support of
the free speech movement in 1964.

Phil Ochs performing at the Anti–Vietnam War Moratorium Day rally in
San Francisco's Golden Gate Park, October 1969.

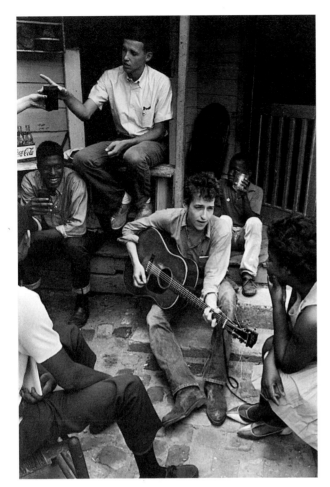

A very young Bob Dylan visiting Greenwood, Mississippi, just after civil rights leader Medgar Evers was assassinated in 1963.

Harry Belafonte, Leon Bibb, and Joan Baez performing on the steps of the state capitol in Montgomery, Alabama, after the march from Selma in 1965.

The March on Washington in August 1963. Joan Baez said, "My knees were shaking. I'd never seen that many people before in my life."

Harry Belafonte (*front right*) was Dr. Martin Luther King's "pointer" for many of the early civil rights rallies and marches. At the 1963 March on Washington, he led a contingent of Hollywood stars, including Charlton Heston, James Garner, Diahann Carroll, and Marlon Brando.

Mahalia Jackson singing "How I Got Over" on the steps of the Lincoln Memorial at the rally following the March on Washington. She reminded "Martin" to "tell them about the dream."

This poster from the John Sinclair Freedom concert in 1971 proves that Sinclair was in jail for more than just "breathing the air."

Graham Nash was just a fan that night, but he still managed to get this stunner shot of George Harrison and Bob Dylan at the Concert for Bangladesh, August 1, 1971.

Joni Mitchell, Richie Havens, and, in white-face makeup, Joan Baez and Bob Dylan at the Night of the Hurricane concert at Madison Square Garden, December 8, 1975.

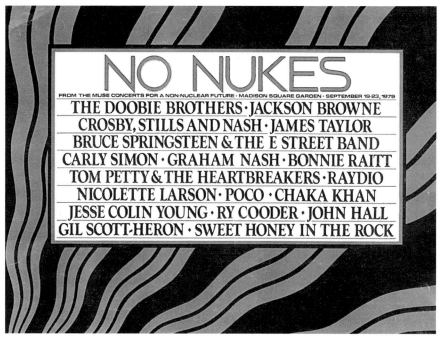

In only one week, Jackson Browne and Graham Nash produced this three-record set from the five nights of No Nukes concerts held at Madison Square Garden in 1979.

From left to right: John Hall, Graham Nash, James Taylor, Jackson Browne, Bonnie Raitt, and Carly Simon performing at a No Nukes concert.

Bruce Springsteen had his thirtieth birthday on stage at a No Nukes concert. Clarence Clemmons helped him celebrate.

Pete Townshend and Paul McCartney are backed by the all-star Rockestra during the finale of the Concerts for the People of Kampuchea at London's Hammersmith Odeon Theatre, December, 1979.

Graham Nash beaming after Bonnie Raitt's performance at Peace Sunday in 1982. More than 100,000 fans filled the Rose Bowl that day and brought his dream to life.

At the end of Peace Sunday, we all came back out on stage and gathered in a big circle around Stevie Wonder. In one of the most electrifying moments I have ever experienced, he started singing "All We Are Saying is Give Peace a Chance."

from the middle of nowhere who didn't really give a shit about politics. Once, when the Vietnam War was just starting to get hot, somebody had the bright idea of asking Janis to tape a public service announcement for the Voice of America, the official propaganda arm of the U.S. government. Although she turned them down, she told her close friend and biographer Myra Friedman that what she would have said was "Drop your guns and run, boys!"

She only did a few songs, the last of which was a rousing version of "Move Over" that had the crowd shouting for more. Because of time constraints (ignoring them would have meant thousands of dollars in overtime costs), Peter pleaded with her to cut her set short. Already very drunk when she arrived, she stormed off the stage and proceeded to get completely hammered. After Shea Stadium, Janis gave only two more public performances. Less than two months later, like Jimi, she was dead.

I loved Janis. She had a good heart. She *cared* about music. She loved a freshly opened bottle of Southern Comfort and anybody who could play the blues. But she was always lonely. She was always wishing that somebody would love her. In the long run, I think the loneliness got her.

The modern benefit concert was born on a rainy afternoon in New York City in the summer of 1971. It was on the first day of August that George Harrison and some "friends" took the stage for the first of two sold-out shows at Madison Square Garden. Harrison had organized the shows to provide aid to the starving people of Bangladesh, the new nation that was formerly East Pakistan. In a desperate effort to maintain control of its former province, the Pakistani government had murdered over a million people in Bangladesh and had driven an estimated ten million more into India as refugees. These were some of the poorest people on the planet and what was happening to them rivaled the Holocaust for sheer brutality and horror.

Ravi Shankar, the Indian master of the sitar, whose music I'd first discovered (and fallen in love with) during my earliest days in the Byrds, was devastated by what he saw: "So many were killed, including my distant relatives, many friends, including Muslim friends, and even people from the family of my Guru; their homes burned, completely destroyed." Shankar couldn't sit idly by. "I was very disturbed and wanted to do something for the people of Bangladesh. I talked with people from many different organizations in the United States and in Europe who wanted me to give a benefit performance. But I thought of doing something on a very large scale that might bring in a lot of money and also, you know, awareness."

(Years before, when I'd first gone to England with the Byrds, I think I was the one who introduced George to the sitar and the music of Ravi Shankar. At least he tells people I did. I know that at the time I was so turned on by Indian music that I played it constantly for anyone and everyone I knew, even the Beatles. Subsequently, George played sitar on "Norwegian Wood" and arranged a meeting with the "master" when Shankar was visiting England.)

Unsure of even how to *begin* to put on a benefit concert, Shankar logically sought out George (who by now was both his sitar student and a close friend) for advice. "I thought I would ask George, even if he could not take part himself, if he could advise me, ask other artists about it, write or talk about it—something. Then maybe we could do a big function where we could raise twenty-five or fifty thousand dollars. So, when I talked with him, he was impressed by my sincerity, and I gave him lots to read and explained the situation. He was very deeply moved and said he would be glad to help in the planning—even to participate."

George Harrison has always been a very good-hearted man, not an elitist, not a racist, not anything that prevented him from being open to the world. He was probably the first guy who understood world beat, because he was one of the first guys who started listening to music from other places; and that, of course, led him to consider the plight of people in other places. He's always been a generous, compassionate human being, so it was only natural that he would respond so immediately—and so completely—to Ravi's pleas for help.

After George agreed to participate in a concert, the idea quickly expanded beyond an event to raise "twenty-five or fifty thousand dollars." Shankar remembers that "Things started moving very fast. George called Ringo in Spain where he was working in a film, and he talked to Leon Russell and all of these wonderful musicians from the West Coast and East Coast who came to play. And, of course, Bob Dylan, as luck would have it, was so wonderful to take part in this cause. In a period of only four or five weeks all of this was done. To conceive, plan, and execute in such a short time must be setting a record in the history of world entertainment."

Looking at it in hindsight, George said, "I think that one of the things that I developed, just by being in the Beatles, was being bold. And I think John had a lot to do with that, because John Lennon, you know, if he felt something strongly, he just did it. And I picked up a lot of that by being a friend of John's. Just that attitude of, Well, we'll just go for it . . . just do it."

The day of the shows (one at 3:30 P.M., the other at 8:00 P.M.) was a typically humid, oppressive midsummer day in New York City. Then the rains came, breaking the humidity and leaving the fifty thousand people who would see both shows with the feeling that they, too, were about to be cleansed by the amazing musical experience awaiting them. The excitement inside the hall was palpable. Rumors swirled: John Lennon was in the house; Paul McCartney was stuck in traffic; Mick Jagger had been spotted at rehearsal the night before.

Apparently, John *had* initially agreed to play, but a few days before the show, he called and asked if "Mother" (his pet name for Yoko) could also perform. George politely told him that she hadn't been invited, and in much the same way that it went down with me and John in the studio, John chose Yoko. The two of them flew to Paris instead.

Paul was also invited but refused, later claiming that he might have played if Allen Klein (who was managing the Beatles instead of Paul's father-in-law, Lee Eastman) hadn't been so heavily involved in putting the concerts together. Paul subsequently told *Rolling Stone* that "I was asked to play George's concert for Bangladesh and I didn't. . . . Klein called a press conference and told everyone I had refused to do it for the Pakistani refugees. . . . It wasn't so. If it wasn't for Klein I might have had thoughts about it."

On the other hand, Mick Jagger, who *had* said yes, couldn't get an American visa because of a pot bust in London a few years earlier. Ultimately, none of this mattered because anyone who saw either show remembers it as one of the most extraordinary musical experiences of their life. Graham Nash, who was in the audience at the first concert, says: "I think it was obvious that something truly momentous was going down. After all, it was the first time George had played live [in America] since the Beatles broke up."

When George first walked out on the stage, a bearded figure bathed in a single spotlight, the applause he received was deafening. Not only was it George's first solo performance ever, it was the first time *any* Beatle had set foot on an American stage in five years. The group had formally disbanded only the year before, so this also marked the first time that Americans could personally express their gratitude for all the Beatles had meant to them. And they did. George, always shy, didn't seem to know how to respond. He stood there for several long minutes just absorbing the adulation and emotion. People wept openly.

Finally, George was able to be heard above the roar, and, thanking everyone for coming, he introduced Ravi Shankar and several other musicians for a set of traditional Indian music. Before beginning, Shankar said simply, "We are not trying to make any politics; we are artists. But through our music we would like you to feel the agony and also the pain and sad happenings in Bangladesh."

After Shankar's set, George, now dressed in a stylish white suit offset by a bright orange shirt, returned to the stage. This time he brought his friends out with him: Eric Clapton (who came out of "retirement" to play), Leon Russell, Billy Preston, Klaus Voorman, Jim Keltner, the entire Badfinger band, a brass section led by Jim Horn, and a large group of backup vocalists. One more friend roused the crowd to a fever pitch when he sat down behind his drum kit: Ringo Starr was in the house.

All of them launched into an energetic electric rendition of "Wah Wah," after which George approached the microphone with only his acoustic guitar. Softly speaking the words *Hare Krishna*, he began to strum the opening chords of "My Sweet Lord," a choice that was met with tremendous approval. Ringo then did "It Don't Come Easy," which left the crowd up and shouting for more. But it was Leon Russell's turn to dazzle, as he joined Harrison on a chillingly powerful version of "Beware of Darkness." Before introducing Eric Clapton, George paid tribute to his fellow artists' selflessness in just showing up: "Everybody here came on very short notice and some people even canceled a few gigs to try and make it and nobody's getting paid for anything."

Clapton, then longhaired and mustachioed, was greeted reverently by the crowd as he and George (reprising their roles on the *White Album*) traded licks on "While My Guitar Gently Weeps."

Doffing his jacket, George then brought Leon Russell back out for a blistering version of the Stones' "Jumpin' Jack Flash" (which included a bluesy cover of "Youngblood" in the middle). There were more tears for George's stunning acoustic performance of his own classic "Here Comes the Sun," a song—perfect for the event—about hope.

Just when everyone thought they'd died and gone to rock 'n' roll heaven, it got better. Once again George came out alone to the microphone and, this time, instead of chanting *Hare Krishna*, he uttered the one name whose power that night was the equivalent of even the greatest Hindu deity: "I'd like to bring on a friend of us all, Mr. Bob Dylan."

Without warning or any advance billing, Bob Dylan walked out onstage for his first New York appearance in four years—and only his fourth public performance since the 1966 motorcycle accident that had left his career shrouded in myth and mystery. He opened with "A Hard Rain's Gonna Fall" (sadly appropriate after torrential rains had caused even further devastation in beleaguered Bangladesh), followed by "It Takes a Lot to Laugh, It Takes a Train to Cry." Then Dylan, Harrison, and Leon Russell all leaned into one microphone to harmonize on "Just Like a Woman," with Ringo on tambourine. "Blowin' in the Wind" and "Tambourine Man" rounded out his brief but unforgettable set, and as quickly as he had

arrived, he was gone. For two solid minutes, the crowd chanted
More! but it was Harrison, not Dylan, who returned. In a final
homage to the Beatles, Harrison chose "Something" as his encore.
Then, picking up the jacket he'd flung down earlier and throwing it
over his shoulder, George and his friends left the stage.

There was one more moment of magic yet to come. To thunderous applause, everyone (except Dylan) came back out for the finale.
George had written a song that had taken the name of an unknown
and desperately suffering nation and turned it into a household
word—and a hit single, all the proceeds of which were to go, as the
chorus says, to "relieve the people of Bangladesh."

> I've never known such distress
> Now please don't turn away, I want to hear you say
> Relieve the people of Bangladesh
> Relieve Bangladesh

After the shows, an exuberant Ravi Shankar said, "With George's
single, 'Bangladesh,' my single, the film that has been made of the
concert, the album coming out and whatever the gate monies are
from this concert . . . it will all add up to a substantial amount.
Though, when you think of the amount being spent on almost eight
million refugees, and so many of them children, of course it is like a
drop in the ocean. Maybe it will take care of them for only two or
three days. But that is not the point. The main issue—beyond the
sum of money we can raise—is that we feel that all the young people
who came to the concerts . . . they were made aware of something
very few of them felt or knew clearly—about Bangla Desh and what
has happened to cause such distress. It is like trying to ignite, trying
to pass on the responsibilities as much as possible to everyone else.
I think this aim has been achieved."

George was just relieved that it was all over: "It was just pure
adrenaline, and it was very lucky that it came off because all the
musicians weren't there for rehearsal. We rehearsed bits and pieces
with different people but we didn't have everybody all on at one

time until the show itself. And we were just very lucky really that it all came together."

Unfortunately, although the concerts themselves had gone off almost miraculously well, their aftermath was far less blessed. The concert album and movie, both of which would account for the vast majority of the $13.5 million raised for the United Nations International Children's Emergency Fund (UNICEF), were also very successful. The album was on the charts for forty-one weeks, rising as high as number two. It even won the Grammy for Album of the Year. This was the good news.

The bad news was that the Internal Revenue Service ruled that since the concerts had not been produced by a nonprofit entity, all proceeds were to be viewed as taxable under the law. Worse, Apple Records was undergoing an audit in the aftermath of the Beatles' breakup. The result was that it took an unbelievable *eleven years* for most of the money to reach UNICEF. Although as Ravi Shankar said, the money was only a few "drops in the ocean," it would have saved many, many more lives had it reached its destination quickly. A UNICEF study estimates that during those eleven years, more than eight million children of Bangladesh died of malnutrition and disease.

This nightmare of bureaucratic indifference left George bitter and disillusioned about the entire process. It would be well over a decade before he would agree to perform at another benefit concert.

I asked Carlos Santana about this and he said something that really moved me: "We musicians have been giving benefits since Bangladesh, you know. And a lot of it doesn't go to where it's supposed to go. It goes to the offices of lawyers or something, but it doesn't mean that we should become cynical and stop. It means we do *more*, because eventually these people will touch their hearts like we do and they'll say, Well, you know, I don't *need* it, I'll just do it out of my own goodness."

Although John Lennon didn't wind up playing at the Concerts for Bangladesh, it definitely wasn't an indication that he'd withdrawn from activism. In fact, at the same time that George was decrying

the politics surrounding the crisis in Bangladesh ("There's a war;
any war is wrong as far as I can see. All I'm trying to do is generate
enough money and make sure the money's distributed in order to
relieve some of the agony. I'm not interested in the politics."), John
was becoming increasingly politicized—and radicalized—in his own
thinking.

After their early forays into antiwar activism with the WAR IS OVER
IF YOU WANT IT billboard campaign and the "bed-ins" for peace,
John and Yoko began to spend more and more time in the United
States, eventually renting an apartment on Bank Street in
Greenwich Village. Part of their reason for taking up residence in
New York City was to bolster Yoko's effort to regain custody of her
daughter from a previous marriage to an American citizen. But it
was also true that the Lennons found the highly volatile political climate of the early seventies very attractive. Just as Greenwich Village
had been the mecca for folk musicians a decade earlier, John and
Yoko's apartment became a magnet for radical activists (particularly Jerry Rubin, the Yippie leader and one of the Chicago Eight
defendants), who figured out that if they wanted real credibility
with the masses, this was the Lennon who could get it for them.

Jerry Rubin quickly became a member of John and Yoko's inner
circle, counseling them on American politics, traveling with them,
even "playing" music with them as a conga player in their band.

I think it's fair to say that as a political activist, John was a brilliant musician. Unfortunately for him, he was essentially tone-deaf
to the nuances of politics, particularly in America. This wasn't
entirely his fault. People like Rubin were consciously influencing
him for their own purposes, and although John wasn't stupid or
naive, it was possible to take advantage of him because he always led
with his heart.

One of the first to try to exploit the Lennons' genuine commitment to peace was a Canadian music promoter named John
Brower. Brower's main claim to fame was that he'd recently produced a pop festival in Toronto where John and Yoko had performed with their Plastic Ono Band. In December of 1969, still

riding the high we all were feeling after Woodstock, John and Yoko announced their intention to stage a "Give Peace a Chance" festival at a Toronto racetrack. At a press conference, John promised a Beatles reunion in combination with performances by Bob Dylan and Elvis. One million people would come to this concert—designed solely to promote world peace. The Lennons asked Brower to pull the show together as a free concert. After only a month of watching Brower's dubious efforts in their name, however, they became highly skeptical of his motives and disavowed the whole event. They sent him a telegram that read: "Have read your report. You have done exactly what we told you not to. We told you we wanted it to be free. We want nothing to do with you or your festival. Yours in disgust, John & Yoko."

Despite their bad experience with the aborted Give Peace a Chance festival, John and Yoko remained open to the idea of performing for a political purpose. It was the Lennons' new American consigliere, Jerry Rubin, who first brought the case of John Sinclair to their attention.

Sinclair was a radical activist in Michigan who for years had maintained a running battle with the police for his outspoken views on marijuana, publicly advocating its legalization and openly flaunting his own use of it. After several arrests and some jail time, he was set up in a sting operation and busted for giving an undercover officer two joints. He was sentenced to twelve and a half *years* in the Southern Michigan Penitentiary in Jackson.

This is where he was in the fall of 1971, serving the third year of his sentence while his case slowly worked its way through the appeals courts. It was at that point that Jerry Rubin first told John Lennon about the plight of their jailed "brother," John Sinclair.

A rally and concert were being planned for "John Sinclair Week" in Michigan, a series of protests designed to coincide with the next appellate court review of Sinclair's case in December. When John and Yoko agreed to play at the Sinclair event (along with Michigan natives Stevie Wonder and Bob Seger), it took on national significance. As the concerts for Bangladesh were for George and Ringo, this would be John Lennon's first American performance since the breakup of the Beatles.

Jerry Rubin was deeply involved in organizing the event. He saw it as the beginning of a series of political concert-rallies that would stretch across the country over the following year, culminating in a gigantic one to be held in proximity to the 1972 Republican National Convention, which was certain to renominate Richard Nixon for a second term as president. (Although poor Nixon wouldn't get to finish his term, Rubin's dream wouldn't materialize either. The FBI became involved when it learned of these "subversive" plans, and many of the potential performing artists were harassed continuously. Phil Ochs, for example, had his phone tapped and was followed around the country. For John Lennon, the government's response was even harsher. Nixon's Immigration and Naturalization Service initiated proceedings to deport John because of an old drug bust in England. Although he ultimately won the right to stay in the United States, the protracted fight soured him on performing for political causes. After a 1972 benefit at Madison Square Garden for mentally handicapped children, John Lennon never performed in public again as a solo artist.)

The Free John Sinclair concert-rally was held on December 10, 1971, at the University of Michigan at Ann Arbor, a campus that prided itself on rivaling Berkeley for the title of "most radical." As soon as Lennon's involvement was announced, the fifteen-thousand-seat Crisler Arena (the university's basketball arena) was immediately sold out. In addition to John and Yoko, Stevie Wonder, Bob Seger, Phil Ochs and Commander Cody & His Lost Planet Airmen were scheduled to perform, as was MC5, the radical rock group that John Sinclair managed before his imprisonment. There would also be readings by Allen Ginsberg and speeches from several of Rubin's Chicago Eight co-conspirators: David Dellinger, Rennie Davis, and the chairman of the Black Panther Party, Bobby Seale.

Shortly after 7:00 P.M., Allen Ginsberg, accompanied by a young longhaired guitarist, came onstage and "sang" his poem written in honor of the event.

Oh Dear John Sinclair
We pray you leave your jailhouse
Oh Dear John Sinclair
We celebrate your liberty tonight
Oh Dear John Sinclair
In your name we are having a party
15,000 people here
Here with no fear

Next up was the hometown hero, Bob Seger, his long dark hair flowing out from underneath a brown felt hat. He opened with a boogie number that got the crowd up and dancing.

Seger's growling vocals were still echoing in the Crisler Arena when a Roman Catholic priest, Father James Groppi, came onstage to condemn Nixon's war policies ("Nixon is killing as many Vietnamese as Hitler killed Jews. What happened there is happening here now."), the first sign that the rally had a larger purpose than John Sinclair's freedom.

If there were any lingering doubts about the rally's scope, they were erased by the next speaker. Black Panther chairman Bobby Seale—now unbound and definitely ungagged—strode confidently out to the microphone (accompanied by four bodyguards) and delivered a blistering attack on what he called the "pollution" of capitalism. In the rhythmic cadence of a preacher, Seale told the crowd that "The only solution to pollution is the people's humane revolution!" Trying to reinforce the connection between music and politics, Seale said, "If you want to dance, if you want to feel the revolutionary spirit of the music . . . we do not have to articulate politics anymore. We're sayin' the music is free, the life is free, the world is free."

After Seale came Phil Ochs, whose friendship with Jerry Rubin was also instrumental in his agreeing to play at the rally. In fact, Rubin had arranged a meeting in New York between John Lennon and Phil before the Sinclair event and the two got on famously. They played several songs for each other, including a new song that Lennon had written specifically about John Sinclair.

Commenting on the crowd's obvious excitement, Ochs observed, "You always generate a lot of energy when you have rallies like this . . ." and then did a short but well-received set, highlighted by a song called "Here's to the State of Richard Nixon." Here's just a sample:

Here's to the laws of Richard Nixon.
Where the wars are fought in secret,
Pearl Harbor every day
He punishes with income tax
That he don't have to pay.

Is it any wonder he was being followed?

Phil Ochs left the stage to a standing ovation, then the crowd grew quiet as a crackling sound came through the speakers. Suddenly, a man's disembodied voice was heard, speaking words that were filled with emotion. It was John Sinclair himself, talking live to the crowd from the prison in Jackson. And, more important to him, he was talking to his four-year-old daughter, Sunny, who was onstage with her mother. "Dad. What are you doing? Hey Dad, what are you doing?" Sinclair, struggling unsuccessfully to keep his composure, managed to say, "I'm trying to get to see you, Sunny." With the exception of the undercover FBI agents who were furiously writing down every word (no joke—years later records obtained through the Freedom of Information Act showed that there were agents all over the hall that night), almost everyone who heard Sinclair talking to his little girl was reduced to tears.

Seven and a half hours into the concert, following a previously scheduled club date, Stevie Wonder and his whole band, including three backup vocalists, came onstage. It was 2:30 A.M. and the arena was still packed. They opened with "For Once in My Life," with Stevie giving special emphasis to the lyric "I'm not alone anymore." With delicious irony, he introduced their next song this way: "This song goes out to any of the undercover agents who might be in the audience. The title of the tune is 'Somebody's Watching You.'"

After that, Stevie gave a truly remarkable speech. You have to remember that in 1971 he was only twenty-one years old, just a kid. With the band playing a gentle, rhythmic beat underneath his words, Stevie addressed the crowd: "I've never been very good at giving speeches because basically what I feel I just say to the people I come in contact with directly or indirectly. Before coming here today I had a lot of things on my mind—a lot of things you don't have to *see* to understand. Seeing that we are in a very troublesome time today in the world, a time in which a man can get twelve years in prison for possession of marijuana and another who can kill four students at Kent State and come out free. What kinda shit is that?" Huge cheers answered Wonder's rhetorical question. Then he finished by saying, "Sometimes I get very disgusted and discouraged. Whenever I do I look up in the sky and I sing the words to a tune I did about a year and a half back":

> Heaven help the child who never had a home,
> Heaven help the girl who walks the street alone
> Heaven help the roses if the bombs begin to fall,
> Heaven help us all.

Finishing the song in a soaring vocal duet with his backup singer, Linda Tucker, each of them singing the line "We need the Lord!" Stevie leaned in to the microphone and said, "Everybody knows [that we need the Lord] and I wish that Nixon and Agnew knew it."

Then, at 3:00 A.M., a roar erupted from the Crisler Arena as the words everyone was still waiting to hear were finally spoken: "John Lennon and Yoko Ono!"

John and Yoko came onstage with their small band (with Jerry Rubin again on the congas) dressed in identical outfits; each wore blue jeans and a black leather jacket worn open, revealing a lavender FREE JOHN SINCLAIR! T-shirt that pictured Sinclair smoking a joint. John had on his trademark round sunglasses with the small blue lenses.

As if his position on pot might not have been clear enough to everyone in the house (including the FBI), John's first words into the microphone were "The Pope smokes dope!"

Their first song was a new one written by John about the recent brutal suppression of riots at Attica state prison in New York. Introducing it, he said, "This is a song called 'Attica State.' It was conceived on my birthday, October 9. It was ad-libbed and then we finished it up." This was followed by another new song, a fun, political tune called "Luck of the Irish," on which John and Yoko traded lead vocals:

> You should have the luck of the Irish
> You'd be sorry and wish you was dead
> You should have the luck of the Irish
> And you'd wish you was English instead

Yoko then did a song she had written "a day before yesterday for sisters in Ann Arbor, Michigan"; it was called "Oh Sister." When she finished, John kissed her, smiling proudly, and told the crowd, "We came here not only to help John [Sinclair] and to spotlight what's going on, but also to show and to say to all of you that apathy isn't it and that we *can* do something. Okay, so flower-power didn't work. So what? We start again. This song I wrote for John Sinclair":

> It ain't fair, John Sinclair, in the stir for breathing air
> Won't you care for John Sinclair, in the stir for breathing air
> Let him be, set him free, let him be like you and me.

After only four songs, all of them new, John and Yoko left the stage, each with an arm raised in the clenched-fist salute of solidarity with the people.

The people, it seemed, were disappointed. Although thrilled to see John, after that long a wait they'd expected something more. According to biographer Michael Schumacher, Phil Ochs wrote about the crowd's disappointment in his journal: "Response not as big as I thought it would be."

Days later, Yoko defended their brief performance this way: "We went back to the original concept of the folk song like a news-paper. The function was to present the message accurately and quickly."

Regardless of its length, the message appeared to get delivered. Two days after the concert, the appellate court freed John Sinclair on bail. An exultant Jerry Rubin said that it was "an incredible trib-ute to the power of the people," and that what was needed now were "Two, three, four . . . many more Ann Arbors!"

Years later Stevie Wonder spoke to a British writer, Robin Denselow, about his appearance at the John Sinclair concert: "We joined in support of him being released. Ultimately, I don't know if I would say 'Everybody smoke grass,' but alcohol for sure has killed more people, and people just accept it . . . "

At the risk of calling into question my own current choice of stay-ing straight, I still believe we were right about acid and we were right about pot. They did blow us loose from the past and they did give us a new perspective, a way of setting ourselves apart from the rest of straight society. There is a kind of knowledge that acid gives you on a cellular level about what's really going on with birth and growth and death and everything else. Like it or not, it's true that psychedelics are a way—not the only way, but clearly an effective way—of gaining tremendous insight into life. The government lied to us about so many things that we just assumed that everything it said was a lie. "If you take that acid, you'll stare at the sun and burn out your eyes." Wrong. "If you take that acid, you'll have bad babies." Wrong. "If you take that acid, you'll immediately think you can fly and jump off a building." Wrong. So, when they said that marijuana was a gateway drug and would lead to harder drugs, we just went, *Right, just like all the other stuff you told us that wasn't true.*

That's where we were wrong. Unfortunately, marijuana was illegal and you had to go to illegal people to get it. Those people would then hand you a gram of cocaine and say, If you think that's fun, try this. And you'd take some and you'd say, Holy shit, energy for free! I feel like I'm ten feet tall, covered with chrome, and I've got wings. This is fantastic! Give me more! Not figuring out that you'd just made one of the worst mistakes of your life. But we didn't know any of that then.

Coincidentally, the very first benefit concert that Graham Nash and I ever did together—just the two of us without either Stephen or Neil—also happened in Michigan, and it was also in that same year, 1971. It was for the Vietnam Veterans Against the War, who were taking tremendous personal risks by trying to expose the American atrocities in Vietnam. At the same time that Lt. William Calley was on trial for his part in the My Lai massacre of Vietnamese civilians, the Vietnam Veterans held a moot court in Detroit (chosen because it represented the heartland of America). Over a three-day period, powerful testimony was given by veterans who recounted their own experiences of officially sanctioned brutality similar to My Lai. They called these hearings the Winter Soldier Investigations, taking the name from Thomas Paine's letter to General Washington's troops: "These are the times that try men's souls. The summer soldier and the sunshine patriot will in this crisis, shrink from the service of his country; but he that stands it now, deserves the love and thanks of man and woman."

Jane Fonda had originally approached Nash and me about doing a concert in Detroit on the eve of the hearings, and we immediately told her yes. We'd been talking about playing together just as a duo for a while, but we'd never done it. So the Winter Soldier benefit became the first time that Crosby and Nash ever played together in public. It was a fantastic event; the crowd was incredibly into the music and stoked at the fact of us being there to show support. I was hoping it would get us on Nixon's Enemies List. I said at the time that I would rather have been on that list than have won a Grammy or an Academy Award. It was the height of my aspirations. Although we didn't perform with him, Phil Ochs also did a Winter Soldier benefit and I believe he actually did make it onto Nixon's list . . .

Nash wrote a song that's on his *Wild Tales* album called "Winter Soldier (Oh! Camil)." It was inspired by the story of Scott Camil who . . . well, let Graham tell it: "I heard this phenomenal story about a gung ho soldier who comes back from a tour of duty in Vietnam to some of his friends who are saying: 'Hey, you're being fucked with here. This is not real. We're dying by the thousands and the government is changing its mind constantly about the truth of what's going on over there.' So he became a leader of the Vietnam Veterans Against the War and was persecuted by the government (he was audited by the IRS). At one point, someone even shot him in the back for his troubles. Later I actually met him and we had tea together up on the top floor of my house in San Francisco. He told me his story personally . . . about getting shot, about getting arrested for his beliefs. I believe Scott Camil was a hero."

Events like the Free John Sinclair concert and the Winter Soldier benefit grew out of our need to respond to misery that was visited on innocent human beings by other not-so-innocent human beings.

Unfortunately, the destruction caused by natural disasters exceeds even mans' seemingly unlimited capacity to do damage to himself and the planet. Two days before Christmas in 1972, Managua, the capital city of Nicaragua, was devastated by an earthquake registering 6.2 on the Richter scale. Six thousand people were killed, more than 20,000 were injured, and 350,000 were left homeless. As with most catastrophes, it usually takes a personal connection to put a human face on something so overwhelming. For Bangladesh, Ravi Shankar was that person, the human connection who first brought the crisis to the attention of the world—and particularly to George Harrison. When the earth shook in Nicaragua, it had an immediate impact on one Nicaraguan-born woman living in London with her husband, a musician who just happened to be Mick Jagger. Bianca Jagger's parents still lived in Managua and because of the almost complete destruction of Nicaragua's infrastructure, their daughter had no way of knowing if they were alive or dead. Desperate for any information, Bianca and Mick quickly flew to Jamaica, where they chartered an airplane to Managua, taking with them badly needed medical aid and personally doing volunteer work with the Red Cross. (It was on a similar mission of mercy that the great Latin baseball player Roberto Clemente lost his life only a few days later when his own plane, overburdened with supplies, went down en route to Nicaragua.) In fact, initial news out of Managua was so sketchy that Mick and Bianca's whereabouts were in doubt after their arrival, leading to a rash of "Is Mick Dead?" stories around the world. For Bianca, at least, the news turned out all right. After Mick arranged for radio appeals asking for information about his wife's parents, they turned up safely in the nearby town of León.

Moved by the enormity of the human tragedy they'd just witnessed firsthand, Mick and Bianca left Nicaragua resolved to find other ways to help relieve the tremendous suffering there. With unprecedented speed and the invaluable help of Bill Graham (who would later produce some of the biggest benefit concerts ever staged, including the U.S. portion of Live Aid and the Amnesty International world tour), a Rolling Stones benefit concert was scheduled in Los Angeles for January 18, 1973, less than a month after the earthquake struck and only a couple of weeks after Mick and Bianca left Nicaragua. Even though at ten, fifteen, and a hundred dollars the ticket prices were higher than for any previous rock concert, almost all of the eighteen thousand seats were snapped up instantly. The show, which would include performances by Santana and Cheech & Chong, was set for the Forum, the still-new basketball arena that was home to the Los Angeles Lakers.

Carlos Santana remembers it as an amazing night: "At the Forum . . . I remember very well because Cheech & Chong followed us, so it was a riot. It was really funny and then the Rolling Stones followed them. When musicians offer their passion, their music, their sound, their vibration, for something more than just another house or paying the rent or the salaries, it always takes on [something special] . . . I guess what I'm trying to say is that musicians always play better when they play for free."

The show began at 8:30 P.M. when Bill Graham came to the microphone to request a minute of silent meditation for the Nicaraguan earthquake victims. Santana opened the musical part of the program with a sleek hour-long set. (Santana also had a strong personal commitment to playing this benefit. The whole family of their timbales player, Jose "Chepito" Areas, was in León, the same town near Managua in which Bianca's parents had been found alive.)

Cheech & Chong were on next. Tommy Chong deadpanned that "We're doing this benefit so if we have an earthquake, Nicaragua will help *us.*" Then, after a forty-five-minute set change, it was time for the Stones.

Writing for *Rolling Stone* magazine, Ben Fong-Torres vividly described Mick's entrance: "Jagger is a caped peacock; peaking already as he holds a rhinestone-studded black costume ball mask up to his face, glitter onto the already glittering body. He giggles and does away with the prop, whirls around and around in a black cape and tosses it aside, flashing violet lining as he does. Now it's just him in short faded Levi jacket and blue velvet pants, silver patterned stars in silvery stripes running diagonally down the left side. And two scarves, a long white one as a sash; a regulation blue for the neck. And this brilliant glow in his hair: it is a thick rhinestone headband, a crown for Little Queenie, changing colors under the bank of reds and whites and blue lights shining."

Opening with "Brown Sugar," the Stones' tight two-hour set included "Bitch," "Gimme Shelter," "It's All Over Now," "Tumbling Dice," "You Can't Always Get What You Want," "Jumpin' Jack Flash," and "Street Fighting Man." It was after 1:00 A.M. when they returned for their encore. Of course at that hour, they had to do "Midnight Rambler." And they did, exiting the stage with eighteen thousand cheering and stomping fans begging for more. (The Stones didn't do a second encore that night, but I don't doubt that Bill Graham tried hard to persuade them. Once at the Fillmore East, after a CSNY concert where we'd already done three encores, Bill came back to our dressing room to ask for just *one more.* We were exhausted; we just wanted to kick back and get high. That's what we'd started to do when suddenly a hundred dollar bill was slid under our locked dressing room door. Then a second one appeared, and a third. Neil picked one up, looked at the door and, smiling, said, "*More,* Bill." After eight hundred dollars we were all laughing hysterically, which shows how smart Bill was. We did another encore.)

I don't mean to take anything away from Mick's efforts for earthquake relief, because his commitment was clearly heartfelt. But the timing and location of the Nicaraguan concert were not accidental. The Stones were about to embark on a world tour and, because of a previous drug bust, they were having all kinds of difficulties getting visas. Despite their incredible popularity in Japan, that country had already banned them. The United States hadn't yet made a decision and a Hawaii date was looming. The Stones' bass player, Bill Wyman, in his book *Stone Alone,* says that "Mick favoured a Los Angeles venue [for the benefit] since this could help our status with the US government." Mick was absolutely right. After the benefit, they all received their U.S. visas and the Stones were permitted to play their gig in Hawaii.

Bill Wyman is understandably a little cynical about the aftermath of the Nicaraguan benefit, at least as far as the rest of the Stones were concerned. A few months later Mick and Bianca flew to Washington to receive an award for their humanitarian efforts and, as Wyman notes, the rest of the Stones "never even got a letter."

Maybe that's why, although each of the Stones has subsequently performed individually at benefits, the Nicaraguan concert still remains the only time the Rolling Stones have performed a benefit show together as a full band.

The bottom line was that almost $500,000 (at the time, the biggest single benefit take in history) was raised for Nicaraguan relief, and that's a very good thing. Unlike the take from the Bangladesh shows, the money got there quickly, owing in large part to Bianca's fierce lobbying of the U.S. government. She obtained a guarantee that Anastasio Somoza, Nicaragua's corrupt dictator, wouldn't get the chance to line his pockets with proceeds from the Stones' show.

As only he can, Carlos Santana sums up the positive impact of the Nicaragua event: "You know, there's a difference between being in the bedroom with somebody naked in bed and being in the kitchen cooking and eating. Each one has its own thing, you know. When people come to this concert and they know it's a benefit and their money—besides watching the Rolling Stones or Santana or Cheech & Chong—they know that their energy vibration, which is money, is going to feed children . . . you have a twinkle in your eye that they have hope and you can say, Look, I also make a difference."

Several months before the Nicaraguan earthquake struck, two other foreign travelers in Latin America, Phil Ochs and Jerry Rubin, had a chance encounter with a young Chilean singer-songwriter named Victor Jara, a man whose life—and death—would one day have a tremendous impact on artist activism around the world.

Ochs's brother Michael remembers that "Jerry Rubin and Phil went down to Chile to check out the Allende Marxist government. I think it was the first freely elected Marxist government, maybe ever. [It was.] And they met Victor Jara, who was a political singer. Jara said, 'If you guys are serious, you want to come down in the mines with me.' And Phil said, 'Definitely.' So they went down into the mines and Phil sang for the miners, and Victor Jara translated it. And when Phil came back he said to me, 'I just met the real thing.' He said, 'Pete Seeger and I are nothing compared to this. I mean here's a man who really *is* what he's saying. We're entertainers. I mean here is the real, real deal.'"

Two years later, with the help of the CIA, the Allende government was overthrown in a military coup. Says Michael: "Allende was killed and Victor Jara was tortured to death in the [sports] stadium. From the reports we heard, they cut off his hands and then said, 'Now play your guitar.' And they cut out his tongue and they said, 'Now sing your songs.' I mean it was just horrific."

A generation later, Peter Gabriel is one of those still affected by the life and death of Victor Jara: "He had great, soulful, simple music that touched the hearts of the people he was playing to and singing for, because in many countries where there is oppression, music is one of the tools through which people can fight. And I think for any musician, it's an amazing story in the sense that a lot of us make very comfortable livings out of the business of writing and performing music. And he lost his life for [doing] exactly the same thing."

Phil Ochs was devastated by the savage murder of his friend. Typically, the outlet for his anger and grief came through taking action. His brother recalls that "Phil tried to raise public consciousness about what happened in Chile and organized an event called An Evening with Salvador Allende.

An Evening with Salvador Allende was held on May 9, 1974, at the Felt Forum in Madison Square Garden. But it almost didn't happen. In addition to Ochs, at first only Pete Seeger, Arlo Guthrie, and Melanie agreed to perform, which wasn't a strong enough lineup to fill the house. A week before the show they'd sold just a thousand tickets, out of the Felt Forum's capacity of forty-five hundred. Ochs had borrowed the money to rent the hall and Ron Delsener, the savvy New York concert promoter who was helping him, advised him to cut his losses and cancel the show. Ochs stubbornly refused, convinced that he could still get one big star to commit to doing the concert in time to sell it out. Incredibly, the first person he tried was *Frank Sinatra*, who didn't take his call (it was probably just as well; Sinatra was by then a Republican who almost certainly would have applauded the CIA's role in the Chilean coup). Then Ochs tried his old friend Joan Baez, who had to turn him down because she was already committed to performing somewhere else that same night. Ochs was crushed.

Finally, at the eleventh hour, fate smiled on the man who once wrote "There but for Fortune." Ochs's desperate pursuit of other acts had taken him down to Greenwich Village to see Buffy Sainte-Marie at the Bottom Line, where he hoped to recruit her for the benefit. Suddenly he heard a familiar nasal voice and turned to see his old friend (and sometime rival) Bob Dylan, the same man who'd forced him out of a taxi ten years earlier for criticizing one of his songs. Dylan was warm. Ochs was psyched, convinced that destiny had just delivered him the one person who could save his Allende show, if he could only persuade Dylan to perform. It wouldn't be easy. Bob hadn't played in New York since the Bangladesh concerts three years before; in fact, in that time, he'd hardly given a live performance anywhere.

A week after their brief meeting, Bob called Ochs and asked if he could come over and visit him in his apartment. Ochs seized the opportunity of having a captive Dylan, and talked nonstop for hours about the political situation in Chile, vividly describing the horrible murder of his friend Victor Jara and detailing the then little known role of the U.S. government in deposing Allende. His passionate oratory was capped by an impromptu reading of Salvador Allende's complete inaugural address. That sealed it. Dylan left the apartment saying that he would almost certainly play (which is as definitive as Bob ever gets). On May 8, the day before the benefit, Ochs went on radio and let it "slip" that Dylan would be the "surprise guest" listed on the poster advertising the show (a poster printed weeks before Ochs had even run into Dylan). All the remaining tickets for An Evening with Salvador Allende were sold out that same day.

Arlo Guthrie says: "And so I went to this concert—they were raising money to help get people out of Chile because things were getting bad and they needed to get money. They were actually bribing people to get people out. The only thing I remember of the event . . . well, I remember a couple of things. I remember most everybody was drunk. That was the first thing I remember. I was too young so that I might have been the only person there that hadn't had anything to drink. But during the show at some point backstage a woman came up to me, beautiful woman, and she handed me a piece of paper and she said, 'This is a poem written about my husband, who has been killed in Chile, in the stadium.' And I'd never heard of the guy. His name was Victor Jara. It was a poem written by an English poet named Adrian Mitchell. And I was so moved by it. I just read it. And I said, 'You know, I don't normally do this.' But I took the piece of paper and I put it on the piano, on the stage, when it was my turn to sing. And I just made up a tune right then and there and sang this thing as best I could. I went on later to finish the song and record it. And it's still one of the most powerful songs I ever recorded."

Yes, it is. Phil Ochs must have had Arlo in mind when he wrote, "A protest song is a song that's so specific that you cannot mistake it for bullshit."

Victor Jara of Chile
Lived like a shooting star
He fought for the people of Chile
With his songs and his guitar
His hands were gentle, his hands were strong
Victor Jara was a peasant
He worked from a few years old
He sat upon his father's plow
And watched the earth unfold
His hands were gentle, his hands were strong
Now when the neighbors had a wedding
Or one of their children died
His mother sang all night for them
With Victor by her side
His hands were gentle, his hands were strong
He grew up to be a fighter
Against the people's wrongs
He listened to their grief and joy
And turned them into songs
His hands were gentle, his hands were strong
He sang about the copper miners
And those who worked the land
He sang about the factory workers
And they knew he was their man
His hands were gentle, his hands were strong
He campaigned for Allende
Working night and day
He sang "Take hold of your brother's hand
You know the future begins today"
His hands were gentle, his hands were strong
Then the generals seized Chile

They arrested Victor then
They caged him in a stadium
With five thousand frightened men
His hands were gentle, his hands were strong
Victor stood in the stadium
His voice was brave and strong
And he sang for his fellow prisoners
Till the guards cut short his song
His hands were gentle, his hands were strong
They broke the bones in both his hands
They beat him on the head
They tore him with electric shocks
And then they shot him dead
His hands were gentle, his hands were strong

I want to say something here about Arlo Guthrie. Early on Arlo absorbed the activist ethic at his father's knee, then studied it under Pete Seeger. He really got it at an early age. And with a sense of outrage tempered by a wonderful wry sense of humor, he was able to do a song like "Alice's Restaurant," which is one of the greatest and subtlest antiwar songs of all time. You still hear it on the radio every Thanksgiving . . . he's turned on several more generations to the idea of questioning authority. He was, and remains, a wonderful example of an activist musician. It's in his blood, and he handles it with great skill and style, *and* he's humble about it. He's just a wonderful cat.

I wasn't at the Allende show, but Ochs's sister Sunny sent me a tape that audibly confirms Arlo's memory of it. In her note she says, "I was really angry at the display of drunken abandon. I felt it was an insult to the Allende family. [Allende's widow was in the audience.] The guys were passing a jug on stage." She also sent along a surprisingly candid press release issued by the event staff the day after the event: "The evening opened with Seeger singing the old Cuban resistance song 'Guantanamera' and Arlo Guthrie playing guitar accompaniment. It concluded, five hours later, with Guthrie singing 'Deportees,' about the Mexican wetbacks, while Bob Dylan, who forgot the words, backed him up on guitar."

That's not to say that there weren't some powerful, even riveting moments during the show. In addition to Arlo's spontaneous tribute to Victor Jara, folksinger Dave Van Ronk did a moving version of our Byrds' song "He Was a Friend of Mine" (which we'd always dedicated to another assassinated president), and there were emotional speeches from Dennis Hopper, Daniel Ellsberg, and Victor Jara's widow, Joan. The weirdest part of the night had to be when the Beach Boys' Michael Love and Dennis Wilson tried to get the crowd to sing along with them on "California Girls." They barely made it offstage alive.

Ochs was both drunk and wired throughout the show, choosing not to perform but rather to act as a master of ceremonies, and an often hostile one at that. Deni Frand, who organized the entire night, says, "Phil got onstage and started screaming at the audience, 'We're not here to fuck the stars, we're here to save the Chilean refugees'. . . It was really just an amazing thing. He didn't care if they [the audience] came for Chile, but once they got there he insisted that they learn while they were there. It was a manic thing but it was also a very important thing to him. It took money and effort to make this [concert] and he wanted everyone to understand what had happened in Chile."

Despite its musical sloppiness, in some ways An Evening with Salvador Allende exceeded even Ochs's grandiose expectations. Not only did the event raise money for the Friends of Chile, but Dylan's presence at it—no matter how brief—brought renewed media attention to the issue of U.S. involvement in Chile and to the CIA's role in toppling a freely elected government.

Initially, the Allende show also appeared to be a great personal victory for Phil Ochs. Its success seemed to validate his abilities as an organizer, and as an unexpected bonus, it temporarily restored his old friendship with Dylan. In fact, a few days after the benefit, Ochs and Dylan set up a meeting with Ron Delsener to discuss their plan to do an entire benefit tour, using the Allende show as a model.

Their idea was to gather a group of like-minded musicians and take them out on the road, playing smaller venues that would require only minimal promotion to sell out. All the proceeds would be divided among charities chosen by the artists. Unfortunately, their plan died on the drawing board. Ochs was still so wired that he couldn't focus long enough to follow through with it. He missed his own meeting with Delsener and by the time he tried to reschedule, it was too late. Bob had moved on to other things and the window of opportunity for a Dylan-Ochs benefit tour had closed.

Only a year later, however, Bob would revive the notion of taking a group of musicians on the road with him, although this time it wasn't planned as a benefit tour. Their original idea was transformed into what became Dylan's now-legendary Rolling Thunder Revue, a tour that included everyone from Joan Baez to Robbie Robertson to Joni Mitchell to Roger McGuinn.

It was a tour that Phil Ochs was never asked to join.

At the same time the Allende concert was going on in New York, Crosby, Stills, Nash & Young were in California getting ready to go out on the road for our first full tour. We were booked into stadiums across America. Although the Beatles had played a few arenas like Shea Stadium and Candlestick Park, this would be the first time that any band had ever done a whole tour in venues of that size. It was a huge logistical undertaking, much like sending an army into battle. There were no blueprints to follow, no Rolling Stones or Grateful Dead tours to study—those wouldn't happen until a lot later. We knew we needed the best possible support, since no one had ever pulled off anything of this magnitude before.

The man we chose to promote that tour was Bill Graham. There was no one else we even considered.

What can I say about Bill? Bill Graham was a feisty, sometimes objectionable, always charismatic, very world-wise, very tough guy, but he was a good man when it came to helping other human beings because he understood hard times. He'd been there himself. I think the best description of Bill Graham I've ever heard was the one Jackson Browne used at his wake: "Bill Graham was a volunteer."

"I met Bill Graham when I was about fifteen or sixteen," recalls Jackson. "My sister was going out with a guy in the San Francisco Mime Troupe. And there was a show called *Jim Crow a Go Go or Civil Rights in a Cracker Barrel*. It was a minstrel show. Half the guys were white and half of them were black, and they were all in blackface. And it was sort of a comedy review about civil rights. This was probably around 1967 in Haight-Ashbury. I met Bill Graham probably a year or two before he started doing shows at the Fillmore. But even then he had a sense of community and a sense of what to do in order to make things happen. I think that his enterprise came out of the impulse to do something for the community . . . to give a party for everybody. He was a really interesting guy. He came to the United States as a refugee fleeing Nazi Germany. He was one of a handful of children on a boat that was not allowed to dock in the United States. In the end, the boat was turned back, but Bill Graham was taken off the boat and got into the United States in the forties sometime during or right after World War II."

Bob Barsotti, the man who now runs Bill Graham Presents, takes up the story: "[Bill] always felt strong about giving back to his community. Coming from his background of a war refugee, escaping the Holocaust in Germany and walking through Europe with a group of kids of which most of them died, including his sister, on the way to Morocco, and then on to Cuba and then to Ellis Island where people kept passing him up because he was kind of an ugly kid. He remembers people coming up and looking [at him] and shaking their heads and going on to the next kid. He said it was pretty disappointing. So when he got to the point where he had something in his life, he felt it was important to give back to the community. And he had a very strong ethic that way."

Carlos Santana loved Bill like a father. It was Bill who gave him his first break as a kid, putting him on a bill at the Fillmore when no one had ever heard of him. "Bill Graham was the Cecil B. DeMille of transforming consciousness for musicians," says Carlos. "[Bill] was the first to have enough cojones to tell the Grateful Dead: 'You're headliners, but Miles Davis is going to open up. Ten years after, you're going to headline but Buddy Rich is going to open up. Santana, you're going to headline but Roland Kirk is going to open up.' What that meant is that the hippies who came to the concert, they would be assaulted, their senses would be assaulted with Miles Davis, Roland Kirk, Buddy Rich. In other words, you can have your dessert, but first you gotta eat your vegetables."

Carlos is right, if there's one thing Bill had in spades, it was cojones. We got into it once about my not being able to get into a gig that I was playing at. *My own gig.* I threatened to kill him, and he said, "You shut the hell up or I'll break your fingers right now."

We were just venting to each other. He wouldn't hurt me and I wouldn't hurt him. We both had tempers, and we weren't afraid to express them, but underneath that white-hot temper, Bill had a huge heart. He was always ready to help if someone came to him with something that really made sense: "Hey, our schools need this" or "Hey, those people over there are getting shafted" or "Hey, this is poisoning where we live . . . "

"Bill had the respect of the industry because he was a very effective concert promoter, *and* he had a great rapport with artists," says Jackson Browne. "Also, he had real street-level experience, experiential wisdom about what the world's about and what's important."

Early in 1975, Bill read an item in a San Francisco newspaper that made him so angry he decided he had to do something about it himself—this time without waiting to be asked. Says Barsotti, "When the San Francisco School District found themselves short of money and they were going to cut out all their sports programs and music programs, [Bill] decided this was absolutely outrageous. So he put together the SNACK concert at Kezar Stadium, and it stood for Students Need Athletics Culture and Kicks."

In his autobiography, written with Robert Greenfield, Bill said that "SNACK really was the first big rock benefit concert ever done. The Bay Area musicians were called to arms and they responded to the call. For me, it represented the use of the drawing power of our artists to address and attempt to solve a social problem." Added

Bill, "We make our living from the youth of San Francisco. This is one way we hope to thank them."

I remember the SNACK concert very well, because I'll never forget the reason I *wasn't* there. The date was March 23, 1975, the day my daughter Donovan was born. Much later I found out that Bill made an announcement of her birth right from the stage and sixty thousand cheering people welcomed Donovan into the world. (I'm still cheering.)

In his book, Bill wrote that "It was one of the few times that I *personally* approached all the artists. The Grateful Dead, Graham Central Station, Jefferson Starship, Tower of Power, the Doobie Brothers, Santana, Mimi Farina, and Neil Young."

The people who worked with Bill had almost never seen him this fired up about an event. Recalls Barsotti, "He didn't often do that, mainly because he was in the business of presenting live concerts and when you start asking artists to work for free, then the next time they come around they'll say, Well, I worked for free last time, so I want more money this time. So his standard answer was, 'You get the artist, I'll produce the show.' [SNACK was] the one big exception to that. And we got all these big bands. He called everyone that he knew and he put together an amazing show. We had a separate stage on the side where we had all the great San Francisco sports stars from over the years. And in front of that stage was a big donation bucket and people could come up onto that stage, get one of the posters of the concert, have their favorite sports hero sign it, and then put a donation into the bucket. And we raised another ten or fifteen thousand dollars that way. That was my first job—I was in charge of that stage. And I got Willie Mays's autograph on my SNACK poster, which was great for me."

By all accounts—and I've talked to a lot of people about that day—SNACK was an absolutely amazing event. The music reviewer for *Melody Maker*, Todd Tolces, called it "the most important musical event San Francisco has ever seen." *After Dark* magazine said it was "a harking-back to times when rock wasn't all hype and money and problems and slick showmanship."

Not that there weren't some problems. The entire week before the show, it rained steadily in San Francisco. All week. Hard. Kezar Stadium was outdoors, so Bill was very worried. The evening before the show, it poured again. Bill was up all night pacing the field, wondering if he'd have to cancel. Canceling meant that it might be months before he could get that same constellation of stars to align itself in one place again, if he ever could. Finally, at about dawn, the rains stopped. The skies cleared and it remained a perfect, sunny day until 6:05 P.M., exactly five minutes after the show ended. Only then did it begin to rain again. Bill said later that "People in the company looked at me in a strange way. They said, 'What did you *do?*'"

Just after 9:00 A.M., Eddie Palmieri, the terrific Latin musician from New York, came onstage to start the daylong show. Carlos says that "Eddie played incredible [and] the Grateful Dead . . . it's the best I ever heard them. They always sound great, but that's the *best* I ever heard them. They went from Mozart to the Grateful Dead to Weather Report to Chuck Berry . . . it was only one breath!"

The Grateful Dead was the first surprise of the day, since the event only advertised a performance by "Jerry Garcia and Friends." At that time, the members of the Dead were on one of their periodic vacations from one another (something I'm pretty familiar with). So when Phil Lesh and Bob Weir came out onstage along with Jerry, the San Francisco crowd went nuts.

Thousands of Deadheads were up and dancing for their whole set, right through the familiar encore of "Johnny B. Goode." Tower of Power was on next, followed by a great performance from home-town favorite Santana. In an unplanned but cool segue from one "black" song to another, Santana's encore of "Black Magic Woman" was followed by the Doobie Brothers' opening up with "Black Water." The Doobies then delivered a high-energy rendition of some of their biggest hits: "Jesus Is Just All Right," "Long Train Runnin'," "Take Me in Your Arms," and "China Grove."

The Doobies' set was followed by a long (and unscheduled) equipment change before the next act, the Jefferson Starship (the seventies' incarnation of the Airplane). The delay was due to the fact that the Starship's bass player, Pete Sears, had somehow gotten himself stuck in crosstown traffic. With nine acts needing to get on and offstage in exactly nine hours, this was not a good thing. There was no margin for error.

Never a patient man, Bill quickly became apoplectic, storming around backstage in a purple rage, threatening to throw the Starship off the show entirely if their bassist didn't "get his ass" out there *immediately*. Just as Bill was about to pull the plug, Sears arrived and, avoiding any eye contact with Bill, rushed right onstage with the rest of the band. Despite these frantic preliminaries, the Starship played a tight, powerful set of their new material—"Ride the Tiger," "Sweeter Than Honey," "Fastbuck Freddie," "Git Fiddler," "Another World," and "Play on Love." They left the stage with Grace's soaring vocals on "Somebody to Love" still echoing in the farthest sections of the stadium. They did return to do one more song, a perfect choice to underscore the spirit of the event: "Volunteers."

All day long a local radio station that was broadcasting the show live had been dropping hints about the possible appearance of an unbilled surprise guest referred to only as "the man from the Fairmont" (presumably because he'd been spotted checking into the San Francisco hotel of the same name). So when Bill introduced a special guest speaker after the Starship set, a lot of people were certain that this had to be the "surprise."

It wasn't. But the crowd of sixty thousand was *very* surprised when Bill leaned into the microphone and said, "Would you please welcome another friend of ours, and certainly a friend of yours, ladies and gentlemen, a man who needs no introduction—Mr. Marlon Brando!" *Rolling Stone* later described him as "Gone a little to paunch, with thinning hair and a neatly trimmed pepper-and-salt beard . . . he spoke in a voice that occasionally dropped into the tones of Vito Corleone but more often reached out unexpectedly passionate, even desperate for communication with this crowd."

Brando told the crowd that "Nobody in history has witnessed an occasion like this. All these brothers up here—blacks, Chicanos, whites, Indians—people! All the brothers out there—that's you—make this possible. They make this spirit possible. . . . We came here today because some people needed some sports equipment. Some people came to hear the sound. But there's another sound, another sound that we have to listen to—because if we don't listen to it, we're not gonna get it together. It's not my generation—I'm doin' five-oh right now—but your generation's gonna catch the shit that my generation and the people before me have laid down for you . . ."

When I asked Carlos what stands out about that day for him, he said, "The highlight for me was Marlon Brando because he went and spoke and he said something very, very soulful and very clear and very relevant and people gave [him] a great ovation. Bill Graham went to talk to him after and Marlon Brando said, 'I can't talk to you right now.' And he went to the side and started crying. And Bill respected his silence and gave him some space, but later on he came back and said, 'What was that about?' And Marlon Brando said to him, 'Look, I'm an actor and people always pay me to act. I wasn't acting and that's the first time people just clapped for me—for me *being* me. I wasn't reading a script and being a character. This was me, and I am not used to people clapping for me, for my views.' That to me was very deep."

With just an acoustic guitar and a voice so beautiful it can make angels weep, Joan Baez came out as the next-to-last performer of the day. The closing act still remained a mystery. Although Neil had always been listed on the bill, he still hadn't played. And it wasn't clear to the audience if he'd be coming out alone or if "others" might be joining him. (*I* knew I wasn't going to make it, but that announcement wasn't made to the crowd until later on.)

So all during Joan's set, which included "All My Trials," "Hard Rain," "Help Me Make It Through the Night," "I Shall Be Released," "Joe Hill," and "The Night They Drove Old Dixie Down," there was a low but insistent murmur from the crowd. Who was it going to be? What "surprise guest" could cap an already unbelievable show?

When Joan had finished, Bill went out and quickly put an end to the speculation. With theatrical flair worthy of his friend Brando, he addressed the expectant crowd: "Thank you for waiting. And now, to close it out, may I introduce: on bass, Rick Danko; on keyboards, Garth Hudson; on drums, Levon Helm; on guitar, Tim Drummond; on pedal-steel, Ben Keith; on harmonica and guitar, *Bob Dylan.* And on guitar and piano, Neil Young!"

At that moment, if a bomb had gone off in nearby Golden Gate Park it couldn't have been heard over the roar of joyous disbelief that completely engulfed Kezar Stadium. All the artists had gathered in the wings to watch the only extended Dylan-Young-Band performance the world would ever see. Joan Baez and Marlon Brando were hugging, and Bill was beaming like a proud father (which is what I had just become at that very moment).

The set opened with Neil at the piano doing "Are You Ready for the Country," backed up by Danko and Helm. Two other Neil songs followed, "Lookin' for a Love" and "Darker Side of Me," with Dylan accompanying him on piano and guitar, respectively. Rick Danko took vocals on the classic Four Tops' song "Lovin' You (Is Sweeter Than Ever)," then Dylan sang the lead on one of his own songs, "I Want You." The crowd shouted its approval when the Band struck up the opening chords of "The Weight." Next, they all did "Helpless," with everyone taking his own instrumental turn. "Helpless" flowed seamlessly into the last song of this brief but historic set, a group version of "Knockin' on Heaven's Door" (which, for reasons known only to him, Dylan had changed to "Knockin' on the Dragon's Door" for this show).

After a quick huddle offstage, they all came back out and, for an encore, did that wonderful old hymn "Will the Circle Be Unbroken." Just as he'd done on "Deportees" at the Allende benefit, Dylan forgot some of the words. After the show, Neil told a reporter, "He just said he'd do it. He didn't ask if we knew the words and we didn't ask if he knew them."

More than $200,000 was raised, the after-school programs were saved, and for Bill Graham, the SNACK concert became "one of the few treasured moments of my life."

Sixteen years later, on a stormy October night in 1991, Bill Graham was killed in a helicopter crash outside the Concord

Pavilion in northern California. According to Carlos Santana, Bill had gone there trying to put together one more benefit. "That's how he died. He died on the helicopter going to see Huey Lewis to ask him to play a benefit for the people who got burned in the Oakland fire. He died with his boots on."

Let me state this for the record: Bill Graham was the most powerful organizer of musicians there ever was—or probably ever will be. And he was my friend. I still miss him.

Enough said.

Even before John and Yoko paid for billboards around the world declaring WAR IS OVER, IF YOU WANT IT, Phil Ochs instinctively understood that popular support for U.S. involvement in Vietnam was largely based on societal inertia I talked about previously: People supported our troops because they were already over there; our troops remained over there because people felt obligated to support them as long as they were in harm's way. Before most Americans had even heard of a place called Vietnam, Phil Ochs figured out that the only way to change the mentality of *We're there because we're there* was simply to deny it. As early as 1967, Ochs organized two War Is Over rallies in Los Angeles and New York.

Michael Ochs recalls that "the War Is Over concept, it was way before John Lennon had it. And it wasn't Phil's idea originally. I believe Phil and Allen Ginsberg were sitting around one night and they said, 'Wouldn't it be great if there was a theater of the absurd and, actually, since it isn't a real war, why don't we just declare it over?' And Phil loved it. I'm not sure if Phil came up with the idea first, or if Ginsberg did, but soon thereafter, Phil said, 'Let's do a 'War Is Over' celebration on both coasts and see what happens.' And they did one in Los Angeles—Lyndon Johnson was in Century City at the time and they did it outside the hotel where Johnson was giving his speech. And the cops rioted and beat up a lot of people. That one was iffy. But the one in New York, I was involved in. And that was great. We started at Greenwich Village and walked all the way to Times Square. And half the people believed us, and the other half hated us. But it sure did get the reaction we wanted."

On April 3o, 1975, as the last U.S. troops were helicoptered off the roof of the American embassy building in Saigon to the strains of the military's typically out-of-touch choice of music, Bing Crosby's "White Christmas" (the troops themselves were playing the Animals' "We Gotta Get Out of This Place" over and over again), Phil Ochs and another leading antiwar activist, Cora Weiss, decided that a third War Is Over rally would be the ideal way to celebrate the fact that this time, finally, the war really *was* over. In a burst of energy, Ochs pulled together a lineup that included veteran opponents of the war like Pete Seeger, Harry Belafonte, and Odetta, and younger artists like Paul Simon. Even Joan Baez, with whom Ochs had been angry for not appearing at An Evening with Salvador Allende, agreed to participate. (Joan was apparently impressed by Ochs's superhuman persistence in pulling off the Allende show, and particularly by his success in persuading her notoriously recalcitrant "Bobby" to play a political show.)

Set for Sunday, May 11, 1975 (Mother's Day, a deliberate choice), the rally and concert drew more than 100,000 people to the Sheep Meadow in New York's Central Park. In less than two weeks, often working without sleep for days at a time, Ochs produced an event that expressed the powerful sense of relief that we all felt after so many years of fighting that insane war. Ochs sang his own song "The War Is Over" and with Baez did an emotional duet of "There but for Fortune," the Ochs composition that she—not he—had turned into a hit a decade earlier. But this wasn't a day for pettiness or old grudges. When they finished singing, Joan kissed Ochs on the cheek and his broad smile was proof that peace had finally arrived.

If measured only by its size and the stature of the performers it attracted, Ochs's final War Is Over event would have to be judged a great victory. But if you look at this rally as marking a watershed moment for music activism in America—this was finally the end of the Vietnam War—it's harder to view it as a success. The biggest problem was that no one seemed to know what to do next. Even Michael Ochs says that it "was one of the strangest events I was ever at. It was like now that the dragon is slain, everybody was lost. I mean everybody was there from Paul Simon to George Harrison to Belafonte, Baez, et cetera. And they were all lost. Belafonte tried to get the crowd involved in Indian rights but got no response. I was talking to Paul Simon and I said, 'What do you think?' He said, 'I don't know. I just brought my kid. It's a gorgeous day in the park.'"

Sadly, almost from that moment on, it was Phil Ochs who would never again find peace in his own life. On April 9, 1976, less than a year after that last War Is Over rally in Central Park, Phil Ochs committed suicide. After a painfully public downward spiral fueled by alcohol and punctuated by disastrous bouts with manic depression, he just gave up. His final enemy wasn't the government, or the media, or big business . . . it was himself.

And it wasn't a fair fight; he had no chance to win.

Arlo Guthrie says: "Later on I remember thinking that Phil got so caught up in these events, whether it was the war in Vietnam, or whatever it was, that he was one of these guys [like it] says in the Bible: What does it gain somebody to gain the whole world and lose your own soul? He was one of these guys who had a vast understanding . . . who had a wit and a way with words to make you understand exactly what was going on, but at the same time got so lost in it that he began to disappear. So when these events became less important to the world, he became less important to the world. When there was no longer any Vietnam, there was no longer any Phil."

In 1966, ten years before Phil Ochs would take his life, the shooting deaths of two men and a woman in a bar in Paterson, New Jersey, would have far-reaching consequences for artist activism—consequences that at the time no one could possibly have foreseen.

Immediately after the murders, a middleweight boxer (and potential championship contender) named Rubin "Hurricane" Carter and his friend John Artis—both black men—were picked up and questioned by the police. Neither of them was identified by any of the other people wounded in the shooting. Both were given a lie detector test, which they passed. The police then released them and said they'd never been suspects.

Four months later, Alfred Bello—a white man with a criminal record who was also a suspect in the killings—swore out a statement placing Carter and Artis in the bar on the night of the shootings. On the basis of Bello's affidavit and the equally dubious testimony of another man, Arthur Bradley, Carter and Artis were arrested and indicted for all three murders. Subsequently, they were both convicted by an all-white jury and each was sentenced to three consecutive life terms in prison.

In 1974, after serving eight years of that life sentence, Rubin Carter wrote a book, *The Sixteenth Round*, meticulously detailing how Bello and Bradley had been pressured by the police to identify him and Artis in return for the reward money, as well as for a reduction of the other criminal charges they were facing. The book also documented how both Bello and Bradley had eventually recanted their sworn testimony.

A year later, Hurricane Carter sent a copy of his book to Bob Dylan because of what he said was Dylan's "prior commitment to the civil rights struggle."

In 1985, Bob gave a rare interview to Bill Flanagan for his book *Written in My Soul*. In it, he recounts how he first got involved with Carter's cause: "The people from the Hurricane Carter movement kept calling me and writing me. And Hurricane sent me his book"— amazingly, somehow, the book actually got to Bob—"which I read and which really touched me. I felt that the man was just innocent, from his writings and knowing that part of the country. So I went to visit him. [I] was really behind him, trying to get a new trial."

Bob explained the plight of Hurricane Carter to lyricist Jacques Levy, with whom he was collaborating at the time, and he said, "Why don't you help me write this song and see if we can do something?" So they wrote 'Hurricane.' This is just part of it:

That's the story of the Hurricane,
But it won't be over till they clear his name

And give him back the time he's done.
Put in a prison cell, but one time he coulda been
The champion of the world.

People magazine described "Hurricane" as "a protest song with the gritty urgency and outrage that had once enflamed a whole American generation." Remember Phil Ochs's definition of a protest song? That it has to be "so specific that you cannot mistake it for bullshit"? There's no mistaking "Hurricane" for anything other than what it is—a brilliant fucking song.

Dylan released it as a single and, defying the conventional music industry "wisdom," which says that a long song about a controversial topic is doomed never to be heard, "Hurricane" became an improbable Top Forty hit.

In the fall of 1975, as "Hurricane" was climbing the charts, Dylan and the Rolling Thunder Revue were crisscrossing New England and Canada, playing everything from college campuses and small theaters all the way up to arena-size venues. The tour was set to end on December 8 at Madison Square Garden, but that final show had now become a benefit for the Hurricane Trust Fund, an organization created to help defray the enormous cost of Rubin Carter's lengthy legal appeals.

On December 7, 1975, the night before the New York benefit, the Rolling Thunder Revue made its way out to northwestern New Jersey for a special, semiprivate performance. It was by far the smallest hall the Revue had played, but for the performers it was one of the most important venues of the entire tour. Their audience was comprised of three hundred male and female inmates who were confined (the males only temporarily) to the New Jersey Correctional Institute for Women, a medium-security facility in the town of Clinton. One of those inmates was Rubin "Hurricane" Carter.

It was a surreal scene. The mostly black prisoners treated Roberta Flack as if *she* were the principal star of Rolling Thunder, with Bob Dylan, Joni Mitchell, and Joan Baez reduced to supporting roles in her show. It must have felt like they'd all gone through to the other side of some bizarre looking glass.

Flack's three-song set of "Killing Me Softly," "This Time I'll Be Sweeter," and "Feel Like Making Love" was greeted enthusiastically by the crowd, while they practically ignored Joni. She didn't like it either, telling the crowd, "We came here to give you love; if you can't handle it, that's your problem." (That sounds like Joni.)

Dylan's reception was somewhat more positive, but still subdued. It wasn't until he and the rest of the Revue did "Hurricane" that the audience gave him its full attention. Of all the white singers, it was Joan Baez who made the strongest connection with the inmates, perhaps because she'd also spent her fair share of time on the inside. When she finished singing, Joan gently chided the prison authorities, thanking them for "making it so easy for us to get in." Then, smiling warmly at her audience—and by this point they were *completely* hers—she added, "I just wish they'd make it a little bit easier for you to get out."

It didn't really matter to Dylan if they got a mixed response from the inmates, because they'd accomplished something valuable just by doing the show. The media accompanied them every step of the way (you don't need to tell *me* about how a rock star in prison makes for a good photo opportunity . . .), and the public was given another vivid reminder of how unjust it was that Rubin Carter remained in prison.

The next night, the members of the Rolling Thunder Revue were back on the more familiar side of the looking glass. The crowd of twenty thousand that filled Madison Square Garden up to the rafters was almost entirely Caucasian, and they'd paid $12.50 a ticket (then top dollar) primarily to see and hear a man who couldn't have been any whiter if he'd tried. As a matter of fact, he *did* try. For the whole show, just as they'd done throughout the entire Rolling Thunder tour, Bob and his band all wore a heavy layer of white-face makeup. Writing about the concert in *Rolling Stone*, Chet Flippo noted that "Someone asked whether the band's white-face makeup signified rock theatrics or social irony; perhaps it was a synthesis of the two."

On this occasion, the irony couldn't have been more pronounced. Billed as The Night of the Hurricane, here was a group of predominantly white musicians railing against the injustice done to a black man primarily because he *was* black, and they were doing it in white-face. Still, it was all for a good cause . . .

The concert opened with Bobby Neuwirth, who welcomed the audience into "our living room" before launching into his own brief set. Neuwirth then brought out Mick Ronson, calling him "the man who invented David Bowie." In keeping with that introduction, Ronson covered the Bowie hit "Life on Mars." Ronee Blakely then joined Neuwirth onstage and the two did a Neuwirth song about Hank Williams, "Alabama Dark." Neuwirth then finished with his version of the Joplin classic "Mercedes Benz," before introducing Joni. This crowd greeted her with considerably more enthusiasm than she'd received the night before, but her short set of material—"Shadows and Light," "Edith and the Kingpin," and "Don't Interrupt the Sorrow"—was largely unfamiliar to the audience (someone called out *Woodstock!* but she pretended not to hear). She left the stage to less applause than she got when she first walked out.

If Rubin Carter was at one time considered a strong contender to someday become "champion of the world," the next person to appear onstage made it abundantly clear that he was, and would always be, the Champ. Muhammad Ali, dressed in a black leisure suit, grabbed a microphone and launched into a rambling statement supposedly meant to show support for his "boxing friend" Rubin Carter. It left most people confused, however, and some of them pissed off, particularly when Ali started introducing political figures he liked personally. He did get off one good line about how the celebrity-studded crowd had "the connection and the complexion to get the protection," but it was all downhill from there. Thankfully, his monologue was cut short by a piped-in phone call from Hurricane Carter, who quoted a line from "It's Alright, Ma (I'm Only Bleeding)": "My brother Bob Dylan wrote a song once that said, 'walk upside–down inside handcuffs, Kick my legs to crash it off, Say okay I have had enough, What else can you show me?'" Before hanging up, Carter told the crowd that "I thank you from my heart. I love you all madly."

Politics over, the Rolling Thunder Revue returned to the stage with short performances from Ramblin' Jack Elliott and my former Byrd-mate, Roger McGuinn. But it was almost exactly halfway into the four-hour show before everything got kicked into high gear. That was when a small, white-faced man, his dark curly hair tucked under a Western hat covered with feathers and daisies, ambled onstage for a duet with Bobby Neuwirth on "When I Paint My Masterpiece."

That was just the first of twenty-one songs that Bob Dylan would do before the night was over, some acoustic and some electric, some of them solo and some of them as duets. They included "It Ain't Me, Babe," "The Lonesome Death of Hattie Carroll," "It Takes a Lot to Laugh, It Takes a Train to Cry," "The Times They Are a-Changin'," "I Shall Be Released," "Just Like a Woman," "Knockin' on Heaven's Door," and, of course, "Hurricane."

Reviewing the show for *New York* magazine, writer Nik Cohn said that "In ten years, I'd never seen him work with more intensity . . . he rasped, he roared, he burned."

Finally, after sets from Joan (who did a stunning a cappella version of "Swing Low Sweet Chariot") and Roberta Flack, and an all-star finale of "This Land Is Your Land," the powerful musical storm that was The Night of the Hurricane finally abated. In its wake, it left behind more than $100,000 for the Hurricane Trust Fund. Even more important, the national wave of publicity generated by the concert about the Hurricane Carter case was now stirring up the waters of the judicial system, just as the Free John Sinclair concert had done in Sinclair's case a few years earlier.

If you're wondering how it all turned out for Hurricane Carter, I'll tell you. Three months after the concert, Carter's and Artis's convictions were overturned on appeal and both men were freed on bail. Incredibly, within a year they were both retried and recon- victed, again receiving life sentences. Although Artis would be paroled five years later, it wasn't until 1985 that a federal district court judge found that the prosecution had committed "grave constitutional violations" in its retrial of Rubin Carter and that his conviction had been based on "racism rather than reason and concealment rather than disclosure." Over the vehement objections of the prosecution, the judge ruled that "human decency mandates his immediate release" and, having now spent nineteen years of his life in New Jersey prisons, Rubin "Hurricane" Carter was finally a free man. He moved to Toronto and eventually became a Canadian citizen (it's hard to blame him). With his life returned to him, Carter decided to use his own painful experience to help others who have been denied their full rights in the criminal justice and judicial systems.

He's become an eloquent advocate for justice: "There is a rush to death in our society, a killing climate of fear," he says. "Fear feeds prejudice and inflames passion. When you fear someone, anything is possible—from slavery to anti-Semitism to racism to the McCarthy witch-hunts. Blinded by our fear of crime, we focus only on the symptoms."

There's one final, almost unbelievable postscript to the story of the Hurricane. This article appeared not long ago in the *Toronto Star:*

Hurricane Carter Arrested by Mistake

A man who has become the subject of book and song for serving time for murders he didn't commit was arrested last night by Metro police—wrongly.

Police said they were looking for a black man wearing a brown and white jacket, and that former boxer Rubin "Hurricane" Carter, who was taken into custody for alleged drug trafficking, fit half that description. Carter was wearing a black and white lumberjack coat.

"I am so furious that what happened happened simply because I was wearing a jacket, and I am black," Carter told the *Star* after being released last night.

"It was a drug buy in a dark area, and he resembled the sus-pect," said 12 division Staff Sergeant Mike Pinfold. "It was a case of mistaken identity."

Pinfold called it an honest mistake.

That's the story of the Hurricane,
But it won't be over till they clear his name
And give him back the time he's done.
Put in a prison cell, but one time he coulda been
The champion of the world.

Political Activism:

"Power to the People"

You can't tell a lie when you're singing. You simply

can't. If you're lying it's very obvious. That act

is a political act. Singing, telling the truth is

a political act, whether you mean it to be or not.

Sting

It's strange how rapidly the world can change, in ways you wouldn't ever have believed unless you'd lived through it. Less than thirty years ago, the establishment regarded most rock 'n' roll musicians as little better than outlaws or revolutionaries. Today we're courted by politicians, banks issue credit cards with our pictures on them, you can invest in us on Wall Street (David Bowie futures are traded on the exchange), and you're much more likely to hear the Beatles' song "Revolution" in a fucking commercial than on the radio. (Had John Lennon lived to see that happen, it would have pissed him off beyond words.)

As much as we might hate to admit it, the simple fact is that we all grew up. People who were children during the Vietnam War protests are running those big corporations now. You can be forty years old and running one of the biggest companies in the world. Look at the Fortune 500. Many of the CEOs of those companies were children when we were doing the Vietnam protests. It's my sincere hope that we got to them and that it's going to affect their decision making somewhere along the way.

"During the sixties and the first part of the seventies," says Don Henley, "I think I was subconsciously or subliminally absorbing the information that simply marching in the streets or joining the SDS or growing my hair long and smoking dope and throwing rocks wasn't going to get the job done; that there was a big system in place that was much bigger than even all the baby-boom activism that was going on in the streets. It was even much bigger than the power of rock 'n' roll music. And that the same corporations and the same banks and the same political factions that had always run the country would continue to be running the country unless we got into the system. I didn't feel like rejecting the system and *not* participating in it was going to bring the walls down. That's when I decided that I was going to get involved in politics, for better or for worse, and participate in the system as much as I could stomach it . . . because I just didn't feel like there was any other way."

My earliest political act was something I did when I was a kid, still singing folk songs in coffeehouses and clubs. In between songs, I used to tell a story called "The Egg Thief," which goes something like this: Once upon a time, there was a planet that was ruled by dinosaurs. There were these little tiny furry guys that lived there too. They were so small, the dinosaurs didn't even notice them. They would step on one—squish!—and they wouldn't even know it. But these little furry guys were determined to survive, so they went around and found out where the dinosaurs' eggs were, and they stole them. And they kept stealing them. Until, one day, there weren't any more dinosaurs left.

I've always been an egg thief, trying to tempt the young away from the dinosaurs with a set of alternative values. Because I never believed in what the dinosaurs were saying. I didn't believe John Wayne was right, that war is glorious. I didn't think that George Wallace was right to stand in that schoolhouse door or that J. Edgar Hoover was right when he found communists under every bed. And so I've always seen myself as one of those little furry guys, sneaking around and stealing eggs . . . luring the young away from the dead ideas of the past. Only I get to do it with music.

Sting told me he was once asked at a press conference in Zimbabwe, "How could musicians possibly affect the way political leaders think? They won't even listen to you, what are you doing?" And he answered them this way: "Well, I doubt very much whether your average right-wing politician listens to my music, I think you're right. He doesn't. But his children do. And his grandchildren do. And you're talking about a political class from where future politicians will be recruited and bred. And if we planted a seed in the minds of those children, those young people, then we've done a good job. And it might bear fruit in twenty, forty, fifty years."

Jimmy Buffett describes what we've all seen at one time or another: "I love to watch politicians come to my shows and be fascinated by how the crowd loves us, because they don't get that. And they want that more than anything. So many times people have asked me, 'How do you do that?' I go, 'Because I tell them the truth. I'm not there to make it up. I'm not asking for their money. I'm just doing it.' It's an amazing thing that what they so desperately want, *we* have. And we have it because we're able to do it from the heart."

Jimmy's absolutely right. Politicians have always wanted to be able to communicate with people as effectively as musicians, and most of the time they just can't do it. So the next best thing they *can* do is to get an artist to appear with them. They'll tell you whatever you want to hear to get your help for whatever project is at hand, which is usually getting themselves reelected. They want money for their campaigns, and they want you standing next to them if you're big enough.

I've done it only rarely. It's a very dicey proposition. A few candidates—Ted Kennedy is one who comes to mind immediately—have stood up for principle (at least the principles that matter to me), and I've never regretted supporting someone like that. Others, like Bill Clinton, talk a pretty good game, but when push comes to shove they find some way to wiggle out of the commitments they've made.

Look at what happened to Melissa Etheridge. She worked for Clinton when he ran the first time in 1992. What started out as a pretty black-and-white choice for her ended up becoming a lot grayer: "When he first ran for President, it was kind of a naive time for me. It was the same time my career was just starting to get going and I felt a power, I felt like I can do *something*. . . I can make a difference, I can make a change. I had just publicly embraced my homosexuality. I've always been out personally, but it was the first time that as an artist I'd stepped forward and said, 'Yes, I'm homosexual and these issues are important to me.' And the whole homosexual community was getting behind Bill Clinton. There was a promise there. I did benefits and performances for him because at least he acknowledged that we existed, which is so much more than any other candidate had done. He would say 'gay' and 'lesbian.' Those words would actually come from his mouth and in a positive manner. It was quite exciting. Then he got into office and changes did come, but the promises fell short. And you sort of learn something. The big promise was the first thing he's going to do when he gets into office is to make a Presidential Order that gays could serve in the military. And he tried. But then you just saw the way the world is and what politics really are. And the whole matter of compromise . . . it was quite a lesson. And now when I'm approached by candidates, I really think long and hard and I haven't endorsed a candidate since then for any office."

REM's Michael Stipe has a similar opinion: "You know, it's no mistake that Clinton, in standing next to me with his arm around me in '92 and again in '96 was, probably in his mind, or in the minds of his advisers, hitting several different communities out there. The queer community, the youth community, the rock community. Who knows what else? And I was a little more reticent about standing there in '96 than I was in '92."

Here was a guy who was promising gay people that he would work for fairness in the law, fairness in the workplace, fairness in the military where tons of gay people have served with honor, and he just found it expedient to ditch them. That's my basic problem with most politicians. You can support them, but their morals are the morals of expediency and their loyalty is the loyalty of expediency. If something turns out not to be popular in the polls, they will drop you like a hot rock, and that's not how I live my life.

My friend Whoopi Goldberg is somewhat less cynical about politicians than I am. She says, "I do them [political benefits]. I do them for the people I believe in. Sometimes they drop the ball. Doesn't mean they're bad people. But I'd rather get out there and try to help somebody raise some money than be faced with the alternative."

When I asked Sting what he thinks about the idea of artists supporting political candidates, he considered the question carefully before answering. Then, as you'd expect from someone who started out as a teacher, he spoke softly but precisely, "There is a downside to celebrity and advocacy. It's not all a bed of roses. You can be abused and used by the wrong people sometimes. You have to be very careful what you attach your name to. Politicians are a certain breed of person. They're usually recruited from the legal community, where the truth is the fallback position. They're tricky. It's best not to get too involved with politicians."

I put the same question to Carly Simon and got almost the exact opposite answer: "I think it is the best way of affecting the most people, by going for the candidate, by becoming active for the candidate who you believe is going to make the changes that you want to have made for the world."

John Mellencamp and Don Henley are about as far apart on this subject as two people can be. When we talked backstage at one of the Farm Aid benefits, Mellencamp was very frank (and very funny) in giving me his take on politicians: "I mean, if there's a worser breed of rock star, it's them—people that will do anything to further

themselves. We've had a few politicians at Farm Aid who were genuinely interested. But, you know, Willie Nelson and I went to D.C.
and testified in front of a Senate subcommittee. And the truth of
the matter is that once they saw Willie didn't have his guitar with
him, most of them left. I looked at him and said, 'We're fucking
monkeys on a string here, man. I'm leaving. You know, if you're
gonna play, they're gonna stay. If you're not gonna play, they're not
gonna listen.'"

Later on, Henley (who wasn't referring to Mellencamp) told me
he gets "very frustrated when people make big, blanket statements
like 'All politicians are corrupt. All politicians are jerks and bad
guys.' They're not. There are some very good people in there, but
like any other system, it's got bad apples in it. But that doesn't
mean that you don't participate. You just simply try to make it
better."

I've known Paul Kantner for almost thirty-five years. We've lived
together, gotten high together, played music together. Other than
me, he's probably the most opinionated guy I know. And one of the
brightest. But don't get him wound up on the subject of politics and
politicians: "They're so . . . politicians are so *smarmy*, you can't
trust them. Why bother with them? Whenever Newt Gingrich would
come on TV, I would make it a philosophical point of reaching for
my remote control and turning the television off, just to get him out.
You know, it's like *Beavis and Butt-Head* when some obnoxious
band comes on and they scream and scream, 'Change it! Change it!
It's going to ruin the pixels, get it off, get it off, get it off!' Within
about six months after I started doing it, Newt Gingrich was in a lot
of trouble. And I like to think it was from me picking up my remote
and turning him off. In a sense I feel sorry for politicians at the end
of this century because there's nothing they can really do about
what's going on. And they're almost pointless to deal with because
they are so removed from reality and the streets that they can't deal
with it on that level. They deal with it on a level of sound bites, they
deal with it on a level of 'How will it affect my next election? How
much money can I raise?' Blah, blah, blah, *blah*. . . . "

For every Paul Kantner, there also seems to be a Bonnie Raitt: "Anybody who decides, from high school on, to take on the stomach-churning job of running for office—the amount of time out of their lives they devote even to running for county supervisor, and then to get to the point where they're going to run for Congress—that's such an incredible arc for a life of service, that the least I can do is give them some support when they feel the same way I do about issues. There are some people, some individual candidates, who in my opinion should almost be elevated to the level of saint. And they deserve my support. So on occasion I do receptions and concerts and make donations to people I think are making a big difference."

Everyone knows that Carlos Santana is a brilliant musician. He's also a deeply spiritual human being who's given considerable thought to the whole question of performing not only for politicians, but for political institutions as well. Says Carlos, "I declined three times to perform for Mr. Clinton. I was invited to go to Cuba many times. For Castro I cannot play. I cannot play for Castro or the President because they represent a different agenda than the highest good for all people. Certain people to me represent a different agenda. And their agenda to me is like wrestling—people scream and they hit each other and they spit at each other and they curse each other, kick each other. But when they go home, they get a check from the same person."

"I was invited to play for the Pope," continues Carlos, "[but] I didn't play there, either. I cannot play for the Pope, knowing that he represents an institution that is worth three trillion dollars, knowing that half of that could feed the world for the next hundred years. It's just that simple. I'll play for the heart of people and for Christ. And I'll give my life. For the institution, *nada.* Because they already have enough. I hear the notes behind the notes. Melodies beyond melodies. And I think that if I play for those people, nothing is going to come out of me because I'm just not going to hear any music. If I go play for free, for the heart of people, I'll hear it."

Even though I share Carlos's view that politicians are very seldom working for the highest good of all the people, to be fair I need to say that my coauthor on this book, David Bender, doesn't agree with me on this. Like Henley, he believes that there are at least as many good apples in politics as there are bad ones. They make a good case, but I'm still not persuaded. . . .

In 1972, David Bender was lucky enough to have a ticket to one of the first and most successful musical benefit concerts ever organized on behalf of a politician. "Four for McGovern" was organized by actor Warren Beatty, one of George McGovern's earliest supporters in his campaign to win the Democratic nomination and challenge Richard Nixon. Beatty had called on everyone he knew in Hollywood and the music industry to help put the event together. The "Four" were Carole King (who had just released *Tapestry*), James Taylor, Quincy Jones, and, in what would be her first public performance in more than six years, Barbra Streisand. Beatty had chosen the Los Angeles Forum as the site of the concert, which would take place on April 15, 1972, six weeks before the crucial California presidential primary election.

Carole King says that "The first time somebody came to me and said 'Let's do a benefit' was for George McGovern, when he was running for president in 1972. They had James Taylor and Barbra Streisand and Quincy Jones set to do this concert to raise money for him. And I really liked his politics. I liked a lot of the things he was saying. He was speaking for me and my generation. I said 'Absolutely.' Plus, it was a chance to play with some great people."

Carole and James Taylor came out onstage together to a tremendous ovation from the sellout crowd, some of whom had paid a hundred dollars for seats on the floor, while others, like the fifteen-year-old David Bender, had paid $5.50 for a seat that was almost within arm's reach of the Forum ceiling. Although he couldn't see their faces clearly, David can still tell you exactly what he heard that night: "Carole King and James Taylor started off by doing a duet on one of her songs, 'Song of Long Ago'; then they did James's 'Close Your Eyes,' a song I love, as did most of the crowd, judging from the response it got. I remember James then did several of his songs: 'Brighten Your Night with My Day,' 'Country

Roads,' 'Let Me Ride,' and 'Mudslide Slim.' He finished up by doing 'Fire and Rain,' and the entire arena was singing along with him on every word."

After James left the stage, Carole did several songs, beginning with one of her biggest hits from *Tapestry*, "It's Too Late." She followed that with "Sweet Season" and "Natural Woman," then James came back out to play guitar on another *Tapestry* favorite, "So Far Away." Their set ended in the only way it could, with a crowd-pleasing Taylor-King duet on "You've Got a Friend." When it was over, eighteen thousand people rose to their feet in a warm show of appreciation.

Reflecting on the unusual intensity of the audience that night, Carole told me, "There's a little different vibe, a little different energy than when they come in just paying to hear the music. They're paying for a little extra something, and it brings everyone more together than just going to see a concert. That was part of the magic. And part of it was just watching the other performers, watching James, who I'd been on the road with a lot anyway. The political energy, the energy of working for something beyond just making music was . . . it kicked it up into the next groove."

During the intermission following Carole and James's performance, many of the Hollywood celebrities recruited by Beatty as VIP "ushers" could be seen milling about on the Forum floor, including Jack Nicholson, James Earl Jones, Goldie Hawn, Gene Hackman, Burt Lancaster, Jon Voight, Cass Elliot, and Carly Simon. There was, however, one very important person who was conspicuously absent. Senator George McGovern, the beneficiary of this event, was nowhere to be seen.

Miles Rubin, who chaired McGovern's presidential campaign in California and who, along with Beatty, was the driving force behind the Four for McGovern concert, recalls that "suddenly it was clear he wasn't going to get there." McGovern had been en route to Los Angeles from the East Coast when he'd been told that Nixon was going to announce a major new bombing campaign of North Vietnam, once more escalating a war he'd spent the last four years promising to end. "They decided it was necessary for him to make an immediate statement, so they got the plane to stop down in Detroit," says Rubin.

Only a few people in the Forum knew about this dramatic turn of events, and they kept it to themselves. In keeping with time-honored tradition, the show went on. Quincy Jones, resplendent in a violet-colored robe, came onstage next, accompanied by a huge ensemble of musicians and singers. "Q" and company proceeded to put some real soul into the evening with "What's Going On" and their power-house rendition of "Oh Happy Day."

Then it was finally time for the person whose mere willingness to appear had transformed Four for McGovern from a concert into a genuine musical "event." Barbra Streisand's notorious stage fright had kept her from performing in public since 1966, and many in the audience could hardly believe that they would finally get to see their reclusive idol in the flesh.

Dressed in a black satin pantsuit and a red tank top, Barbra Streisand walked out onto the Forum stage to an instant standing ovation. Opening with "Sing," the *Sesame Street* favorite, Barbra told the audience that it was a request from her young son, Jason. She then moved effortlessly into "Make Your Own Kind of Music" and "Starting Here, Starting Now," before launching into a high-voltage rendition of her show-stopping number from *Funny Girl*, "Don't Rain on My Parade."

After another standing ovation, Barbra paused to chat with the crowd. Sipping tea from a small cup, she told them how she was coping with her jittery nerves: "I've got to tell you this funny thing . . . well, it's not so funny . . . but talking about being scared. I was even more scared till I spoke to friends of mine, also performers you know, and they were telling me . . . that in order to conquer their fear . . . well, some of them drink. But I really hate the taste of liquor, so I can't do that. And some of them . . . take pills. But I can't even swallow *aspirin*, so I can't do that. But, more important than that, I have found, and I believe, that performers should be very strong, you know . . ." At that moment she took an exaggerated drag off of what appeared to be a joint (but wasn't), a move that brought laughter and considerable applause from the huge crowd. In mock surprise, she asked, "It's still illegal?" Then, taking another big "toke," she spoke through clenched teeth and said, "We should face our problems head on."

As the laughter and applause were still dying down, Streisand slowly began to sing once more: "On a clear day . . ." This was followed by a rollicking "Sweet Inspiration," which wove right into her own version of Carole King's "Where You Lead." Changing tempo again, she took the audience into emotional territory only she could reach with her sweet, soulful readings of "Didn't We" and "My Man." Then, in the spirit of the democratic process that had brought them all together, she offered the crowd an opportunity to vote on her next song: either "Second Hand Rose" or her rock hit "Stoney End." It was no contest. If the Streisand fans were divided, the King-Taylor-Jones constituency was not; their votes easily put "Stoney End" over the top.

A reprise of her son's favorite song from *Sesame Street* turned into a slow, almost mournful version of that old political rally song "Happy Days Are Here Again." (Perhaps Barbra had been told about the renewed bombing of North Vietnam. If so, she didn't let on.)

David Bender says, "When Streisand did 'Happy Days Are Here Again,' you could've heard a pin drop in the Forum, even from where I was sitting. Like a lot of people, I'd gone there that night primarily to see Carole King and James Taylor, and they were great. But Streisand was . . . *mesmerizing.* By the time she left the stage, the entire crowd was in the palm of her hand. And when she finally came back out and did 'People,' the whole place just erupted all over again."

As she received the last of her six standing ovations that night, Streisand turned to see George McGovern striding toward her onstage. He'd made it after all. Miles Rubin says that after the stopover in Detroit, "he got back on the plane and the concert was well under way and it wasn't clear at all that we'd get him there [in time]. So I decided to leave the concert, which I did, and get out to the airport. And I had a couple of police cars as an escort. We got him there, literally, as it came to an end."

Wisely, McGovern spoke only very briefly, thanking the artists and the audience. Then, with perfect political pitch, he struck the evening's final note by quoting "The Beatles [who] sang, two years ago, 'Here comes the sun and it's gonna be all right.' We'll be back in California soon, and I think we're going to see the sun again."

"I always say the concert in California was a cause," says Miles Rubin today. "That's the best way to describe it. You're talking about a unique concert; people were going crazy and it was a very, very high evening. There have been lots of concerts since then, but I don't think any of them quite married the artists, the enthusiasm, and the cause itself . . . it all came together at that point."

(Over the next twenty years, Streisand would perform again on only a handful of occasions, almost all of them for political candidates. In 1986, she hosted and performed at a spectacular fund-raising concert in her Malibu backyard for the Hollywood Women's Political Committee, a political action group formed by women in the entertainment industry to support progressive candidates. The event brought in more than a million dollars in one night. Later broadcast as a television special and released on CD, Streisand's One Voice concert added $7 million more to its take, making it one of the most successful political concerts in history.)

My partner Stephen Stills has always been very politically aware and involved. So I remember paying attention when he started talking to me about this obscure former governor of Georgia named Jimmy Carter, who Stephen said had a good shot at becoming the next president of the United States. That was in early 1975, almost a year before most people had even heard of Carter. Although I didn't know it, Carter was already running hard, moving around the country, raising money, trying to get himself on the map.

Almost from the beginning Jimmy Carter recognized that recruiting support from the music community would provide his campaign with a big boost of both money and visibility. Stephen, who later got very involved in the Carter campaign, says that it was one of Carter's sons who helped inspire the idea: "I heard a story that the whole thing resulted from when Chip Carter was living on a commune down in southern Georgia. Jimmy Carter went down there and realized early one morning, as he was talking to these kids in the commune about their concerns, that young people had played a large part in his decision to run in the first place. And so he reached out and asked for these people's involvement way early on, musicians who could help him connect with young people. Because if you remember the seventies, we were still very disconnected about that war, and peace with honor, and their entire generation just flat refusing—in the face of horrifying evidence—to admit that we'd made a mistake. And so an entire generation had completely disassociated itself from the political process. And wisely, Jimmy looked to the music and to the arts to try and reconnect with young people."

At about the same time, Phil Walden, who ran the Capricorn Records label, became a close adviser and supporter of Carter's. One of the biggest Capricorn acts happened to be a Georgia band named the Allman Brothers (supposedly Carter's favorite group). The Carter campaign was really struggling for money in the fall of 1975 when Walden agreed to put together several benefit concerts for it, including a big event in Providence, Rhode Island, headlined by the Allmans. Those events helped bring in more than $400,000 (which was doubled by federal matching funds), and that money, along with the national attention he received from having the Allman Brothers' support, almost certainly carried Jimmy Carter through to victory in the New Hampshire primary. Strange but true: Jimmy Carter might never have been president without the Allman Brothers behind him.

It's often been said that no good deed goes unpunished. While the campaign was still under way, Gregg Allman was threatened with indictment by a federal grand jury unless he testified against one of the band's employees in a drug investigation. The guy wound up getting seventy-five years in prison, and the other band members felt that Gregg had betrayed them. At the time, Dickie Betts said, "There is no way we can work with Gregg again, ever." Fittingly, it was Carter's inauguration in 1977 that gave them an opportunity to bury the hatchet. Dickie later said he'd come to believe they were "set up by a Republican administration that was trying to discredit Jimmy Carter through his connection with Phil Walden and us."

After Carter was elected, Crosby, Stills & Nash were invited to the White House, kind of as a thank-you to Stephen for all of his help during the campaign. It was a funny time because it was sort of the Drug Culture meets the Peanut People. There was certainly not a lot of common ground there, but Carter was very nice to us. The one really dumb thing was that one of the guys who was managing some of us at the time thought it would make for a great story if he could say he'd lit up a joint in the Oval Office. And he actually started to light one. So I put my hand over it quickly and whispered to him, "Don't you have *any* conception of the fact that there are cameras and microphones all over the place, you stupid fool!" I told him if he didn't stop immediately, I was going to kill him on the spot. He stopped.

I firmly believe that Jimmy Carter was a far better president than most people gave him credit for at the time. Although he didn't have a very successful presidency, I believe he's a tremendously sincere and decent man. He's proved what a wonderful human being he is by being even more effective after he got out of the presidency than he was when he was in it. His work of monitoring elections around the world to ensure their fairness is wonderful. When you see someone who's been president of the United States hammering nails to build houses for low-income families, that's quite a guy. And he doesn't just do it when the cameras are on; he does it all day long.

When Jerry Brown ran for president in 1980 (against Jimmy Carter), he had one asset no other candidate could claim: he was going out with Linda Ronstadt. And Linda just happened to have some good friends who were in a band called the Eagles. Together they did two benefit concerts that filled arenas in San Diego and Las Vegas.

Don Henley remembers the Brown concerts, along with a concert for then California Senator Alan Cranston, as being pivotal events in the Eagles' history as a band: "We did make the mistake of doing a couple of political benefits in the Eagles. I say it was a mistake. It was a mistake because the band members didn't all agree that it was a good thing to do. We did one for Jerry Brown. That was basically at the behest of Linda Ronstadt. And our last show before we broke up was for Senator Alan Cranston, who I still think was a good man and a good senator. And we broke up onstage during that show. We have some great footage. We filmed it and recorded it, and you can hear Frey and Felder threatening each other on the microphone and under their breath, [saying things] like, 'I'm gonna kick your ass as soon as we get offstage.' 'Oh yeah? Come on then, motherfucker.' Stuff like that. You can hear them muttering that stuff in between songs, while they're smiling at the audience, you know, with their guitars in their hands. Felder smashed a Takamini or some Japanese guitar. It wasn't a big deal. But we all sort of swore off political benefits after that."

As a solo performer Don has gone on to become one of the most politically active and effective musicians around. He knows more about a politician's stance on an issue than most reporters do. Before he commits—and he's a major contributor of both time and money to political candidates—he studies their records, he knows where they stand, he knows how they vote, and nothing gets by him. He can really rake a politician over the coals, but that's a good thing.

By the eighties most politicians were falling all over themselves trying to appear hip enough to have a rock star in their corner. Probably the most ridiculous example of a politician blatantly attempting to exploit the popularity of a musician came in 1984, when that epitome of hip, Ronald Reagan, tried to ride Bruce Springsteen's coattails back into the White House for a second term. In a speech in New Jersey, Reagan said, "America's future rests in a thousand dreams inside your hearts. It rests in the message of hope in the songs of a man so many young Americans admire: New Jersey's own Bruce Springsteen. And helping you

make those dreams come true is what this job of mine is all about."
Bruce quickly made it clear that he wasn't a Reagan supporter,
which opened the door for Reagan's Democratic opponent, Walter
Mondale, to suggest that Bruce was in fact supporting *him*. He
wasn't, and Bruce had to issue another statement disassociating
himself from Mondale as well.

Neil says, "If you back somebody on one thing, people think you
back them on everything. And you can't put that kind of stigma on
your music or people won't believe what you're singing. And then
the music's no good. So this certain thing has to be protected about
the music, the believability factor. You've got to know that the person who's singing to you is actually singing something that matters.
That's the problem."

A perfect example of what Neil is talking about happened in 1991
when the members of REM, all of whom are from Georgia, hosted a
fund-raising party for their incumbent senator, a Democrat named
Wyche Fowler who was in a close race for reelection. His campaign
really needed the money, and REM's hosting this party was an
important contribution. What happened, though, was that a few
weeks after the event, Wyche Fowler became one of the only
Democrats to vote to confirm Clarence Thomas for a lifetime seat
on the Supreme Court. Fowler had previously led his supporters to
think that he wouldn't vote for Thomas, so when he did, many of
them were furious. Fowler lost his seat anyway, but the fact is, REM
was still left with having thrown their credibility behind this guy.
That's why I have a problem with working for candidates: you're
working for a person rather than a principle. Which is why, even
when I'm involved in politics, I much prefer to work with issue
groups like Rock the Vote or Voters for Choice, rather than for an
individual candidate.

Rock the Vote started out in 1990 as a way for members of the
recording industry to fight right-wing attempts to censor music and
restrict artistic freedom. A year later, recognizing that young people
were its natural base of support for that agenda, Rock the Vote committed itself "to the political empowerment of young Americans."

One of its biggest accomplishments so far has been to lobby suc-cessfully for the passage of the motor voter bill (now the National Voter Registration Act of 1993), which allows people to register to vote when they get a driver's license. This particularly encourages young people to register. A lot of younger artists have been very involved with Rock the Vote, including Jewel, Pearl Jam, Chuck D of Public Enemy, Hootie & the Blowfish, Queen Latifah, Sheryl Crow, LL Cool J, and REM.

"I joined onto the board of advisers for Rock the Vote," Michael Stipe says, "largely because I felt really strongly that the motor voter bill was something that needed to be passed. When I went and got my driver's license a month later, the woman who took my picture and filled out the form asked me if I'd like to register to vote. She was doing about thirty or forty people an hour. That made me feel really good."

Since the Vietnam War ended, there's been only one political issue in America that's evoked the same passion on both sides, and it's been the issue of a woman's right to choose an abortion. It seems crazy to me that there's any debate about this at all, but what's even worse is that it's become a political football for candidates to use as a way to score points with powerful right-wing groups like the Christian Coalition. Realizing that there wasn't any equivalent pro-choice group, Gloria Steinem organized Voters for Choice to sup-port politicians who had the guts to stand up and say, "This is a civil rights issue; it's not our place to legislate morality."

Graham Nash and I were among the first male musicians to offer our support to Voters for Choice. No other men were touching it with a ten-foot pole; it was seen as a "chick thing." So rather than waiting to be asked, which is the way it usually works, we went to them and volunteered our services. They were stunned, but very grateful. And we kicked off an event that now happens every year at Constitution Hall in Washington, D.C.

My friend Tom Campbell organizes these Voters for Choice events through his production company, Avocado. Tom is an amaz-ingly dedicated activist who, as far as I know, is the only person in the country whose full-time job is putting together benefit concerts for worthwhile causes. Artists trust him completely because he follows every nickel as if it were his own, plus he knows the issues inside and out.

For that first show in 1991, I called the Indigo Girls, Emily Saliers and Amy Ray, with whom I'd just made a record. They immediately agreed to appear. After that, the show gained a momentum of its own. Tom remembers that "the Republican chair of Voters for Choice happened to know Mary-Chapin Carpenter's mother, so she came on the show. And here's the beauty, an unsolicited proposal. I had never worked with Melissa Etheridge before. I didn't know anybody who knew her to speak for me before. We said, 'We're doing this pro-choice show.' I sent a fax over to her office. Then Bill Leopold [her manager] calls and says 'Melissa's there.'"

I asked Melissa why this issue was so important to her and, as always, she was very honest in her answer: "I think I was eighteen or nineteen and I [had] just graduated and my sister already had a child. And my parents were doing okay. They had enough money to make us comfortable. My sister was still working and trying. And she got pregnant again. I had to take her to have an abortion—I actually paid for it because I'd been making money performing and singing. And it was quite an intense experience that I won't forget. We had to go to Missouri to get it done because we were living in Kansas, and it wasn't legal in Kansas. And this happens all the time. This happens today. And I remember that feeling of having to drive so far. And afterwards, with her still drugged from the procedure, us having to drive back all that way. And thinking how crazy it all was. That affected me personally. That's when you find your causes."

"So we had this incredible first night in Washington, D.C.," recalls Tom. "It was really a mind-boggler. And now we've done them every year for the last eight years. But that's how things start and how things happen. One person says, 'Well, take a look at this . . . ,' and then someone else says something and someone calls someone, and suddenly we've got a whole bunch of benefit concerts that are being done about this issue, including people like Pearl Jam and Phish and Natalie Merchant and Ani DiFranco."

In January 1995, the fourth Voters for Choice concert (actually there were two shows, held on successive nights) was headlined by Pearl Jam and Neil Young. For Pearl Jam, then at the height of their tremendous popularity, this was their first live performance in almost a year. And in the thirty-five-hundred-seat Constitution Hall, even with two shows, the demand for tickets was far greater than the supply. Campbell made the tickets available through a lottery system, and they received more than 175,000 postcards.

On the morning of the first show, the streets around Constitution Hall were closed to everyone except those who had a winning lottery number. Security was tight, not only because of the overwhelming excitement surrounding Pearl Jam's appearance (people were coming in from all over the country), but also because there was a legitimate concern that some pro-life lunatics might attack the concert in the same way they'd been attacking abortion clinics.

At a press conference with Gloria Steinem before the show, Eddie Vedder said, "It is a weird position as an artist . . . to blatantly enter the political ring. We don't come from that space . . . [but] I know what it is not to be heard, so if I can raise my hand and speak out for some of these people who don't have a voice at the moment, then I almost feel a responsibility."

A singer-songwriter named Lisa Germano opened the five-hour show with a short, well-received set. She was followed to the stage by the high-energy, all-female group from Los Angeles, L7, who'd started a pro-choice effort, Rock for Choice, in the alternative music scene. Their set included the not-for-radio number "Shit, Goddamn, Get Off Your Fuckin Ass and Jam," and was made memorable by their bassist playing topless on the last song.

Neil and Crazy Horse came out next, and although this was obviously a Pearl Jam crowd, they were won over quickly with songs like "I Am a Child," "Cortez the Killer," and "Hey Hey, My My" (a song that particularly touched a lot of the Pearl Jam fans who were still mourning the death of Kurt Cobain eight months earlier; Neil's line

"Better to burn out, than to fade away" had been quoted by Cobain in his suicide note). Neil introduced a new song that night called "Act of Love," with lyrics that seemed written for the occasion: "Have your baby / have your life," "You said baby / I said maybe," "Don't wanna have your baby / don't wanna leave your baby," and the last lines:

I know I said I'd help
Here's my wallet
Call me later

When Pearl Jam finally took the stage, it was after midnight. The capacity crowd, if it even knew what time it was, clearly didn't care. This was what they'd been waiting for all night. They weren't disappointed. Starting off with "Release" from its first album, Pearl Jam roared through five songs from the just-released *Vitalogy*: "Spin the Black Circle," "Last Exit," "Tremor Christ," "Corduroy," and "Not for You." Reviewing the show for the *Los Angeles Times*, Robert Hilburn wrote that the "pairing of 'Corduroy' and 'Not for You' . . . ranks alongside the great concert moments of any decade."

The rest of Pearl Jam's high-octane set included "Daughter" (with the appropriate new lyrics "My body's nobody's body but mine"), "Glorified G," "Go," "Deep," "Black," "Rearviewmirror," and "Immortality." Neil joined them for an encore, reprising "Act of Love," a fitting ending to a powerful and purposeful night.

Like most of the greatest political benefits, the Voters for Choice concert was an excellent show for an important cause. But it's absurd, bordering on criminal, that it remains necessary to raise that kind of money in order to have a voice in the political process. The real threat to our democracy isn't the right wing; it's the fact that elections can be bought for the price of a bunch of thirty-second TV spots.

Bonnie Raitt has worked hard for Voters for Choice, as well as for a lot of other political groups and candidates. And she's as angry as I am that we still have to do it: "The zillions of dollars that are thrown out the window for good or bad candidates is so disgusting to me. What about those people who work hard at two jobs, who are two-income families? They're barely able to support their kids, let alone send them to college. You know, just hardworking people who put together thirty-five dollars to come to one of our concerts. That's seventy dollars, then parking, baby-sitters. How many hours did they have to work to give us that money that we then give to [a candidate], who then spends it in a second, *in a second*, on a TV ad? You know, I never saw the money in the first place. I funnel it. But those people who worked to make the money to come to the show, I owe it to them to work for campaign finance reform, because all of us could be doing better things with this time and with our money."

CHAPTER 5

The Antinuclear Crusade:

"We Almost Lost Detroit"

The reason music works so well to fuel a popular

movement is that you don't need everybody's

permission to make music, and everybody

recognizes the value of a really good song.

Jackson Browne

Both the civil rights movement and the antiwar movement grew out of problems that got right up in our faces every day and stayed there until we dealt with them. We couldn't ignore lunch counters and fire hoses and Rosa Parks and Schwerner, Cheney, and Goodman, any more than we could deny seeing body counts and secret bombings, My Lai or Kent State. We had to deal with them as a country and, painful as it was, we did.

But by the mid-seventies, when the issues of nuclear energy and nuclear weapons first started getting a lot of attention in the media, it was a completely different situation. The antinuclear activists, most of whom were the same people who had previously fought for civil rights and against the war, now discovered that they had a much tougher job. They'd been doing exactly the same things they'd done before—organizing, marching, getting arrested . . . but this time it wasn't working.

It's not that the issue wasn't clear. Very few people (except maybe the big power companies and their shareholders) really wanted nuclear power. We didn't want nuclear meltdowns; we didn't want nuclear waste. And we absolutely didn't want nuclear bombs. We didn't *want* any of it. We knew it and we were a pretty sizable portion of the population by the time the antinuclear movement first started coming together.

Of course, not *everyone* felt the same way about the nuclear issue. Neil Young, for one, is a guy who always likes to swim upstream. When almost everyone else started attacking nuclear power, Neil wanted to find a way to go in the other direction, if he possibly could. He's a very contrary guy. Here's Neil's take on it: "Every time I think of nuclear power, I think of the *dream* of nuclear power and the energy, the clean energy that it could be. At one point in my life I even thought—of course, this might have been in the days when I was getting high a lot—I thought that maybe I should have gone to school and learned all about nuclear physics." Neil is also a very smart guy and he's studied a lot of science, so he knew that if you *could* produce nuclear power from cold fusion instead of fission, you'd be able to run the entire eastern seaboard on a teacup full of seawater with absolutely no radioactive waste. (Unfortunately, cold fusion doesn't exist yet, and unless Neil *does* get a degree in nuclear physics, it probably never will.)

Personally, the antinuclear movement made me feel like I'd come home again. To me it absolutely felt the way it had in the sixties and early seventies at the civil rights rallies and the moratoriums against the war. But unlike racism or the war in Vietnam, nuclear power was still only a theoretical problem to most people. Because of that, it was much harder to motivate them to try to do something about it. Sure, everyone had seen the pictures of Hiroshima, but that was thirty years ago and, anyway, the bomb was dropped on *them*, not us. We also knew the potential danger of having that kind of energy generated right in our own backyards, because we'd put human beings just as fallible as we were in charge of it. There *is* no such thing as foolproof. Foolproof doesn't exist. We've got fools who are dumb enough to screw up anything. A nuclear power plant is a bad idea simply because there's so much force that can be unleashed from only one mistake. I predicted it when they first started building them. I always believed that sooner or later one would melt down completely to a full China syndrome, to windward of a major population center. Thankfully it hasn't happened yet, but if it ever does we will lose two or three million people in one day. And that's just in the first die-off. After that, we'd have people dying horrible deaths from leukemia and other cancers for the next twenty years.

To most people in the seventies, all of this was just the stuff of scary science-fiction novels. It wasn't a real problem to them yet. They didn't take it seriously. And why should they? The government didn't. George Bush, who was then head of the CIA and getting ready to run for president, actually told a reporter what he really believed about "winning" a nuclear war: "I don't believe there is no such thing as a winner in a nuclear exchange. You have a survivability of command and control, survivability of industrial potential, protection of a percentage of your citizens and you have a capability that inflicts more damage on the opposition than it can inflict on you."

What people like Bush really mean when they use words like *survivability* is this: "We're prepared to see our cities destroyed and our babies deformed, as long as the other guy gets it worse than we do." *Jesus.*

What was obviously missing from the antinuclear movement was one popular figure who could get the message out, who could tell the people how criminally insane it was to be using words like *surviv-*

ability. The earlier movements all had their charismatic minstrels—Woody Guthrie for the migrant workers, Pete Seeger against McCarthyism, Harry Belafonte for civil rights, Joan Baez against the war. Each of them had captured certain moments—snapshots in time—with their words, their songs, their presence.

All it takes is a single voice.

The antinuclear movement found that voice in a brilliant black musician named Gil Scott-Heron. Gil is many things, a poet, a novelist, a jazz musician . . . some people call him the Father of Rap. On the subject of nuclear power, he was also a prophet. In 1977, two years before most people had ever heard of Three Mile Island, Gil wrote a song called "We Almost Lost Detroit." It's about an accident in 1966 at a nuclear power plant just outside Detroit that triggered a partial meltdown of the fuel in the reactor core. They caught it in time, but Gil heard about it and he couldn't stop thinking about what might have happened if they hadn't. He was staggered by how close his whole city had come to being blown away by an *accident.* Plans were actually being made to evacuate the entire metropolitan area around Detroit. Unable to put those images out of his mind, he did what singer-songwriters do—he processed his own fears by writing a song:

> We're maybe seconds from annihilation
> But no one stopped to think about the people
> Or just how they would survive
> And we almost lost Detroit, this time

Gil was out front on the nuclear issue before anybody, and he's rightfully proud of it now: "After Three Mile Island a whole lot of sons of bitches went antinuke because it scared the shit out of them. It scared me in advance!" And although Gil Scott-Heron may have been the first musician with a sizable following to write about nuclear power (his song "Barnwell," about a nuclear plant in South Carolina, was written in 1975, two years before "We Almost Lost Detroit"), he certainly wouldn't be the last.

In 1978, after organizing a concert to benefit the family of Karen Silkwood, the woman in Oklahoma who I believe certainly was murdered for talking to the press about the hazards at the nuclear power plant where she worked, Bonnie Raitt decided she needed to do something else. And something bigger. Bonnie says: "It started after the Silkwood concert when John Hall and myself and James Taylor, Carly Simon, and Jackson Browne, and some people got together and decided that it was imperative that we organize something more than isolated concerts here and there. That's when we had the idea of doing something larger in the major media center of the world, which is New York City. And that's why we picked Madison Square Garden."

For a lot of us, doing another benefit concert at Madison Square Garden felt like returning to the scene of a crime. Although seven years had now passed since the concerts for Bangladesh, it was still the yardstick by which all big benefit concerts were measured— which was exactly the problem. Given that we all knew how the proceeds from the Bangladesh shows were still tied up in IRS hassles, most of us (and particularly our managers) were very reluctant to commit ourselves to doing another benefit concert on that scale ever again.

The most zealous activists didn't care about any of that. They still kept dreaming of these huge benefit shows as the solution to all their problems. We'd get these requests literally twenty-four hours a day. When Crosby, Stills, Nash & Young were touring America in 1974, I used to get notes slipped under my hotel room door in the middle of the night, sometimes at three or four in the morning. The notes were interchangeable, and they always went something like: "Dear Mr. Crosby, please forgive me for writing you this note but you are the only person who can help us. We need to raise a million dollars by next week to (feed the world, house the homeless, clothe the whales). Will you do a concert for us? And will you ask all your friends to do it with you? It's only one night and it will make a huge difference to (the world, the homeless, the whales). Thanks in advance for saying yes."

We'd get at least one of those letters a day, every day. And that was only what got through. But nothing happened until Bonnie, Jackson, and a certain single-minded Brit named Nash really became persuaded that the cause of stopping nuclear power was so vital, so important to everything we cared about, that they decided it was time to ignore the risks and just go for it. And they took a big risk. They started planning not just one, but *five* shows at Madison Square Garden. Along with a dozen other antinuclear activists, including musician John Hall and a big redheaded organizer from California named Tom Campbell (who had already established a specialty of doing only benefit concerts), they formed an organization called MUSE, or Musicians United for Safe Energy. Their strategy was brilliant in its simplicity: cut out the middlemen. To avoid the mistakes that had marred the Bangladesh benefits, the MUSE board, which was evenly divided between musicians and antinuclear activists, took direct control of all aspects of the planning and execution of what we were already calling the No Nukes concerts.

I have to admit that when Graham, Bonnie, and Jackson (who are some of my best friends in the world) first told me about their plans for doing five consecutive shows at Madison Square Garden, I immediately thought of that old expression "Fools rush in where angels fear to tread." Not because they're foolish; exactly the opposite is true. These are three of the smartest people I know. It's just that I was aware of the long odds they were up against and what a chance they were taking, both personally and professionally, if they failed to pull this off.

But if you know anything at all about these three individuals, you know they had no choice. These are people for whom not acting on personal conviction is no more of an option than not breathing.

Graham Nash was one of the first people I knew who really *got* nuclear power, who really understood what a potential for disaster there was and what an enemy of life it was. To him, it was a very personal threat. Nuclear power and nuclear weapons were like a guy standing outside his house with a shotgun, blazing away at his kids' bedroom. This was not some distant, mythical thing to him.

Remember, he came over here from a country that actually experienced what it was like to be bombed. During World War II, he was one of thousands of kids who got shipped out of England's cities for safety, with only a name tag for identification. Many of them later returned home to find their entire neighborhoods burned to the ground.

Graham recalls that he was still a teenager when he first became aware of—and frightened by—nuclear weapons: "I remember seeing Lord Bertrand Russell walk with thousands of people from Aldermaston to London in protest of the deployment of U.S. nuclear submarines. But when I was sixteen or seventeen, I didn't have any power to do anything about it."

The antinuclear movement started happening at a time in Graham's life when he was very frustrated artistically by the fact that there were two other guys in his group (and remember this was a *trio*) who couldn't keep their shit together for more than five minutes. So instead of sitting around and complaining, he was able to put that energy and anger into fighting something he saw as pure evil, what he called "nuclear madness." He just wasn't able to sit idly by and let the big corporations get away with perpetrating that shit all over the world.

Don't get me wrong, Graham's not a violent guy, but he *is* a very strong personality. He's not willing to take no for an answer, which makes him very much the archetypal activist. The late Bill Graham, our friend, once said that "When Graham Nash is concerned about something, he doesn't just talk, he *does*. He takes action. Graham is an organizer. He's not a follower." Amen to that.

Now in Bonnie's case, she comes out of an environment that taught her you had to have social responsibility and that war was not an option in the first place. As a Quaker she learned this very early on and it obviously took. She says, "When I was a kid, I used to go to the principal's office instead of diving under the desk during air raid drills at school because somehow it seemed that to participate would mean accepting the inevitability of nuclear war." By the time she was eleven or twelve years old, she had become, in her words, "a self-appointed Joan Baez clone." She'd sit around the campfire and "sing songs about changing the world. Joan Baez was my absolute hero because she was Quaker as well." She was also deeply influenced by Bob Dylan and Pete Seeger and their activist work: "I kept my eyes peeled to the TV about Ban the Bomb marches and the civil rights movement. So all the artists that were involved in that, people that would sing at those rallies, were all people I just loved because I liked them as people as well as I liked their music. I liked what they stood for."

One of the things I most admire about Bonnie is that she's willing to listen to the other side. She's not dogmatic. That takes guts and a real strength in one's convictions, which Bonnie has in spades. She thinks that even if she doesn't change anybody's mind, if she has created a dialogue with people, she's won. And I vote for Bonnie. I say that's absolutely the truth.

Bonnie is a news junkie, she reads everything. So she knew early on just how evil the people behind these nuclear plants really were: "I first became aware of how dangerous the nuclear industry had become when I read about Karen Silkwood's death in 1974. Sometime later, the Supporters of Silkwood approached me about doing a benefit to raise funds for the family's case against the Kerr-McGee plutonium company, which they believed was responsible for her death. Ironically, tickets to a concert Jackson Browne and I were giving a few days later in Oklahoma City were found in her car when she died."

Jackson will tell you that his own antinuclear activism started at the precise moment he first realized that politicians lie. "It was around the time that Lyndon Johnson was running for president," says Jackson. "He was already president because of the Kennedy assassination and he was running against Goldwater for a full term and my father asked me to help him canvass for votes, which meant going around and getting people to register as Democrats. My father said, 'If Goldwater wins, he's going to bomb North Vietnam. Johnson won't do that.' So we canvassed the neighborhood for votes. And I explained all this to people. 'See, Goldwater wants to bomb North Vietnam. Lyndon Johnson won't. There will be other ways of resolving this.' Johnson won and he bombed North Vietnam. That was the beginning of my education about electoral politics."

This is a truly brilliant man; an informed, conscious human being who does nothing unthinkingly. Jackson's perfectly aware of his emotions and is willing to feel things to the max, but he doesn't ever just disengage his brain and ignore what's going on around him. And so he's very powerful because of that combination. He's incredibly articulate and he has the passion of having had an uphill fight the entire time. A lot of people said to Jackson then (and still say it now), "Tone down this activism shit, you're hurting your career." Many *business* people have leveled that criticism at Jackson because they felt he was destined to be one of the biggest stars of his generation. They felt that he would be a wonderful and manipulatable star whom they could use to earn tons of money. But right from the beginning, he made it clear that he had his own purposes, his own life, his own direction, and his own values. And they really didn't dig that. The music *business* didn't dig Jackson's approach. Not the people. The people who love Jackson—like me—appreciate the hell out of what he's done.

Jackson's career was at its commercial peak in the second half of the seventies, so his activism involved making some of the greatest sacrifices of anybody. He did antinuclear concerts everywhere, including a tour of California in early 1979 with Nash to try to stop the construction of a nuclear plant at Diablo Canyon near San Luis Obispo—only miles from an active earthquake fault. He was arrested a bunch of times and rearrested when he refused to promise the judge that he wouldn't protest at the same site again.

At about that same time, Michael Douglas made a film called *The China Syndrome* about a nuclear power plant that narrowly averts a meltdown, and when it was released everybody said, "Great movie! We're sure glad that can't happen *here*." Then, bang, life imitates art in this eerie way, and virtually the exact same thing that happens in the movie happened in real life at Three Mile Island in Pennsylvania.

Suddenly, the whole country had to face its denial and deal with the fact that these accidents really *can* happen.

"Between the time we started to plan these shows and when they actually happened, Three Mile Island melted down," says Jackson, describing the momentum that was starting to build behind the No Nukes concerts. "Within weeks of that you had this movie come out, *The China Syndrome.* By the time the concerts were being planned, people already knew a lot and they were pretty much lined up in favor of doing something. So the focus of the concerts became—they went from initially being a call to arms to actually [being] a way of fueling these grassroots antinuclear organizations."

Those two events, because they happened only a few weeks apart in 1979, immediately gave the antinuclear movement more credibility than it ever had before. Now artists were calling up and *asking* to play at No Nukes. For Bonnie this was a great thing, but also a little ironic: "Since Three Mile Island, all of a sudden everybody was more than eager to get involved."

James Taylor and Carly Simon were committed to playing No Nukes right from the beginning, having already agreed to do something big after the Silkwood concert the year before. The Doobie Brothers, Tom Petty, Chaka Khan, and, of course, Gil Scott-Heron all jumped in pretty quickly too. I remember *Rolling Stone* started calling it "a Woodstock for the eighties."

At the time Carly said, "I think people become involved in causes if there is a personal danger to them or there is a personal involvement. The fact that I have children may have increased my involvement. You think, 'I am here. I could die from this, I could get cancer, my children could be affected for the rest of their lives by radiation poisoning.'" Years later, looking back at it (and having now survived her own experience with breast cancer), she told me she felt like "we were all out there together. We were all doing it for this thing that we believed in from our hearts."

But it wasn't until we heard that Bruce Springsteen had agreed to play on the third and fourth nights that the excitement around the No Nukes shows turned into something bordering on hysteria.

Tom Campbell, who has enough enthusiasm and passion about the nuclear issue to be an alternative energy source himself, had the job of confirming Bruce Springsteen for No Nukes. He remembers how it went down: "Jackson told me, 'We really need to have Bruce Springsteen. I've kinda talked to him and [his manager] Jon Landau about it and I think it's pretty well set up. You just need to go down there to Bruce's hotel and mop up for me, Tom.' So, I went down there and I gave him my big speech about how horrible nuclear power was and how important he was to these shows in New York. I got a little *excited*, as I do sometimes, but I figured, 'What the hell, Jackson says he's already in.' And Bruce listened to me for a while without saying much, then he just smiled and said, 'Yeah, we'll do it. We'll do the film, we'll do the record, and we'll do the two nights. Whatever you want, wild man. No problem at all.' It wasn't until about two years later that I found out Jackson hadn't talked to Bruce about it at all, that he had just shipped me in there cold."

(Things like this happen to Tom Campbell. One night during No Nukes—I think James and Carly were onstage—Tom was standing off to the side making sure everything was running smoothly, which was his job, and there's nobody better at it. Suddenly, this little guy walks by him and heads right for the stage. Tom immediately sees that this guy has no credentials—security was very tight, everybody had to have a pass—so he reacts on pure instinct and adrenaline. He reaches down and grabs the guy, who has to be at least a foot shorter than Tom, only about five feet tall. He grabs this guy by the collar and the back of the shirt and just *hurls* him into the wings. Just as he lets go, it dawns on Tom that the guy he's sent flying through the air is *Paul Simon*. Tom doesn't know I knew this story. Now he does.)

However Springsteen was persuaded to do No Nukes, it was a major coup for MUSE to get him. At that time, he was as big a star as you could find in America. He had legions of devoted fans who showed up in droves on the two nights he played. It got a little weird for the rest of us, just because we *weren't* Bruce. I remember Chaka Khan leaving the stage in tears after her set (which immediately preceded his) because she thought that twenty thousand people were booing her—when what they were really yelling was *Brooce! Brooce!* We all felt really sorry for her because she had no idea what was happening.

After a long set change and a lot more chanting, Bruce finally came onstage, bringing the whole E Street Band with him: Clarence, Little Steven, everybody. I remember that Bruce had his thirtieth birthday that night and he was so pumped up he just threw his cake at the audience, who literally ate it up. That was also the first night that Bruce had ever performed "The River" live onstage, and you could hear the echoes of his voice off the back walls of the Garden, it got that quiet.

I've since heard that some of the more self-righteous of the antinuke activists had the balls to be critical of Springsteen because he wasn't personally "committed" enough to the issue, and because they believed his fans weren't really activists. What a load of politically correct crap. Sure, his fans were ardent and maybe they were a little rowdy. So what? If some of Bruce's fans weren't aware of the nuclear issue coming in, they sure as hell were when they left those shows. Nobody left that building without knowing there was something very wrong with nuclear power. Information got passed along, a lot of money was handed over, and Bruce's involvement greatly expanded the number of people who supported the cause. Let me tell you this: the idiots who were complaining that he didn't really care about the nuclear issue obviously weren't listening to his music at all. After Three Mile Island, Bruce wrote a song called "Roulette" that tells the story of a man who somehow makes it through a nuclear meltdown and then has to find a way to survive in the broken world that's left. These are a few lines from it:

We left the toys out in the yard
I took my wife and kids and left my home unguarded
. . . .
There's a shadow in my backyard
I've got a house full of things that I can't touch

If he can't communicate something that really matters to him, Bruce truly believes that there's no point in even performing: "If you don't have that, stay home or something. If you have some ideas to exchange, that's what it's about. That's at the heart of it. I just wouldn't go out and tour unless I had that. There wouldn't be a reason. The reason is you have some idea you wanna say. You have an idea about things, an opinion, a feeling about the way things are or the way things could be. You wanna go out and tell people about it. You wanna tell people, well, if everybody did this or if people thought this, maybe it would be better."

One more thing about Bruce Springsteen: after playing the MUSE shows, he started saying yes to doing a lot more political work. I've always said it's not just the audience that's affected by these events. None of us is ever the same after we do them.

Even though they had Springsteen, MUSE still had one major problem left. They didn't have an act to headline the fifth night and the tickets for it were about to go on sale. This put Graham in a very uncomfortable position. He needed Crosby, Stills & Nash, but he really didn't want us to play. I'll let him tell it: "I'd done a lot of shows in my life, so I knew that the first three nights cover expenses and the fourth and fifth nights are the gravy, the profit. So I was determined not to cancel the fifth night." Nash says it was Jackson who finally confronted him, "He came up to me in the dressing room and said, 'You know we have no one to headline this fifth night . . . you know what I'm gonna ask . . . what do you think?' Prior to that, I'd totally refused to consider Crosby, Stills & Nash because I didn't feel we had anything to contribute. Our music depends on our personal feelings for each other, and when it's not there, we can't perform. It's that simple. But I knew Jackson was right. I thought about it for about seven seconds—and I went through all the changes by the microsecond. I went through *everything*."

I actually don't remember who got called first or how it happened. I just know that at the time they desperately needed Crosby, Stills & Nash as drawing power. Now I can't speak for anybody else, but I know they didn't want to deal with me. I'm sure if Nash could've pulled it off without having CSN, he would have, and I personally wouldn't have blamed him. At the time I was still very much in the grip of my addiction, and they didn't want me around or even want me associated with the event because I could be detrimental to the image of the cause. If he asked me to play at No Nukes, Graham would have to deal with the fact that I couldn't extend myself, that I didn't really function the way the rest of them did. Those were people who were fully functional at the time. I wasn't. Still, Nash finally bit the bullet: "I figured this cause was greater than whatever personal differences might exist between us. So I called them up and they were gung ho to be there. And the No Nukes concerts turned out to be a high point of our benefit life."

When I first showed up, the vibe was a little weird. It felt as if they had to trot me out like some cigar-store Indian and prop me up and say, *See, we've got the Crosby thing going. Okay, that's done.* It was like *I* was radioactive and everybody else could see it but me (almost true—I had so many chemicals in me in those days that they *should* have declared me a toxic waste dump). Then, when we were rehearsing backstage, something happened that completely turned my head around about being there. It was this accidental moment when some photographer was trying to get everyone close enough together to fit into a group photo, and there were a lot of us hanging out: me, Graham and Stephen, Bruce, Bonnie, James, Carly, all of the Doobies . . . a lot of people. So this guy keeps saying "Get closer. Get closer. Get *closer,*" until we all wound up actually *leaning* on each other. Then Bonnie just starts to sing that old Bill Withers song "Lean on Me." You know how it goes: *Lean on me, / when you're not strong / and I'll be your friend, / I'll help you carry on. . . .* And then all of us started harmonizing with her, singing and laughing and falling on each other. It was at exactly that moment that everything just hit me and I got really, really clear. I suddenly knew that this was the one place in the entire universe where I was absolutely supposed to be, where I *needed* to be. I wish I could say that experience was all it took to keep me sober, but it wasn't. What it did do was show me something I kept choosing to forget, that the music and those people would still get me higher than the best drugs I could ever score. Moments like that are made out of unobtanium. They don't exist anywhere else.

I think the other emotional high point of No Nukes for me—and everyone I've talked to says this too—was when all of us went down to the tip of Manhattan for this massive outdoor rally. I remember being completely astounded at the size of it. We *filled* Battery Park. There must have been a quarter of a million people there, and I remember looking out and seeing Pete Seeger's sloop, the *Clearwater*, cruising up and down slowly, right out in the Hudson River. I think it had a big peace flag on it . . . it was just beautiful. People brought these handmade signs that said things like HELL NO, WE WON'T GLOW and BETTER ACTIVE TODAY THAN RADIOACTIVE TOMOR-ROW. There were great speeches from Ralph Nader and Jane Fonda—and, of course, there was Pete. When he sang "If I Had a Hammer," thousands of the kids sang the words with him, even if some of them didn't know for sure who he was.

Funny how that can work out. Adam Yauch of the Beastie Boys told me he was there that day too. He was only about fourteen years old, just handing out leaflets as a volunteer. But he really *got it* that day, really understood that this was something musicians could do. And he never forgot. Two decades later, Yauch became so personally committed to stopping the Chinese atrocities in Tibet that he didn't hesitate for a second. He organized the Tibetan Freedom concerts—huge events in San Francisco, New York, and Washington, D.C., with Pearl Jam, Smashing Pumpkins, REM, and a lot of others. And because of those shows, there are now hundreds of Free Tibet groups on college campuses across the country. There's no question in my mind that this torch is always being passed, sometimes in ways that we aren't even aware of at the time.

After No Nukes, public opinion overwhelmingly turned against the use of nuclear power, and no new plants were built. I wish I could say that the reason nuclear power failed was that we succeeded in making a compelling moral case to save life on the planet.

It wasn't. Maybe that argument would have worked eventually, I don't know. What really happened, though, was that the people running those plants read their bottom line and started shutting them down or selling them off because they were proving far too costly to operate. A lot of that expense came from the massive cost overruns that occurred during construction. Greed created nuclear power in America and greed killed it. It's as simple as that.

Unfortunately, this didn't mean that the antinuclear movement could fold its tent and go home. Not yet. We now had a new president, Ronald Reagan, who'd previously made his living by shilling for General Electric, so we all understood exactly where he was coming from on the issue of nuclear power. Remember, this is the same guy who once said that trees cause pollution. But when Reagan started calling the Soviet Union an evil empire, all of a sudden the issue became far bigger than just nuclear energy. Reagan's rhetoric was heating up the Cold War, which now meant that the antinuclear movement needed to take on the fight against nuclear weapons too. This was a real problem for the antinuclear activists who remembered being branded as traitors and communists during the antiwar movement. They could read the handwriting on the wall: if they opposed Reagan and his massive nuclear weapons buildup, they risked the entire antinuclear movement being labeled as un-American. Some, like Jane Fonda and Joan Baez, didn't miss a step. They'd been hit so hard for so long ("Hanoi Jane" and "Joanie Phoney") that they didn't care what anybody said about them. They just spoke the truth, with courage and eloquence. And the terrifying truth was that we now had a guy in charge of a nuclear arsenal big enough to destroy the planet whose only experience of war came from acting in World War II movies, and who told stories from those movies as if they had actually *happened* to him.

It was Nash who figured out the plan that would give the antinuclear movement the respectability needed to prevent Reagan from using it as a political scapegoat. Graham heard that a group of religious leaders in Los Angeles had reserved the Rose Bowl for a spectacular gathering of church choirs all singing for world peace. Their concert was planned for a Sunday in June of 1982—timed to coincide with a United Nations special session on disarmament that would be convening in New York. Now on paper this might have seemed like a good idea, but the reality was that the Rose Bowl is one of the largest football stadiums in the country and these good people had no idea how to fill it.

Graham did. It literally came to him in a dream. One night in early January of '82, he sat bolt upright in bed, grabbed the notebook he kept on his nightstand, and quickly sketched out his vision of an event he called Sing for Your Life. The pages of his notebook are amazingly accurate in describing what, six months later, would become Peace Sunday—at that point, the largest one-day benefit event ever held anywhere on the planet. His journal entry has it all written down, including the names of the performers (most of whom *did* play) and a sketch of the Rose Bowl filled to capacity. Maybe it's only for me, but he calls the dream his "deja pre-vu."

Having the dream was one thing. Making it real was a lot harder. Nash needed all his powers of persuasion (and they're considerable, believe me) to sell his vision to the religious leaders, who were deeply suspicious of rock 'n' roll. He laughs—now—when he tells the story: "I said, I don't think you stand a chance of filling the Rose Bowl with just a religious slant. I told them, If you really, seriously want to fill the Rose Bowl, why don't we pool our sensibilities—the antinuclear forces and the religious Peace Through Justice movement—why don't we combine the two and put rock 'n' rollers on the bill? They didn't trust me at first. One of them actually asked me, 'Well, what's God's cut?'"

Eventually the religious leaders went along with Graham, who then brought in our friend Tim Sexton (the associate producer of the No Nukes shows) to produce Peace Sunday. Tim knew that filling the Rose Bowl wasn't going to be easy: "We needed an artist who could draw a huge crowd (like Springsteen at the MUSE concerts) and who could also reach people who hadn't come to those shows—particularly the black community, which had never really been involved in the antinuclear movement. There was only one name that made any sense at the time: Stevie Wonder."

Jackson had already tried, unsuccessfully, to get Stevie involved in the antinuclear effort. Three years earlier, he'd approached him about doing No Nukes, and he'd been turned down. But it's Nash's favorite thing in life to be audacious, so he just said, "Why *can't* we get Stevie Wonder for Peace Sunday? I bet we could. What do you mean you can't get his number? I bet *I* can get his number. Let me see here." And with the help of the wonderful photographer Lisa Law, he got on the phone and wound up talking to Stevie Wonder.

Jackson says that when he first heard about Graham approaching Stevie Wonder for Peace Sunday, he was totally skeptical: "I said, Yeah, *right.* Good luck. And he just went and convinced him. And I was really knocked out when I heard that Stevie was in."

Stevie showed up at Peace Sunday with his entire band dressed in military fatigues. It was a big band and they were all in very high spirits before they went on, stomping and clapping and chanting. He told a reporter, "We're dressed like this because we are all in a war—a peaceful war—against *all* war. We are the ones who are responsible. And we have to rid ourselves of the barriers that for the most part do not exist in the world of song."

I remember meeting Stevie for the first time over by the side of the stage before he went on. Somebody introduced me, probably Graham, and I remember how soft his hand was. He has a very soft hand, a very delicate touch. He doesn't squeeze your hand, he just touches it. And he has this soft voice and he was smiling. I think he was enjoying himself. I remember thinking, *He's remarkably aware of everything that's going on around him in more ways than just being able to hear the words that are spoken or the music that's played. He knows what's going on here.* And then he played and he was unbelievable.

After Stevie came Joan Baez, who finished her set and then turned to the side of the stage and asked a friend of hers to come out—Dylan. The crowd went crazy because nobody knew he was there. I remember him walking over to Joan, covering his mouth with his hand and whispering something to her. Later on I found out he said, "Let's do 'Blowin' in the Wind' and get the hell out of here."

Looking back on it now, Joan says, "I remember he wanted me to sing 'Black Is the Color of My True Love's Hair.' Because he's nuts, you know. Anyway, we sang something else, and he had the words written on his wrist. . . . I love singing with him. It's such a dynamic thing that doesn't happen with anyone else I know. To a lot of the young ones down front, I think we were some sort of aging myth. But I think the main part of the audience knew something special was happening."

Peace Sunday became this incredible parade of musicians that started at noon and lasted until almost midnight. Linda Ronstadt, Stevie Nicks, Tom Petty, Jackson, Bonnie, and even Bette Midler (who had my favorite line of the night: she told the crowd not to "eat the green acid . . . the green acid makes you talk like you're from Encino") were just some of the ones who performed, and there were stirring speeches from people like Muhammad Ali, Jane Fonda, and Jesse Jackson, who was part preacher and part musician. As always, his voice had the power of a great gospel singer: "The peace movement lives again in America. Today is the signal of revival of a peace movement that has been interrupted now for a decade. This time we will not stop marching with the end of one particular war. We shall march until there is no more war and no more weapons. We want peace *now* and we want peace *forever.*"

I was so proud of Graham, because he'd done it. He *made* Peace Sunday happen through the sheer force of his will and the power of his imagination. He was actually in tears when he stood onstage for the first time and saw the entire Rose Bowl filled with almost a hundred thousand people.

At the end of that very long day—more than twelve hours of music and speeches—everybody who was still there came back out onstage and lined up in a big circle around Stevie Wonder. It was so many people that the circle went clear to the back of the stage. It wound all the way around from one corner of the stage, around to the back, and then all the way around again to the other corner because there were that many performers. I thought I remembered Stevie somehow just walking out there by himself to the microphone. Jackson says *he* led him out there. It doesn't matter. All I know is that Stevie somehow got to the microphone and in one of the most electrifying moments I've ever experienced at any gig, but especially at any benefit, he walked out and the whole audience—this giant bowl of humanity—fell quiet. And he gave it a couple of beats to let it sink in that they were *being* quiet, then he started singing *"All we are saying, is give peace a chance."* When he was halfway through it the second time, tens of thousands of voices were singing it with him. I've never heard anything like it, I've never felt anything like it. It was an absolutely transcendent moment of communication and of activism, of it all *working*, of what we felt in our hearts actually being returned to us as real as a piece of fruit on a plate. There it was. Bang. You could taste it. These people were all singing that song and they all really meant it . . . and, you know, it was as if John Lennon was standing on the stage with us and the whole thing was just unbelievably fine. It was a moment to hold on to forever. You would never want to lose that moment.

So, in the end, were the No Nukes and Peace Sunday concerts successful? It depends on how you measure success. They certainly raised a lot of money. And both events significantly raised the level of public awareness around the whole nuclear issue. In the twenty years since the No Nukes shows, MUSE has raised and contributed more than $1 million to antinuclear groups around the country, much of it through proceeds from the three-record set that Graham and Jackson produced. You can still find the *No Nukes* movie playing on television—and now it's a whole different generation that's getting to see it. Peace Sunday raised $200,000 (and this was in *1982* dollars) in a single day, which it gave to grassroots groups promoting "peace with justice." Five months after Peace Sunday, the people of California voted to support a freeze on the further development of all nuclear weapons. Unfortunately, their votes were nonbinding, so Reagan and the Congress pretty much ignored them. It would take another decade before we'd get to the point we're at today—no Soviet Union and the actual dismantling of at least part of our nuclear stockpile.

Graham sees those events—and the antinuclear movement in general—as having achieved a clear-cut victory: "I think those concerts had a lasting effect on the nuclear power industry, on the policy of this country. Even as late as last week, they were showing the *No Nukes* movie on public television. In certain cases it's necessary to drive the issue home deeply enough that it's felt for a long time and people get invigorated and energized to carry on the work for many years."

Bonnie looks at those same events and has a slightly different take on them than Graham. On the one hand, she says, "In all the years of activism, that particular week [of No Nukes concerts] was the most powerful and exciting thing. When I look back at my life, that's the thing I'm most proud of, hands down." But for Bonnie, the glass still remains half-empty: "At the time, we thought the *No Nukes* movie was going to come to everybody's town and get people into the theaters to see their stars and learn about nuclear power. Well, guess what? The corporate politics of the movie industry is that you don't have to promote it. Just because you get a movie deal doesn't mean they're going to open it in the cities you want it to open in. And I learned my lesson. As happy as I was to have a three-record set that did so well, the movie's lack of promotion was my first big lesson in how this so-called liberal film industry really *isn't* liberal at all. And when it comes to bucking the system, they're going to open *No Nukes* in the elderly Jewish section of Miami and the poor black section in Houston and go, *See, nobody wanted to see it. I guess it's not doing well. Let's pull it.* It couldn't have been that it was just a little *too* political. So for all the good that the film did, it was heartbreaking and it didn't raise any money. And it didn't get shown, and twenty years later it's on VH–1 at one in the morning and there's *still* nuclear power."

Here's the deal: I think they're both right. These events worked on more than one level. First, they communicated the message that nuclear power was too dangerous. On the face of it, people obviously went home and told other people, "Jeez, the music was so fantastic, we were all there and we were all making a stand about this, and it really felt great"; and they couldn't help but talk about it to their friends, so that each antinuclear flyer got read three or four times. That multiplies the effort. And so does the movie, even at one in the morning. Sure, it would have been better if more people had seen it, but at least it's out there. Second, No Nukes and Peace Sunday showed people that they could do something about a particular problem. That's the underlying truth of every one of these events: that you are not alone and you are not powerless. That message is as important as the primary message, because it means that down the road somebody else will step up to bat and take a swing at the next rotten thing that comes along.

Which is why in 1997, eighteen years after the first No Nukes concerts, Bonnie, Jackson, Graham, Dan Fogelberg, and I went back out and did a series of small benefits in New Mexico and Nevada to oppose a new plan to bring in nuclear waste from all over the country and dump it in remote areas of those states. They pick small states with not too much political clout and put the radioactive waste in the ground near where a few poor people live, or better still, where some *Indians* live. Who's going to notice? Bonnie said it for all of us when we did those shows: "This is just disgusting that we're still doing it, but we walk it like we talk it. I'd rather be record-ing new songs and touring. We've all got better things to do than to do these benefits, but they still need to be done."

And finally, I think there's a higher way that all of these events work. For some reason—and I can't prove this—but for some reason I think truth has its own sustaining resonance; that somehow if you say true things, they go out like ripples in a pond and they don't decrease as they go out . . . they somehow sustain, in a way that lies don't. I don't know why that is and I can't explain it, but I believe it absolutely. At events like No Nukes and Peace Sunday, when we stuck very scrupulously to the truth, to the facts rather than to rhetoric, I think a resonance went out very strongly and kept spreading. That's just what I believe.

To be fair, I have to say that Jackson thinks my viewpoint is naive. What he really thinks is that it's bullshit—at least that's what he told me late one night when he was tired and his guard was down. He believes that we need to keep asking ourselves this "agonizing, soul-searching question, Did any of this mean a fucking thing?"

For Jackson, who fought hard for years to prove that the Reagan-Bush administration had been illegally running guns to the contras in Nicaragua, the answer he gets back sometimes can be painful to hear: "I'd always believed that if people really knew what was going on in Nicaragua, if you told them the truth, that people in the United States are really *decent* people and would do something about it. If you showed them without a doubt that what was being said by the Reagan administration was a *lie,* that they'd do something about it. And what did they do? They fuckin' elected the guy who broke the law. And they forgave the doddering old son-of-a-bitch who gave them all the go-ahead. What does that tell you? It tells you that if you tell people the truth, *it does not necessarily follow* that they'll do anything about it at all." At the end of this tirade, Jackson got very quiet. His voice dropped down to a whisper, and I had to strain to hear him: "Let me just say that I really believe in the things we do. And I don't think I have a choice to do anything else."

And that's the point. Even if Jackson is right and people don't listen or don't care, that doesn't mean we get to stop. We *can't* stop. As he says, we have no choice. We're hardwired this way. I'll give Bonnie the last word here, because she always says it better than anybody else: "I don't know if we can ever be innocent again, but we can still be awake and be vital and make a difference. And if I can get that message out in the benefits that I do, then I'm giving it to myself too, because I get discouraged. When I do those concerts and we sing together, I think, *'This* is what it's about.'"

CHAPTER 6

Global Activism:

"We Are the World"

Music sets an atmosphere for reason to occur in

conjunction with passion.

Stephen Stills

It started out as a con. Someone pretending to represent then secretary-general of the United Nations, Kurt Waldheim, had written very convincing letters to some of Britain's top musicians, including Paul McCartney and George Harrison, asking them to do a benefit for the massive number of new refugees from war-torn Kampuchea, the former Cambodia. Millions of people had been slaughtered or driven from their homes by the butcher of Phnom Penh, the communist dictator Pol Pot. Joan Baez went there to see for herself. "The list of atrocities was grim as hell," she told a reporter.

Many artists quickly agreed to participate in this "United Nations concert" until, as McCartney subsequently explained to *Rolling Stone*, "a letter came from Kurt Waldheim saying 'I have *never* authorized anyone to ask on my behalf if you'd do anything. There seems to be someone going around, [and] it is a hoax. . . . But seeing as you're involved now, would you do something?' We sent back a telegram saying 'Yes, we'd do a show.'"

The year was 1979. With the just-completed No Nukes shows for a model, Harvey Goldsmith, Britain's Bill Graham, decided to put together four consecutive benefit concerts at the three-thousand-seat Hammersmith Odeon in London during the week after Christmas. Even more than to raise relief money, the purpose of these shows would be to call international attention to the dire plight of the people of Kampuchea.

To that end, Goldsmith recruited an unbelievable lineup of talent, including Paul McCartney and Wings, the Clash, the Who, Queen, Elvis Costello, and the Pretenders. *Rolling Stone* wasn't exaggerating in calling the Concerts for the People of Kampuchea "the greatest superstar jam for charity London has ever seen." December 26 is Boxing Day, a national holiday in England. So in honor of the occasion, it was only fitting that the first concert for the people of Kampuchea was given exclusively by Queen. (Even if Harvey Goldsmith had wanted to put a second act on the bill, he couldn't have. Queen's grand theatrics required so much setup and equipment that there just wasn't room for another band to play.) The second night's concert was assembled by Ian ("Hit Me with Your Rhythm Stick") Dury, who brought along his band, the Blockheads. But the evening unquestionably belonged to the Clash, whose just-released record *London Calling* had taken the British music scene by storm.

Those people lucky enough to score tickets on the third night (scalpers were doing land-office business) saw an unforgettable show: the Pretenders and the Specials, followed by a two-and-a-half-hour, take-no-prisoners set from the Who. Pete Townshend, by his own admission half-drunk, still gave a spectacular performance of twenty-three Who songs—everything from "Behind Blue Eyes" to "Pinball Wizard" to "My Generation" (although in a moment of liquid candor he did ask the audience, "Aren't you glad that you live in London and not in poxy Kampuchea?").

In anticipation of the last show—Paul McCartney's night—overwrought Beatlemaniacs again became delusional, just as they had eight years earlier at the Concerts for Bangladesh. John Lennon was "spotted" in the house by more than one fanatic, even though he was in New York at the time. A few months before, the *Washington Post* had quoted a UN official as saying that Paul, George, and Ringo had agreed to give a New York concert for the Vietnamese boat people and that John was still thinking about it. Another paper said that John would appear only if he were billed separately, not as part of the Beatles. One of the British papers made it worse by printing as fact a story that the Beatles would *definitely* reunite for the Kampuchea show. An irritated Paul didn't deny it; when pressed, he just refused to name the "special guest stars" advertised on the bill along with him.

Regardless of the Beatles rumors, the fourth and final Concert for the People of Kampuchea was like an indoor fireworks display, with one musician after the next dazzling the audience simply by appearing onstage—Rockpile (fronted by Dave Edmunds and Nick Lowe), Elvis Costello and the Attractions, Paul McCartney and Wings, and then those unnamed "friends" of Paul's who, as it turned out, were *not* the other Beatles: John Paul Jones and John Bonham of Led Zeppelin, Pete Townshend and Kenney Jones from the Who, Pink Floyd's David Gilmour, and Ronnie Lane of the Rolling Stones, all reprising their studio roles as members of "Rockestra," the all-star band assembled by Paul earlier that year for his album *Back to the Egg.* And for Rockestra's first live performance ever, the part of Eric Clapton would be played by Robert Plant. Not a bad understudy.

For the finale, the full Rockestra, all clad in silver coats and gold top hats, backed Paul on a sweeping, majestic performance of "Let It Be."

"It was conceived as a week of concerts at an urban venue," Paul later told Timothy White, "and it wasn't internationally satellited. Musically, the album turned out all right, but I hated the show itself. I think that the show was the last thing we did with Wings and a lot of it was the fault of the monitors on stage, because if you can't hear yourself, you think you've done a terrible show. My bass sounded like a *squeak*. It gave me the cold sweats."

Even though Paul's experience wasn't a great one, the Concerts for the People of Kampuchea served their purpose very well. Several million dollars were raised through the sale of an album compiled from all four shows and, even more important, millions of people were exposed to the enormity of the human tragedy in Kampuchea.

Joan Baez hadn't stopped working on the crisis since her return from Southeast Asia. She founded the Humanitas International Human Rights Committee, an organization she would lead for the next thirteen years. One of Humanitas's first acts was to publish an "Open Letter to the Socialist Republic of Vietnam" in five major U.S. newspapers, protesting the human rights violations in the new People's Republic of Vietnam. This left Joan's right-wing critics speechless. How could that "commie" Joan Baez ("Joaney Phoney" in Al Capp's cartoons) criticize a communist government? Easy. What people who caricatured Joan never wanted to see was that she was *always* consistent in her opposition to violence—no matter who was responsible for it.

"Humanitas started with going over to Southeast Asia to talk to boat people," says Joan, "and bring recognition to the fact that people were walking out of Laos and there were people being slaughtered in Cambodia. And that wasn't really known much yet. So we spent some time at the border of Cambodia and it was a little risky, too." One of her proudest achievements was persuading Jimmy Carter to send the Seventh Fleet over to rescue thousands of "boat people" who were adrift in the waters off Vietnam.

In the weeks following the London events, Joan, with the support of a San Francisco television station and one of its newspapers (and with the help of—who else?—Bill Graham), organized a series of Kampuchean benefit concerts in the Bay Area. Two shows by Linda Ronstadt and friends, including Baez, Hoyt Axton, J. D. Souther, and Nicolette Larson, and two by James Taylor, were held in the Warfield Theater, a twenty-two-hundred-seat venue in San Francisco. Across the bay in Oakland, in the fourteen-thousand-seat Oakland Coliseum Arena, Joan assembled the Grateful Dead, the Beach Boys, Santana, and the Jefferson Starship for one giant extravaganza.

It was a marathon show, lasting six and a half hours (no surprise with the Dead on the bill), and even the reviewer for the newspaper that *wasn't* sponsoring the show called it "[a] chapter in Bay Area music history." Between the concerts and Humanitas's other fund-raising, more than a million dollars in emergency aid for Kampuchea was raised in less than a few months' time.

Afterward, Jerry Garcia said it was "a lot of fun. The magic of this affair is that we can help someone." Paul Kantner remarked, "I think the eighties portend more of this."

Paul was more prophetic than he could possibly have imagined. Although no one realized it at the time, the concerts for Kampuchea on either side of the Atlantic were merely a trial run for what, five years later, would become the single greatest benefit concert the world has ever seen.

On Sunday, November 25, 1984, three dozen of the top artists from Britain and Ireland gathered in the SARM studio in London to record "Do They Know It's Christmas (Feed the World)." The song was cowritten by Midge Ure of Ultravox and a scruffy, thirty-one-year-old Irishman named Bob Geldof, lead singer of a band called the Boomtown Rats. Its purpose was to raise money to buy food and supplies for the starving people of drought-stricken Africa, particularly in Ethiopia and the Sudan. The idea for doing it had sprung from Geldof's fevered brain only a month before, shortly after he'd seen a powerful television documentary on the situation in Africa, a crisis the narrator described as "biblical" in its horrific proportions.

"It showed very graphically exactly what was happening and how it came into being," says Harry Belafonte, "and it first showed in England and caught the fancy of Bob Geldof."

Unable to think of anything else, Geldof's first instinct was to donate the royalties from his band's new record. Unfortunately for him, the prospect of there *being* royalties was not terribly great, as three singles released from the album had already stiffed. So Geldof figured if his own record couldn't raise enough money to do any good, maybe some of his musician friends could help out by gathering together and singing collectively on one song.

That seemingly simple idea would completely consume Geldof's life for the better part of the next two years, effectively ending the career of the Boomtown Rats, and eventually raising almost $150 million for African famine relief.

My first awareness of Bob Geldof came in 1974 when CSNY were touring in Canada. He was then a twenty-two-year-old journalist, writing music reviews under the byline "Rob Geldof" for an alternative Vancouver newspaper called *Georgia Straight.* He didn't like us much:

> I used to think that stars shone and twinkled and that superstars positively hummed and glowed with brilliance. The dull, flickering gleam of Crosby, Stills, Nash & Young last Wednesday night was more equitable to black holes than any other astral body that comes to mind.

Nice. I particularly liked the phrase *dull, flickering gleam.* Back then, I certainly wouldn't have called him "Saint Bob," a nickname he'd be given by the media only a decade later.

"Geldof's a great friend of mine," says Sting. "I've known him since the late seventies, middle of the seventies actually. He was the leader of the Boomtown Rats, a great singer. He called me one day and said, 'I've just seen the television. I've seen the fucking television and they're fucking starving in fucking Africa. We've got to fucking do something.' I said, 'Well, I saw it too. What do we do?' He said, 'I've written a fucking song.' He said, 'Will you come and fucking sing it?' I said, 'Yeah. I'll fucking come and sing your fucking song.'"

(I know, I know. *Sting.* Former teacher. Articulate. Thoughtful. But he's no stiff. Sting's got this deliciously British sense of humor. I've had a Brit as a partner for thirty years, so I know about this. They invented the language and they can do any damn thing with it they please.)

Geldof became a man on a mission. He rarely slept. He forgot to eat. Fully aware of the irony, he chose to call his effort Band Aid ("you can't put a sticking plaster on a gaping wound"), and he went after all the biggest musicians he knew—and many he didn't. Nobody was safe from his pressure and pleading. In this exchange from his autobiography, *Is That It?*, Geldof recounts how he literally talked Boy George out of bed—in New York:

> "George, it's Geldof, where the fuck are you?" It was 6 A.M. in George's bedroom.
> "What? Er . . . I'm in New York," he yawned.
> "What the fuck are you doing in New York?"
> "Er . . ."
> "You're meant to be here."
> "Who's there?" the sleepy voice asked.
> "Everybody. Sting is here, and Paul Young, the Spandaus, the Durans, Marilyn, Bono, [Status] Quo, Bananarama, Kool and the Gang, George Michael, [Paul] Weller, Heaven 17. Everybody is here. Everybody except you. There's a Concorde leaving at 9 A.M. Get up and come."
> "I'll try."
> "Don't fucking try. It's important. Get up now and get on with it."

Phil Collins remembers Geldof calling him up out of the blue and saying, "I don't know any famous drummers, so will you do it?" And Phil, always ready to help in a good cause, said, "Sure, that sounds like a bit of fun . . . so I went to the studio on that day and by that time he'd asked everybody else. And we did the 'Band Aid/Do They Know It's Christmas?' song."

In addition to Phil, Sting, and Geldof, Band Aid was made up of Annie Lennox, Bono and Adam Clayton from U2, George Michael, Marilyn, Boy George and Jon Moss of Culture Club, Jody Watley, Paul Weller, and Paul Young, as well as the members of Bananarama, the Boomtown Rats, Duran Duran, Frankie Goes to Hollywood, Heaven 17, Kool & the Gang, Spandau Ballet, and Ultravox. Several of them were asked to do a lead vocal or duet:

(Paul Young)
It's Christmas time
There's no need to be afraid
At Christmas time
We let in light and we banish shade
(Boy George)
And in our world of plenty
We can spread a smile of joy
Throw your arms around the world
At Christmas time
(George Michael)
But say a prayer
Pray for the other ones
At Christmas time it's hard
(Simon Le Bon)
But when you're having fun
There's a world outside your window
(George Michael)
And it's a world of dread and fear
Where the only water flowing is
(George Michael and Bono)
The bitter sting of tears
And the Christmas bells that are ringing
Are clanging chimes of doom
(Bono)
Well, tonight thank God it's them instead of you.
(Band Aid)
And there won't be snow in Africa this Christmas time.
The greatest gift they'll get this year is life
Where nothing ever grows
No rain or rivers flow
Do they know it's Christmas time at all?
Feed the world
Let them know it's Christmas time
Feed the world

The 1985 recording session for "We Are The World" featured forty-five of the top artists in popular music, including Michael Jackson (*front row, third from left*) and Lionel Richie (*front row, seventh from left*) who co-wrote the song.

One of my stand-out memories from Live Aid is Tina Turner's sexy duet with Mick Jagger on "It's Only Rock and Roll."

I knew that we'd done right at Live Aid when I turned and saw Mick applauding us from the side of the stage.

Bono and U2 electrified
the Live Aid crowd at
Wembley Stadium,
July 13, 1985.

Bob Geldof at the microphone after the all-star finale of
"Do They Know It's Christmas" at Live Aid in London.

Bob later said that he was
"embarrassed but intensely
proud" to be held aloft by
Paul McCartney and Pete
Townshend at the end of
Live Aid.

Willie Nelson at the first Farm Aid
concert in Champaign, Illinois, 1985.

John Mellencamp (*right*) at a Farm Aid
concert. There's only one John
Mellencamp. Period.

A Farm Aid T-shirt displays the musical line-up.

"Teach Your Children" was the perfect choice for our encore at the first Bridge School benefit in 1986. *From left to right:* Stephen Stills, Timothy B. Schmit, Graham Nash, Tom Petty, Don Henley, J. D. Souther, Neil Young, Bruce Springsteen, me, and Robin Williams. My short haircut was courtesy of the barbershop in the Texas State Penitentiary.

Bruce Springsteen and Neil Young sharing vocals at the first Bridge School benefit. There are musical combinations at benefits that you'll never see anywhere else.

From left to right: Peter Gabriel, Tracy Chapman, Youssou N'Dour, Sting, Joan Baez, and Bruce Springsteen were part of a series of concerts benefiting Amnesty International in 1988.

This 1990 Amnesty International concert was held in the same stadium in Chile where, twenty years earlier, thousands of political prisoners had been tortured and killed.

Sean Lennon spoke eloquently about China's brutal oppression of the peaceful Tibetan people at a rally following the 1998 Tibetan Freedom Concert in Washington, D.C.

Adam Yauch of the Beastie Boys at a press conference before the Tibetan Freedom concert.

Sean and I performing at the Free Tibet rally in Washington, D.C.

Do they know it's Christmas time at all?
(Paul Young)
Here's to you
Raise a glass for everyone
Here's to them
Underneath that burning sun
Do they know it's Christmas time at all?
(Band Aid)
Feed the world
Feed the world
Feed the world
Let them know it's Christmas time again

"It was great camaraderie," recalls Phil. "I mean everybody was in the studio watching everybody else sing or play the drums or play the guitar. They mixed it that night and the next day it was on the radio, in the shops by the following Friday and sold millions of copies."

No less an activist than Harry Belafonte was deeply impressed: "A lot of people mobilized doing a thing called Band Aid, which I thought was a magnificent use of artists coming to a cause and a need in the human family."

Typically, Geldof was blunt and to the point: "Band Aid was a moral issue: whether you were of the right or left was irrelevant. It transcended local politics because the issue was global."

"Do They Know It's Christmas/Feed The World" entered the UK charts at number one and stayed there for five weeks, eventually selling more than three million copies worldwide. Artists in many other countries made plans to follow Britain's lead by recording their own songs for African relief. Particularly noteworthy among them was the Canadian effort, a song called "Tears Are Not Enough." It featured, among others, Neil Young, Joni Mitchell, and Bryan Adams, all recording as the group Northern Lights.

The big question was what would the Americans do?

The answer started with a phone call from Harry Belafonte to Ken Kragen on December 20, 1984. Kragen is a well-respected artist manager whose clients at the time included Lionel Richie and Kenny Rogers.

"I'm sitting in my office about noontime and my secretary says, 'Harry Belafonte's on the line,'" recalls Kragen, whose kind eyes always seem larger behind the bottle-thick glasses he wears. "I'd only met him once before and not under the most auspicious circumstances. I didn't know him well and he said, 'Have you seen those pictures on television, those pictures of those kids in Africa dying?' And we'd all seen them—Tom Brokaw had been responsible here for putting them on the air despite the fact that the brass at NBC really didn't want him to. And it had moved Americans already. Every night you'd turn on the TV and see another horrible picture of kids dying and people starving in Africa. And Harry wanted to do something about it. He'd read where Bob Geldof had organized Band Aid in England. And he'd read how so many artists had come together there to raise what turned out to be about $10 million. And it bothered him that the African American artists here in America, who are so successful, were not doing anything at this point and he felt something should be done."

Belafonte *was* angry that black artists in America hadn't stepped up to help: "What I did not understand was black America indifference and black America insensitivity to what was going on in the African continent. We have so much linkage, so much history . . . so many reasons to be far more attentive to what was going on than was evidenced. And this lethargic absence, this mindlessness that was going on, I thought had to be repaired. So I took the question to my fellow artists on a moral basis with 'How can you sit so comfortably with the indifference that you're evidencing with this tragedy, when you could, in fact, take some part of that tragedy and fix it and make a difference? Not all of it. Don't sit there and be overwhelmed by the enormity of the problem. Just pick out that portion which is yours, and kick butt. Go out there and make a difference. Change it. Change it. *Change it.*'"

"So Harry called me," continues Kragen, "and we talked for a long time about it. By the end of the call I'd convinced him that we should do what Geldof had done but organize it in an even bigger sense. Not to try to do a concert. I'd been trying to do that with great futility for six months. I said, 'Let's do a record. Geldof has shown us the way.' And so we went to work on a record. And within thirty-six hours I was able to call Harry back and say, 'I've got a song being written by Lionel Richie and Michael Jackson (and actually, at that point, Stevie Wonder). I've got Quincy Jones producing it. In addition, I've got Kenny Rogers and Kim Cairns and Lindsey Buckingham (who all were clients of mine at that time) to perform.' I said, 'I've had thirty-six hours; give me another two weeks and I'll have it done.' And I think I kind of blew him away. He actually left and went to Europe for the next few weeks, and when he came back we had this thing pretty well in hand. But Harry Belafonte was the inspiration, the driving force, the spokesperson, the motivator, the spirit of it. I'd have to say the two greatest influences on everything I've done and on much of America would be, for me, Harry Chapin and Harry Belafonte, the two Harry's in my life."

Singer-songwriter Harry Chapin had several hit songs in the seventies, "Taxi," "Cat's in the Cradle," and "W*O*L*D," before he was killed in an auto accident in 1981. When asked to describe what he did, however, he always called himself an activist first, then a musician. Way ahead of any other artist, Chapin identified the issue of world hunger and made it his own, even forming his own organization, World Hunger Year.

"Harry Chapin was probably the greatest humanitarian in the entertainment field in his time," says Ken Kragen of his old friend and client. ". . . here he was at the end of the seventies, the most active person in trying to fight the evils of hunger and homelessness here in America. I happened to be very lucky to take on his management at that point. And he was a total inspiration. I mean, you couldn't keep up with the man on the street. He walked faster than you. Everything in his life moved at a reckless speed. He was trying . . . I think he believed he was going to die [young] and he was trying to basically accomplish everything in this very short life that he saw before him. And he did everything in a huge hurry. This enormous, energetic, charismatic human being who devoted almost every waking hour to some aspect of charity."

Until I began work on this book, I didn't really appreciate the influence Harry Chapin had on so many artists, including my partner Graham Nash. He and Bruce Springsteen performed at a 1987 memorial concert to Chapin in Carnegie Hall, on what would have been Chapin's forty-fifth birthday. Remembering him that night, Bruce said, "Harry instinctively knew that it was gonna take a lot more than just love to survive. That it was gonna take a strong sense of purpose, of duty, and a good, clear eye on the dirty ways of the world."

When Harry Belafonte was honored at the American Music Awards for his role in "We Are the World," he used his acceptance speech as a platform to let the world know who he thought was *really* responsible: "Harry Chapin died five years ago. But he'd thrown a pebble into a pond and I saw the ripples. It reached Geldof. It reached me. It reached Willie Nelson. It reached millions of people around the world."

Even with Harry Chapin as its guardian angel, "We Are the World" almost didn't happen. The day before the recording session, the whole thing was almost called off. Kragen shudders at the memory. "The night before the event—the very night before the event— one of the managers of one of the artists came to me and said, 'The rockers don't want to be part of it. They don't like the song that much. They don't really want to stand next to the nonrockers.' You know, Lionel Richie has a phrase *You are who you hug*, and everybody in our business wants to hug somebody more important [than they are]. And the rockers didn't want to be associated with the people who weren't rock stars. It wasn't true of all of them. The key thing was Bruce Springsteen, who said 'I'm not going to have any part of that, I'm staying.' And he was the most important rock star of them all at that point. Since he was going to stay, they all would have looked foolish if they'd backed out. But here I was, the night before the recording, faced with the possibility that the event might not happen or that some of the major stars that had committed would now not participate. And there was nothing to do about it. I figured fate would take its place and it was a blessed project. And it was."

"We Are the World" was recorded on the night of January 28, 1985, at the A&M studios in Hollywood. Kragen and Quincy Jones had carefully picked that date to coincide with the American Music Awards, when a lot of musicians would already be in Los Angeles. The session was scheduled to begin immediately after the awards were over.

"Quincy Jones did all the arrangements and everything for 'We Are the World,'" says Willie Nelson, "and I think he was instrumental in putting together a lot of the acts that were there. He sort of envisioned who he wanted on this record, and we came in there and learned the words and smiled a lot."

A total of forty-five artists passed through the huge wrought-iron gates of the studio, some in limousines, some in Bentleys or Mercedes, one even on foot. (Springsteen stunned everyone by renting a car at the airport and driving himself to the studio. He parked outside on the street.) Lionel Richie came directly over from hosting the American Music Awards, as did Tina Turner and Cyndi Lauper, both of whom had also performed. As they entered the studio, they all saw the now-famous sign placed there by Quincy Jones: CHECK YOUR EGO AT THE DOOR.

Inside, Diana Ross was already getting psyched up. "This is some powerful magic gonna happen tonight," she said. "I can feel it."

Appropriately, Bob Geldof had been flown in to be part of the choir. Before they started, Quincy Jones introduced him to the assembled artists by saying, "First I'd like you to meet Bob Geldof, who is really the inspiration for this whole thing. He just came back from Ethiopia and he'd like to talk to you."

Even in this heady situation, the tart-tongued Geldof couldn't resist a comeback. "Oh, *would* I?" he said, smiling. Then he turned serious. Rubbing his eyes, he spoke off-the-cuff, his Irish brogue somehow conveying the global significance of what had drawn them all together.

"I think it's best to remember that the price of a life this year is a piece of plastic seven inches wide with a hole in the middle. And that I think is an indictment of us. And I think what's happening in Africa is a crime of historic proportions. And the crime is that the Western world has got billions of tons of grain bursting in its silos and we're not releasing it to people who are dying of hunger. And I don't know if we in particular can conceive of nothing, but nothing is not having a cardboard box to sleep under in minus ten degrees; nothing is not having any drink to get drunk on, not having water. And you walk into one of the corrugated iron huts and you see meningitis and malaria and typhoid buzzing around in the air, and you see dead bodies lying side by side with the live ones, and on a good day you can only see 120 people die slowly in front of you. And in some of the camps you see fifteen bags of flour for twenty-seven and a half thousand people."

As he spoke, Geldof sometimes shut his eyes, as if to recall more vividly the horrors he'd seen—and do them justice for these people who had gathered there to help.

"And it's that that we're here for. And I don't want to bring anybody down, but maybe it's the best way of making what you really feel and why you're really here tonight come out through this song. So thanks a lot everybody and let's hope it works."

Nothing could follow him except what they'd all come there to do. See if you can still hear it:

LIONEL RICHIE: There comes a time when we heed a certain call
LIONEL RICHIE & STEVIE WONDER: When the world must come together as one
STEVIE WONDER: There are people dying
PAUL SIMON: Oh and it's time to lend a hand, to life
PAUL SIMON & KENNY ROGERS: The greatest gift of all
KENNY ROGERS: We can't go on pretending day by day
JAMES INGRAM: That someone, somewhere, will soon make a change
TINA TURNER: We are all a part of God's great big family
BILLY JOEL: And the truth
TINA TURNER & BILLY JOEL: You know love is all we need.

MICHAEL JACKSON: We are the world, we are the children,
We are the ones who make a brighter day, so let's start giving
DIANA ROSS: There's a choice we're making, we're saving our
   own lives, it's true
DIANA ROSS & MICHAEL JACKSON: We'll make a better day just you
   and me
DIONNE WARWICK: Well, send them your heart, so they know that
   someone cares
DIONNE WARWICK & WILLIE NELSON: And their lives will be
   stronger and free
WILLIE NELSON: As God has shown us by turning stone to bread
AL JARREAU: And so we all must lend a helping hand
BRUCE SPRINGSTEEN: We are the world, we are the children
KENNY LOGGINS: We are the ones who make a brighter day, so
   let's start giving
STEVE PERRY: There's a choice we're making, we're saving our
   own lives
DARRYL HALL: It's true we'll make a better day, just you and me
MICHAEL JACKSON: When you're down and out and there seems
   no hope at all
HUEY LEWIS: But if you just believe, there's no way we can fall
CYNDI LAUPER: Well, well, well, well, let us realize that a change
   can only come
KIM CARNES: When we
KIM CARNES & CYNDI LAUPER & HUEY LEWIS: Stand together as one.
CHOIR: We are the world, we are the children, we are the ones
   who make a brighter day, so let's start giving
BOB DYLAN: There's a choice we're making, we're saving our own
   lives, it's true we'll make a better day, just you and me

"We Are the World" took all night to record, and the principal
vocalists stayed until well after 6:00 A.M. When it was done, all the
sheet music was passed around furiously for autographs. Although
everyone in the room was a star, it was impossible not to be excited
by *somebody*.

Even Ray Charles was impressed: "All the people that are here are ultra in their own right and of course I'm just so happy to get to see them." (That *is* what he said. . . .)

Still, nobody forgot why they were there. "When something like this comes along," said Paul Simon, "that allows everyone to participate and feel that they're making a contribution, you rush to do it because otherwise you feel that you're just a witness to a tragedy." Added Springsteen, "I think anytime somebody asks you to take one night of your time to keep people from starving to death some place, it's pretty hard . . . you can't say no."

"It was one that worked," says Harry Belafonte today. "It was hugely, hugely beneficial. I mean the arts community showed themselves off very well then."

Three months after its release, in an unprecedented show of global unity, "We Are the World" was played simultaneously on eight thousand radio stations around the world. It reached number one on the U.S. charts and, including merchandising and video sales, raised more than $50 million for USA for Africa (United Artists Support for Africa), the American counterpart of Band Aid.

"Do They Know It's Christmas?" and "We Are the World" were both written for a particular moment in time. By listening to those songs, people got to connect to another part of themselves, a better part. We all have an experience in our lives with a song that made a difference to us, a song we heard early on that affected us and that we've never forgotten. "Strange Fruit" was that kind of song for me. When a song is actually designed to get people enlisted in a cause, it has a double impact. You're not just providing pleasure, you're doing something important, both by raising money and by getting people to listen to the message of the song. What Geldof did, what Lionel Richie and Michael Jackson did, led to a lot of things that are now standard. Someone will write a song about a painful situation. It may raise money or awareness. Then it becomes a song that's about more than just pain; it's about the possibilities that can come out of that pain.

Bob Geldof still wasn't satisfied. He'd gone to Africa with the first shipment of Band Aid assistance and came back convinced he needed to do something more. That something was Live Aid, Geldof's grandiose plan to stage two all-star benefit concerts simultaneously, one in London and the other in Philadelphia, and then for good measure, link them together via satellite and create the first worldwide fundraising telethon.

"I heard about this concert that Geldof was trying to organize," remembers Phil Collins, "this global thing . . . and I just didn't see it happening, you know, getting all those bands together with all the egos involved and all the management and all the kind of things that can be . . . the spam that can be put in the works to sort of slow these things up."

"I came to discover that I didn't really have to sell the idea at all to the artists," Geldof wrote in his memoir. "If I got through to them direct, the response was always positive. But if I got through to the managers, their attitude was often negative. . . . It is irritating when managers assume the moral guardianship of their charges. Often they are simply obstructive in the misguided notion that they are 'doing their job.'"

Among the first to sign on to Geldof's next crusade were Band Aid participants like Sting, Phil Collins, U2, George Michael, Ultravox, Spandau Ballet, and Paul Young. Duran Duran, then one of the most popular acts in the world, had effectively become two groups at that point, with half the members splitting off to form a new band, Power Station. Somehow the persuasive Geldof was able to convince both bands to appear, and the Duran Duran set at Live Aid would be their last live performance ever.

Some groups, including the Who, Led Zeppelin, Black Sabbath, and Status Quo reunited just for the occasion. (So did Crosby, Stills, Nash & Young, but I'll get to that in a minute.) Paul McCartney, David Bowie, Elton John, Queen, and Dire Straits were confirmed for England. In fact, the lineup there got so crowded that the Pretenders, Simple Minds, and the Thompson Twins were sent to Philadelphia to join a roster that already included Bob Dylan, Mick Jagger, Eric Clapton, and Tom Petty.

Geldof was now calling this a "Global Jukebox," and he told everyone that the most important thing was not if an artist or group was musically "significant" but whether they could sell a million records. Hits, pure and simple, determined whether a band was asked to play. On the face of it, Geldof's reasoning was sound: if more people watched, more money would be contributed and more lives would be saved. That explained Adam Ant and Rick Springfield.

To be honest, in 1985 that rationale didn't guarantee a place in the lineup for Crosby, Stills & Nash. Our last Top Ten hit had been Nash's "Wasted on the Way," three years earlier. And even though we were in the middle of a very successful tour, I wasn't sure we'd be invited at all. To make matters worse, neither Stephen nor I were in particularly good shape.

Nash says: "Crosby, Stills & Nash at that particular point were feeling a little estranged from each other. David was a little out and so was Stephen, and therefore I was too. Because if any one of us is falling, we're all falling as far as I'm concerned, no matter how much and how strong any individual member is or is not at the time."

If there was any question about whether we'd get asked to do Live Aid, it was firmly resolved by the show's American producer, Bill Graham: "People like Crosby, Stills and Nash deserve to be in the show," he told *Rolling Stone*. "Creatively, they have a right, and they've also been there for all the positive movements over the last twenty years. How could you *not* put them in the show?" Thanks, Bill.

Not everyone wanted to be a part of Live Aid. John Mellencamp told me, "If something feels natural, if something feels organic to me, then I don't mind doing it. But I've been asked to do a lot of stuff and I just don't like to do it. I feel funny . . . it embarrasses me to do it, quite honestly. It would have been embarrassing for me to do Live Aid. I would have been embarrassed to be there . . . all the infighting . . . the people that I do business with day to day in the music business are involved in all that shit. So the first thing I hear is, 'Well, the prime-time TV'. . . Huh? The prime-time TV time is what time? Not a time for me. So go ahead and put other acts you manage on there, because I don't give a shit, you know, if it's about prime-time TV time and what time most satellites are gonna hook up and you're gonna be seen all over the world. Go ahead and put one of your other acts on there, because I'm not gonna do it. And that's just pretty much how I felt about it. So I stayed in Indiana that day."

"When you went to Live Aid," says Peter Yarrow, "for some people it was absolutely authentic, a commitment to do something they believed in, whereas other people were saying, 'How much time do I get on the bill?' 'What am I going to get to do with whom?' 'How much press am I going to get?'"

Peter learned this painfully for himself. He and Mary and Noel (Paul) arrived in Philadelphia early on the day of the show expecting to sing "Blowin' in the Wind" with Dylan, only to find out that it wasn't happening. Dylan *was* singing it, but not with them. They were left out of the show until the finale, when they got to come out and sing in the chorus along with everyone else. If there was one blatant injustice about Live Aid, it was the omission of Peter, Paul & Mary. Nobody deserved to be there more. Not us. Not anyone.

Live Aid was as remarkable for who wasn't there as for who was. Michael Jackson had a "major commitment." Stevie Wonder was announced, then his people said it was never definite. The artist still known as Prince had just "retired." Bruce Springsteen had only recently been married and had spent almost no time with his new bride because of a heavy touring schedule. Billy Joel couldn't get his band together. According to Geldof, Paul Simon and Willie Nelson were both treated badly by Bill Graham and they decided not to play.

Bill was dealing with other problems, some not of his own making. After Live Aid was over, he revealed one in particular: "As the show grew, Bob Geldof had a certain number of acts which had committed to him. He had no black acts. It was obvious to me right away. Certain major black acts were not available. People could say, 'They should be available for their brothers and sisters in Ethiopia.' That was not for me to say. What I could say was that I contacted every single major black artist. I won't name them because I'm still in the business. But they all turned down Live Aid. I also turn things down.

That doesn't mean they didn't care. But all the major black artists? All the biggest ones? You name them. They all turned Live Aid down."

With the help of the Philadelphia promoter, Larry Magid, Bill was eventually able to add the Four Tops, Teddy Pendergrass, Ashford & Simpson, and Patti LaBelle to the Philadelphia lineup. And although it seemed impossible at first, Tina Turner eventually re-arranged her tour schedule to make it there as well.

It wasn't smooth sailing yet. Two weeks before the event, Huey Lewis & the News, who had been announced in the initial press release, pulled out. Huey said he had "questions as to whether the food is actually getting to the starving people or not."

Harry Belafonte, who'd just returned from Africa, was angered by Lewis's statement, as he made very clear to a Philadelphia reporter: "I would suggest that Mr. Lewis get his facts together, that he stop being disruptive and divisive. If he is such a hotshot with his mouth, let him get on a plane and go sit in a camp. . . . For him to sit back here and send out information based on hearsay is unfair to his col-leagues and very unfair to the victims."

In the end, all the politics and posturing didn't really matter. Everything had come down to just one day: July 13, 1985.

According to Hal Uplinger, who produced Live Aid for American television, "It was a worldwide 16-hour television broadcast utiliz-ing 13 satellites and 22 transponders. It was shown live to a total of 110 countries. For 45 countries without downlink capabilities, we sent a videotape of the show to be played within a two-week period. So, it was broadcast in a total of 155 countries with an estimated audience of two billion viewers plus one billion listeners on radio."

The newly reunited Status Quo kicked off Live Aid in Wembley Stadium at two minutes after noon with the well-chosen "Rockin' Around the World." At the same time, Style Council was waiting on a second stage that would revolve into place as soon as Status Quo finished its set, while on yet a third stage, Geldof and his band, the Boomtown Rats, were just setting up their equipment. This routine would be continued throughout the concert, with one band performing on Stage A, a second band ready to go on Stage B, and a third band loading in on Stage C. A turn of the giant wheel, and the first band would jump offstage, only to be replaced by a new third-act-in-waiting. It was a brilliant design and it worked perfectly.

You know that huge atomic clock that measures time down to the millisecond? It's the best way I can think of to explain just how precisely everything was scheduled. Take the story of my friend Phil Collins, the only musician who played both ends of Live Aid, in London *and* Philadelphia.

"I wanted to play drums with somebody rather than just sing. And it seemed that the people, close friends of mine at the time, Eric Clapton and Robert Plant, were both playing in America. And they said, 'Yeah, we'd love you to come along and play with us.' In fact, Robert Plant said, 'Why don't you, me, and Jimmy Page do something?' So I said 'Yeah, great!' because I'd been on tour with Robert Plant as his drummer just prior to that. And of course that became the Led Zeppelin reunion.

"Harvey Goldsmith, who was organizing the English one, said, 'You know, if you get on Concorde, you could actually be there in time for the evening show in Philadelphia. And I think a few other people may be trying to do that. So you'd be part of a group of people doing it.' I didn't want to be the *only* one . . . it's like showing off, you know. So, I think Duran Duran were doing England and Power Station were doing America and they've got some of the same guys in those two bands. So I do the gig in Wembley with Sting and then I go to the airport, get on Concorde, and of course there's nobody else. It's just me, because one of the bands has pulled out in America or England, one of the two. So there's just me and a whole bunch of journalists. And so I got to Philadelphia; we go to New York and then got the helicopter to Philadelphia. I ran around the dressing room saying hello to Plant and Page because I had been listening to what I was going to do with Zeppelin on the plane and Eric's stuff I knew anyway. So I got there, went up onstage, checked the piano, checked the drums, the curtain went open and I sang my two songs, the same two songs I just sang in England. Then I found out when I got back to New York that I was the only person that had done it and that it was a link of the two concerts." (The irony of this is that Phil's not a glory hound. There are some people who just can't do good things without hogging the spotlight—like me—but some guys do it very gracefully, and he's one of the best at it.)

"One of the things that ABC was so concerned about was that they wanted the last three hours of the broadcast to air at eight o'clock eastern time exactly," recalls producer Hal Uplinger. "They wanted Phil Collins sitting down at the piano after we were thirteen hours into the broadcast. This was how they were going to begin the ABC coverage in America. . . . When you do a one-hour show, you can pretty well control it. As the second hand was coming up toward eight o'clock—*exactly*—Phil Collins sat down at the piano bench, and the ABC people absolutely couldn't believe it. Now we were lucky he was sitting down right at the second. You can't control those things that close. It was funny."

"I was trying to make up time all day long," Bill Graham later wrote. "If I lost a minute here or there, I would ask an act to drop a song. This got me into problems with the Thompson Twins' manager. I even asked Bob Dylan to drop a song but he wouldn't do it."

Joan Baez (who opened the American half of Live Aid exactly two hours to the minute after Status Quo walked onstage in London) says, "It was *not* Woodstock. I mean it was funny . . . when Woodstock ended it was something like eighteen hours late. When Live Aid ended, it was two minutes late. Times had changed."

They had. Only CSNY, Joan, Santana, and the Who played at both Woodstock and Live Aid.

Joan was introduced to the crowd in Philadelphia by the man who Bill Graham had chosen as the American equivalent of British royalty: Jack Nicholson. Says Joan, "I was the bridge really between the current rock 'n' roll and the social movements. . . . and so I said, 'I don't want any more than six minutes because I wouldn't be able to last with those kids.' Never mind who was out there, on television there would be the older people saying, 'Oh, there's Joan. I remember her.' But the young ones, what would I do? Well, 'We Are the

World'—'You Are the World—'You Are the Children'—and I said something about how this was their Woodstock."

Here's exactly what she said, eloquent as always: "Good morning, children of the eighties! This is your Woodstock, and it's long overdue. And it's nice to know the money out of your pockets will go for food to feed hungry children. I can think of no more glorious way of starting our part of the day than by saying grace together, which means that we thank, each of us, his and her own God for the many blessings that we have in a world in which so many people have nothing. And when we say this grace, we also reach deep in our hearts and our souls and say that we will move a little from the comfort of our lives to understand their hurt, their pain, and their discomfort. And that will make their lives richer and it will make our lives real." And with that she began to sing *"Amazing Grace . . ."*

Joan was laughing when she described her Live Aid experience to me: "And I heard that Bill Graham was offstage saying, 'There she *goes* again. Tell her to shut her mouth. Shut up. Don't talk. Just sing.' He always had it with me and the talking. But I felt to be that bridge I would do what I could."

Although they were not yet linked up by satellite, the two shows were now running on parallel tracks. In Wembley, Elvis Costello was leading the audience in a mass sing-along on what he introduced as "an old northern English folk song," the Beatles' "All You Need Is Love." A few minutes later the Hooters were onstage in JFK. Then it was back to London for Nik Kershaw, over to Philadelphia for the Four Tops, then to Billy Ocean in England, and back again to America for Ozzie Osbourne and Black Sabbath.

Even on acid you couldn't have dreamed up a more bizarre lineup than Ozzie Osbourne followed by Sade followed by Run-DMC. Fortunately, they were all separated by the Atlantic Ocean.

Sting's brief set was next up in Wembley, where it was now 3:30 P.M. An acoustic version of "Message in a Bottle" prompted the second crowd sing-along of the day, and then Sting was joined by Phil Collins for his final song, "Every Breath You Take."

Sometimes the trains overlapped. Rick Springfield went onstage in Philadelphia at the precise moment that Phil Collins began his solo set in London. (Although I was in Philadelphia, who do you think I watched? Good guess.)

Phil has a not-so-happy memory of his two songs at Wembley: "I played 'In the Air Tonight.' And then I made a terrible mistake. I've never been able to play 'Against All Odds' since I wrote it, and I didn't play it on the record because it was made on tour, and I've never really been able to play it since I wrote it. And I tried at Live Aid and I'll never forget . . . my finger slipped off this keyboard because it was very hot in London. And it just semitoned out, and it was horrible. I could hear seventy thousand people go *Arrgh!* and millions of people around the world were going *Arrgh!*"

Immediately after finishing his set, Phil was whisked away from Wembley by helicopter and taken directly to Heathrow airport. Getting permission for the helicopter to make an unprecedented landing next to the Concorde had required the direct intervention of Buckingham Palace. (Prince Charles and Princess Diana attended the opening of Live Aid but had to leave early for lunch with his mother.) As Phil's helicopter approached the airport, it was sent directly onto the field, landing right in between two jumbo jets. The best part happened as Phil was being escorted to the plane—a plane that was being held for *him*—and a British Airways employee stopped him and said, "Excuse me, sir. May I see your passport?"

Just as Phil was boarding the Concorde in London, we were going onstage in Philadelphia. It was about 11:00 A.M. and the day was already a scorcher. We wanted to do a sound check first, but we were told there wasn't time. I told Bill we weren't ready and he and I started to go at it, until he said "You're ready *now*" and opened the curtain. Suddenly we were onstage in front of eighty thousand people, ready or not. We just looked at each other, shrugged, and did "Southern Cross" and "Teach Your Children." It must have been okay, because the crowd response was great. As we were leaving the stage I saw Mick Jagger, who'd been watching us play, and he was applauding enthusiastically. You can't hate that.

At five o'clock in London, noon in Philadelphia, Bob Geldof walked out on the Wembley stage, grabbed the microphone from a slightly startled but amused Paul Young (still in the middle of a duet with Allison Moyet), and announced the live satellite linkup between the two concerts: "Wembley, will you please welcome America to Live Aid day—Hello America, welcome to the world!"

Thirty-five hundred miles away, Bryan Adams replied, "Hey Philadelphia, hello London, hello world!" before launching into his hit "Summer of '69."

With the whole world watching, the next band to take the stage was also one of the most eagerly anticipated—U2. Like a lot of people, I'd heard of them but hadn't yet seen them. They'd just come off a nine-month world tour, but if they were tired they sure didn't show it at Live Aid. Bono was like a man possessed, from the opening chords of their anthem "Sunday Bloody Sunday" (an incredibly powerful song about the infamous Bloody Sunday massacre, when British troops killed thirteen unarmed Irish protesters on a Sunday in 1972; it was the same kind of gut reaction to inhumanity that brought forth "Ohio"), through a runaway rendition of "Bad" that included bits of the Stones' "Ruby Tuesday" and "Sympathy for the Devil," and Lou Reed's "Walk on the Wild Side."

During "Bad," Bono jumped down from the ten-foot stage into the photography pit, pulled a girl out of the crowd, and, eyes closed as if he were in a trance, began dancing with her. I remember watching him on one of the monitors in Philadelphia and thinking, *Who is this guy?* After Live Aid, everybody knew.

"Out of the hours of Live Aid that I saw by the end of the day," Joan Baez says in her autobiography, *And a Voice to Sing With,* "the high point was witnessing the magic of U2. They moved me as nothing else moved me. They moved me in their newness, their youth, and their tenderness."

Following us, Dire Straits did "Brothers in Arms" and "Money for Nothing," with its tongue-in-cheek chorus of "I Want My MTV" bouncing off the satellite and landing everywhere from Brooklyn to Bombay. Perhaps someday they, too, would get their MTV. Back in

Philadelphia, George Thorogood followed with twelve minutes of down-and-dirty blues-rock before giving way to one of the few acts in the world that could make it seem like they appeared before two billion people every day.

Wearing a white tank top, too-tight blue jeans, and a studded leather armband, Freddie Mercury seized the Wembley stage and claimed it as his own. No band at Live Aid was better suited than Queen to fulfill Geldof's dream of a global jukebox. Blasting out a medley of their hits, from "Bohemian Rhapsody," "Radio Ga Ga," and "We Will Rock You" through "We Are the Champions," Mercury and his mates showed the world just how popular they were on their home turf. Traditional British reserve was forgotten as seventy thousand frenzied fans shouted and stomped along with every song, thundering back on the refrain of "We Will Rock You" with such fervor that it actually shook the steel and concrete supports of Wembley Stadium.

"It was a good morale booster for us," said Queen's bassist, John Deacon, ". . . it showed us the strength of support we had in England, and it showed us what we had to offer as a band."

One of rock's few married couples, Jim Kerr and Chrissie Hynde, led their respective bands, Simple Minds and the Pretenders, through back-to-back sets in JFK Stadium, then returned to their trailer to care for their infant daughter. In between those performances, one of Bob Geldof's biggest boosters was onstage in England. When someone first approached David Bowie about doing Live Aid, his immediate response was to ask if Geldof was involved. Said Bowie, "I only want to do Geldof's thing."

Now, at "Geldof's thing," the dapper Bowie wore a light suit and yellow tie, every inch the Thin White Duke. He did "Rebel, Rebel" and "Heroes" ("We can be heroes, just for one day . . . "), before asking the crowd to watch a powerful video documentary of the famine in Ethiopia. Its stark images of children with distended bellies were underscored by the Cars' song "Drive." "God bless you," said Bowie. "You're the heroes of this concert. Lest we forget why we're here, I'd like to introduce a video made by CBC television. The subject speaks for itself." For the first time all day, both stadiums were almost completely quiet. The crowds were stunned at the images they saw on those giant screens, as were the two billion people watching Live Aid around the world. Just as Bob Geldof was unable to ignore what he'd seen on television nine months before, this footage had a measurably similar effect on the global television audience. Every time the video was played during the remainder of the broadcast, the phone lines were jammed, with some people waiting up to seven hours just to make their contribution. In 1985 the power of music and imagery was still pretty much a new phenomenon; at that point, MTV wasn't even five years old. If Live Aid proved one thing, it was how potent that combination could be—particularly as a force for good.

Bob Geldof later described the Who reunion at Live Aid as "like getting one man's four ex-wives together." Before he would even consider playing, Pete Townshend grilled Geldof on the phone for over an hour, asking him detailed questions about the Band Aid Trust—who administered it and *exactly* where the money went. "I thought that was really cool," says Geldof.

After all the effort it took to get the Who just to show up at Live Aid, it's ironic that their set was plagued by technical problems. During their opening song, "My Generation," all the power went out in Wembley. Even though it was quickly restored, the satellite transmission remained spotty for the rest of their set, preventing the rest of the world from seeing much of it. But the crowd inside Wembley didn't know and didn't care that the Who was now playing largely just for them. Roger Daltrey's voice was strong, and he looked as if he hadn't aged a day in the sixteen years since Woodstock.

The Who rocked so hard at Live Aid that they completely ignored the multicolored warning lights at the foot of the stage. Every other band that day stayed within the tight twenty-minute time restriction, but the Who played for twenty-five. When the red warning light started flashing, Pete just smashed it with his boot.

In Philadelphia, Carlos Santana did a short set with another great guitarist, Pat Metheny. Carlos believes Live Aid was a transformational day: "It's great to see the whole world get involved, you know? One person has this idea and it probably comes to him in his dreams like most great things do anyway. And he created a snowball effect. Playing with Mr. Pat Metheny, and playing with all the great bands . . . that's like a plus. But to know that so many people on this planet are watching on worldwide TV . . . for a common cause . . . it's a real turn-on when you can see all of us becoming like one body mechanism in this planet."

The next-to-last performer at Live Aid in London was Elton John, who came out in one of his typically understated outfits: a Russian-style felt hat adorned with feathers and a long black-and-silver coat. Sitting down at the piano, he launched into "Rocket Man," then later did a duet with Kiki Dee on their hit "Don't Go Breakin' My Heart." At the end of his set, Elton was joined onstage by the two members of Wham!, Andrew Ridgeley and George Michael. They did "Don't Let the Sun Go Down on Me," during which it rained for the only time that day, a welcome relief to the sweltering crowd.

Back at JFK, Teddy Pendergrass (along with Ashford & Simpson) made his first concert appearance since suffering a near-fatal automobile accident that left him paralyzed from the waist down. I'll never forget when he emerged from his trailer: all the frenetic backstage activity literally stopped; then, after a brief, emotional moment, all the other artists rose and gave him a standing ovation. In yet another of the bizarre segues that by now were the order of the day at Live Aid, Pendergrass was followed to the U.S. stage by someone Bette Midler introduced as "a woman who pulled herself up by her bra straps." Wearing huge metallic hoop earrings, an auburn-haired Madonna danced and sang her way through a three-song set of "Into the Groove," "Holiday," and "Love Makes the World Go Round."

Natalie Merchant, for one, was offended. She told *Rolling Stone*, "A lot of people who were involved didn't devote a lot of attention to the cause through their art. For instance, it was a hypocrisy for Madonna to perform at Live Aid. It seemed almost grotesque to see her singing 'Holiday' and then to see live telecasts of starving children in the desert."

I'll say this much for Madonna: at least she showed up at Live Aid. But she also came with attitude. Our road manager, Mac Holbert, was walking through the tunnels beneath the stadium when one of the Material Girl's bodyguards approached him and instructed him to look away because Madonna was coming through. Says Mac, "There was an entourage of about fifteen to twenty people. I looked at the guy like he was out of his mind and just walked on, but they really tried to do this, to make me avert my eyes."

It was 10:00 P.M. in England when, as Paul McCartney later described it, "I just wandered in and said, 'Where's the piano?'" Unfortunately for him, he didn't ask, "Where's the microphone?"

Paul's mike was stone-dead, a problem caused by that brief rain-storm during Elton's set. At first, he didn't realize it. Then, as he continued to sing "Let It Be," it became all too clear that nobody could hear him. People started booing, but Paul just kept on play-ing. Eventually some of the audience figured out what was happen-ing and started to fill in for him. They sang "There will be an answer" until, at last, the answer came. The huge crowd roared when Paul's unmistakable voice finally came through the speakers. Then, as one, seventy thousand more voices joined in to finish the song with him: "*Let it be . . .*"

In his book, Geldof described what happened next: "At the end Townshend and McCartney had decided they'd get behind me and grab hold of my legs and hoist me onto their shoulders. I nearly died of embarrassment. It was terrible. These people were pop greats. 'Please put me down. I really don't want this.' I remember thinking, it may not mean much to someone not interested in pop, but looking back, I am still embarrassed but intensely proud that I was carried on Paul McCartney's and Pete Townshend's shoulders."

For the finale of Live Aid in Wembley, only one song was possible. Geldof warned the crowd that it might be a bit rough since some of them didn't know the words: "There might be a bit of a cock-up, but if you're going to cock it up, you might as well cock it up in front of two billion people." Then, everyone who remained, including McCartney, Bono, Elton, Bowie, Freddie Mercury, Pete Townshend, and George Michael, joined in for "Do They Know It's Christmas?" Even though it was July, this Christmas song still worked.

In the United States, there were still quite a few more "presents" left. Tom Petty and the Heartbreakers gave the crowd a tight version of "Refugee." The Cars offered a live "Drive." Neil's gifts included "Sugar Mountain," "Helpless," "Needle and the Damage Done," "Nothing Is Perfect," and "Powderfinger."

Power Station did a short set, followed by the Thompson Twins, who did "Hold Me Now" and "Stay with Me." What I remember most about them was their female percussionist. Her shock of blonde hair was so huge it could easily have been a nesting place for the entire Flock of Seagulls. There was a lot of hair at Live Aid. In the sixties, ours was just long; in the eighties, it was long and *high*.

Then it was time to rock. Eric Clapton blew the doors off JFK Stadium with "White Room" and "She's Waiting." Then, just as the hot Philadelphia sun finally began to fade, Phil Collins arrived onstage in time to back Clapton on drums for a crowd-thrilling version of "Layla."

Showing no apparent ill effects from his trans-Atlantic sprint, Phil settled in at the piano and proceeded to play the exact same songs, "In the Air Tonight" and "Against All Odds," that he'd played earlier that day in London. In between them, he turned to the crowd and with a little half-smile uttered what would become the signature line of Live Aid: "I was in England this afternoon . . . funny old world, innit?" This time he did "Against All Odds" flawlessly.

Says Phil: "So I tried it again in Philadelphia and I got it right in Philadelphia, but that was the last time I actually played the song. It was the same two songs, so I thought I would try to play them right at one of the events." He really *is* a genuinely modest guy.

After his two-song set, Phil went to the microphone and, in one of the most highly anticipated moments of the day, brought out three friends: John Paul Jones, Jimmy Page, and Robert Plant. For all intents and purposes, this was the first Led Zeppelin performance in more than five years. (Phil stayed and sat in on drums, in place of Zeppelin's late drummer, John Bonham.)

When he grabbed the mike and asked the crowd if it had any requests, Plant drove the already hysterical crowd into a near-frenzy. Not waiting for a reply, he started singing "Rock and Roll." Even with little time to rehearse, the band sounded strong. Plant's vocals were rough, but the adoring Philadelphia fans couldn't have cared less. The second tune was "Whole Lotta Love," with Plant and Page sharing a single microphone on the vocals.

Plant later told *Rolling Stone*, "It was very odd. Everyone was congratulating themselves for being there because that's what they'd always wanted. Yet there are a lot more important things to want than Page and I staggering around in Philadelphia, me hoarse and him out of tune."

Of course it was their final song that everyone was waiting—and hoping—to hear. It's always stunning to see an entire audience following along on every word of a particular song, down to the precise phrasing of each line. We've had it happen with "Ohio" and "Teach Your Children," but there was something almost worshipful in the way the fans at Live Aid responded to "Stairway to Heaven." That's really the only way I can describe it; it was like a secular revival meeting with eighty thousand participants. For the length of that one song, "Heaven" was happening right there on earth.

There was one more reunion yet to come.

A couple of days before Live Aid, we'd gotten word from Neil's manager, Elliot Roberts, that Neil (who already had his own place in the lineup) might want to do a few songs with us as CSNY. We hadn't played live together as a group in eleven years, so this would be a very big deal. When word leaked about the possibility of a reunion, the media were all over us with questions. The fact is, we couldn't say anything because we didn't know ourselves.

Live Aid was also toward the end of my days of really being blitzed. I was very excited about the prospect of doing something with the four of us, but I was also very nervous about seeing Neil. I realized he'd know how completely out of it I was. I didn't really want him to see me like that . . . but it happened anyway.

The day of the show, after we'd done our set and before Neil was due to go on, we got together in a trailer and tried to rehearse. We sang "Only Love Can Break Your Heart" and I blew his mind because I remembered it—I remembered exactly what to do, and I sang great. Neil got this look on his face like, *Whoa . . . this is pretty good. What the hell? I thought Crosby was supposed to be dead. What's going on here?* The rehearsal went better than we could have imagined, so I felt very encouraged.

Then we went out there. I said, "Surprise!" and, even on the heels of the Zeppelin set, we got a thunderous ovation. But the surprise was on us. Somebody had crossed the monitors—Stephen's monitor feed was over on our side and Neil's monitor feed was on Stephen's side—and nobody could hear what they were doing. I was stupefied anyway, so I just stood there and *looked* stupefied. We finished with "Daylight Again/Find the Cost of Freedom," changing the lyric to "I think about all the things we said / *Will the world be fed?*" No matter how *we* thought we did, the crowd still went crazy. (It sometimes makes you question all applause. What are they *hearing?*) It wasn't an inspiring experience, even though our intent was good. Neil said later that "the CSNY reunion was terrible, the worst thing I've ever seen. It was totally untogether. We sounded much better in the trailer when we were rehearsing. I'm glad we did it, but we didn't do it very well."

Meanwhile, Bill Graham was fuming at the network television coverage. They wanted pop, not rock. Bill later wrote that "ABC cut away from artists in the middle of songs. They didn't show the Crosby, Stills, Nash, and Young reunion or the Led Zeppelin set. In defense of themselves, ABC said, 'We have a business to run. We have electric bills to pay.' They were actually quoted as saying that in the *New York Times.*" (At the time I didn't know the network had cut away. They may have done us a favor.)

Not by accident, Duran Duran was the first band to perform on ABC's broadcast of Live Aid. They opened with "A View to a Kill," then the number-one single in America. Simon Le Bon's image was magnified a thousandfold on the giant screens. Unfortunately for him, this only made it easier for people to notice when he completely blew out his voice on the line "It's all we *neeeeed.*" He sounded like a kid going through puberty. Poor guy, I knew how he felt. I'd just been there.

No matter how high (or loud) Patti LaBelle sings, she never seems to blow out *her* voice. Her set and the one that followed it (Hall & Oates playing with David Ruffin and Eddie Kendricks of the Temptations) were both tremendous, high-energy performances.

At 10:15 P.M., Bette Midler introduced "my friend and everybody's idol, Mr. Mick Jagger." This was a sleek, simple Mick. Tight blue T-shirt and jeans, no pretense. Backed by Hall and Oates and their band, he opened with "Lonely at the Top" before asking the crowd, "Hey! You still got some energy left?" When eighty thousand people shouted *Yes!!!* he responded with rockin' versions of "Just Another Night" and "Miss You."

What happened next was one of the standout moments of Live Aid. I got to see it right from the side of the stage. After "Miss You," Mick wiped his brow and said, "Thank you everyone for staying all day in this hot weather. All right, where's *Tina?!*"

On cue, Tina Turner strutted across the stage toward Mick, all hair and high heels, wearing only a very tight, very short black dress. With Mick on his knees in front of Tina, they did a sexy duet on "State of Shock," followed by an even bawdier performance on "It's Only Rock & Roll." In the middle of the song, Mick's shirt came off and his pants started to come down too, before he grabbed them and—still singing—raced to the side of the stage and made a complete costume change, never missing a beat.

Although he still only rarely performs at benefits, Mick explained to *Rolling Stone* why he'd made an exception for Live Aid: "I don't believe in being a charity queen. To make the likely rounds, turning up at charity balls and dinners wearing my diamonds. There are very few people in rock & roll who set themselves up as charity queens. But this event has got most everyone in rock & roll—I mean, Jimmy Page isn't known for his charity."

At 10:40 P.M., almost sixteen hours after the event had begun in England, Jack Nicholson stepped to the microphone to make the final introduction of Live Aid. And since Jack *wasn't* wearing his trademark sunglasses, everybody knew it had to be someone special: "Some artists' work speaks for itself, some artists' work speaks for his generation. It's my deep personal pleasure to present to you one of America's great voices of freedom. It can only be one man. The transcendent Bob Dylan!"

Bob strolled out, accompanied by an unlikely pair of musicians he'd run into in a New York club only a few days earlier: Keith Richards and Ron Wood. Although they'd all played together before, this was the first time they'd ever done so in front of an audience. Unfortunately, it showed. They were evidently a little tight (and I don't mean musically), and Keith's and Ron's unfamiliarity with Dylan's songs only compounded the problem. At one point, Wood tuned his guitar *during* a song; at another, he simply played air guitar.

Dylan later told Robert Hilburn of the *Los Angeles Times* that "They screwed around with us. We didn't even have any [sound] monitors out there. When they threw in the grand finale at the last moment, they took all the settings off and set the stage up for the thirty people who were standing behind the curtain. We couldn't even hear our own voices [out front], and when you can't hear, you can't play; you don't have any timing. It's like proceeding on radar."

Whatever the reason, Dylan and friends struggled through the first two songs, "When the Ship Comes In" and "The Ballad of Hollis Brown." Then Bob did something very unusual for him: he addressed the crowd directly.

"I thought that was a fitting song for such an important occasion like this," mumbled Bob. "And while I'm here I hope . . . I'd just like to say I hope that some of the money that's for all the people in Africa, maybe they can just take a little bit of it, maybe one or two million maybe, and use it, say, to pay the mortgages on some of the farms that the farmers owe to the banks."

Now I didn't hear him say it. Although over in England, watching on a huge television screen in a bar, Bob Geldof *did* hear him and he was royally pissed. "He displayed a complete lack of understanding of the issues raised by Live Aid. . . . Live Aid was about people losing their lives. There is a radical difference between losing your livelihood and losing your life . . . it was a crass, stupid, and nationalistic thing to say."

I think Geldof was overreacting, although it's easy to understand why. At that point, he was totally focused on only one thing, the famine in Africa, which was how he had succeeded in pulling off an event that everyone had told him could never happen. But I don't believe Dylan's remarks detracted in any way from the purpose of Live Aid. If anything, I think Bob intuitively seized the moment when our consciousness was raised to communicate something even more important than the plight of the farmers. In his offhand way, I think Bob was saying that Live Aid shouldn't be seen as an end point, but rather as the beginning of a road we're all on together.

Dylan, Richards, and Wood finished up with a ragged version of "Blowin' in the Wind," before huge curtains behind them opened and the artists who had remained throughout the long day came back out. They were led by a new and somewhat surprising arrival. Lionel Richie, one of the black superstars who'd originally declined to be part of Live Aid, had made his way to Philadelphia after all.

It was an incredible scene, everybody onstage at once. Hall & Oates. Chrissie Hynde. Pat Benatar. Kenny Loggins. Tina Turner. Patti LaBelle. Peter, Paul & Mary (finally). Bill Graham became the ultimate roadie, rushing around getting more microphones for all the additional people who were flooding onto the stage. Off to one side, Joan Baez was boogying with Mick Jagger. Cher appeared, seemingly from out of nowhere. (I later learned that she'd been on the Concorde with Phil. After seeing all the cameras that were waiting for *him*, she apparently decided that Philadelphia was the place for her too.)

Just as "Do They Know It's Christmas" had been the only choice to end the concert in London, only one song could serve as the perfect finale to Live Aid in America. A beaming Lionel Richie conducted a choir of eighty thousand voices as they sang the now-familiar words that he'd written with Michael Jackson just six months earlier: *"There's a choice we're making, / we're saving our own lives, / it's true we'll make a better day, / just you and me. . . ."*

"This is the ultimate day that pop music can give," said a happy, but plainly relieved Bob Geldof when it was all over. "I heard David [Bowie] say that we should do it again next year. Is he gonna give up six months of his life? If so, I'll be there on the day."

"Historically, George's Bangladesh show was the real forerunner of ideas like Live Aid," Paul McCartney told an interviewer, ". . . which was great too, fabulous. It was nice to see the music guys [at Live Aid] that you thought were just wallys being so concerned." (I asked Nash. A "wally" is a doofus.)

Added Paul, "Often you find your musicians do more bloody good than your government does. Certainly on Live Aid, they did."

Paul is right. I find myself thinking over and over again that we shouldn't have to do these. If our governments answered to the people who elected them, to our wishes and our needs, we could be working at trying to make things measurably *better*, instead of just not so bad. We keep having to play catch-up ball with hunger and disease and poverty and disasters while our governments waste billions of dollars of our money on things we don't believe in.

In 1992, having raised a staggering $144,124,694, the Band Aid Trust was shut down permanently. Forty-nine percent went directly for relief. Another 49 percent went to fund development. Only 2 *percent* had gone to administration. Bob Geldof had always pledged not to build an institution, and he'd kept his word.

The final press release was vintage Geldof, passionate and poetic: "It seems so long ago that we asked for your help. Seven years. It was only meant to last seven weeks, but I hadn't counted on the fact that hundreds of millions of people would respond and I hadn't reckoned on over $100 million. Seven years. You can count them now in trees and dams and fields and cows and camels and trucks and schools and health clinics, medicines, tents, blankets, clothes, toys, ships, planes, tools, wheat, sorghum, beans, research grants, workshops. Seven years ago I said I did not want to create an institution, but I did not want the idea of Band Aid to die. I did not want the potential of it to cease. There were a few dozen aid agencies and they do great work, but that was not our function. Our idea was to open the avenues of possibility. The possibilities of ending hunger in Africa are there. There can be other Band Aids; there must be others, in new times, in different ways. I once said that we would be more powerful in memory than in reality. Now we are that memory."

CHAPTER 7

Lending a Hand:

"That's What Friends Are For"

Music is the universal language. It has the tiniest

little hands that go into people's hearts and make

them discover their own empathy, their own pain.

Paula Cole

As fate would have it, Bill Graham's allegedly rude treatment of Willie Nelson before Live Aid turned out to be one of the greatest gifts to the American farmer since the invention of the tractor. If Bill supposedly hadn't made things so unpleasant for him, Willie wouldn't have been at home listening when Dylan made his off-the-cuff remark about diverting some of the Live Aid money to America's farmers.

"Live Aid was going on and I was watching it," recalls Willie. "I saw Bob Dylan talking and he said, 'Wouldn't it be great if some of this money that we're sending to the rest of the world could stay here to help the family farmer?' And I wasn't aware that there was a big problem. I was raised on farms and worked on farms all my life, and I knew they didn't make any money. But I didn't know that it was any worse than usual. So I started talking to some of my friends and farmers and ranchers in Texas, and they told me, 'Well, it hasn't got that bad here yet, but in the Midwest and in the farm belts, it's really bad.' So I started checking around. And sure enough, at one time we had eight million small family farms. Now we're down to fewer than two million and we're still losing five hundred a week. It's incredible that this can be going on in America and the powers that be have managed to keep it under the surface so that nobody knows. They keep everybody so busy trying to pay the rent and buy groceries in the big towns that there's no time to worry about what's going on out in the countryside. And they've managed to keep us blinded until they took over the whole countryside."

Willie immediately took up Dylan's unintentional challenge. "It *was* Dylan's idea," says one of the cofounders of Farm Aid, Neil Young. We're sitting on Neil's bus in Columbia, South Carolina, the site of Farm Aid '96. And Willie acted on it . . . he put out the word and I got the word real fast and I got right over there and told him, Listen, I'm on your side. I want to help you do this . . . how can I fit into this where I can bring something to the table and continue to do it for a long time?"

"If there hadn't been a Live Aid, there wouldn't have been a Farm Aid," agrees Willie. "You see someone else doing something and that leads to your having to decide whether you want to do something or you want to do nothing. That's really the whole deal . . . once you find out about the farm situation in this country, you either have to decide that 'I'm gonna do something about it' or 'I can't do anything about it.' It's a black eye to America that we have to do something for the farmers. Everyone used to tell me when I was growing up that the farmers were the backbone of our country. Where along the way did we forget that?"

John Mellencamp never forgot. He says, "I grew up and still live in Indiana, in a rural community, and I was able to see firsthand . . . the demise of the small town. Like when I say small town, I mean 350 people, with a general store and a gas station. Well, they don't exist anymore, those towns. When I was a kid they were all there.

There was hundreds of them, and now there's none. And it's just because corporate farming has absolutely driven the small family farmer out of business. And that was what I noticed in the mid and early eighties."

I think Mellencamp is one of the real independent spirits in this country. As an artist, he defies easy classification, and I admire him for that. There's only one John Mellencamp. Period. And he's very honest about his love of Americana; you can hear it in his songs, you can see it in his videos.

"It never occurred to me until Willie Nelson called me," says Mellencamp, "because I've always been by myself. I'm with *me*, you know? I'm not with this. I'm not with that. I don't want to be a part of anything. So when Willie called and said, 'Hey, would you like to do this? I understand you're concerned about this' (I had just made a record called "Scarecrow," that dealt with these things) . . . this was like '85. And so it seemed very natural to me to do [Farm Aid]. There wasn't anything fake or phony or forced about it. . . . It never occurred to me to do anything except be a guy in a bar in a band until this happened."

Everybody believes Willie Nelson and believes *in* Willie Nelson. Everything's donated. And they do a fantastic job. Farm Aid puts 82 percent of what they raise back out the door, and they run the organization on the rest. Only *18 percent* for administration. That's why Farm Aid is regarded as the cleanest machine in the benefit business.

"It's either a benefit or it *isn't* a benefit," says Willie, "and this one is a real benefit, because everyone who comes here pays their own way, pays their plane ticket in or gasoline expenses in, pays for their motel, pays for their food."

These three guys—Willie, Neil, and John Mellencamp—have made an ongoing annual commitment to Farm Aid since launching it with a concert in Champaign, Illinois, on October 22, 1985. They were joined at that memorable first event by, among others, Bob Dylan (of course), Billy Joel, B. B. King, Loretta Lynn, Roy Orbison, Tom Petty, and John Fogerty (who, after years of legal hassles, gave his first public performance in more than thirteen years, telling the eighty thousand in attendance, "It's nice to be back"). That first concert raised more than $7 million to support Farm Aid programs like crisis hot lines, job retraining, and legal aid. Subsequent Farm Aid events have been held almost every year since, and nearly everyone in rock, pop, and country music has played at one or more of them. It's an amazing list: Garth Brooks, Bonnie Raitt, Elton John, Don Henley, Phish, Paul Simon, Mary-Chapin Carpenter, the Highwaymen, Lorrie Morgan, Hootie & the Blowfish, Beck, the Allman Brothers Band, Leon Russell, the Dave Matthews Band, Vince Gill, Lyle Lovett, John Denver, Alabama, Stevie Ray Vaughn, the Beach Boys, Michelle Shocked, Tracy Chapman, Bruce Hornsby, Bryan Adams, Ringo Starr, Martina McBride, Dwight Yoakam, and Crosby, Stills & Nash. One year the Grateful Dead even performed live via satellite (although I'm not sure that isn't a contradiction in terms). I've played at a couple of Farm Aids and there's always a wonderful vibe happening. Doing something that's doing some good rather than just lining your own pocket is the most wonderful part of it. Plus getting to play music and share spirits with other people of like mind whom you greatly admire . . . that's beyond price.

Says Willie, "All these people are lending their talents and their names to do something about it. It's not because they need the publicity. It's because they're really, genuinely concerned."

"At every Farm Aid concert," adds Willie, "I count on Neil to speak his mind. Neil doesn't hold back when he blasts factory farms for polluting the water and soil. He's not afraid to point out Washington's farm policy failures. He's got courage."

Neil is like the éminence grise of Farm Aid, the power behind the throne. He swings a lot of weight, but Willie is the one everybody associates with the event. And Neil wants it that way. He's not looking for glory; he's looking to do good. He says, "The credit for the conception of it and everything is totally Willie's. He puts together these bizarre, unique casts of characters. A lot of the people are chosen from his palette of friends, which he has so many of. Those crazy musicians, the different kinds of musicians. The first couple of Farm Aids, there were like sixty performers in a day, and it just went on and on and on and there were just tribes of people coming in and out and they did the funkiest things you've ever seen."

"I was a part of Farm Aid consistently for years and years and years," says Arlo Guthrie. "Always proud to show up. Always supported those kinds of things. I thought my dad would approve, you know. I think he had a special affinity to people who were living on the land . . . his ancestors had been booted off essentially because of hard times or Wall Street or sort of the convergence of Mother Nature and business together. And so I've always had a special place in my heart for those families that wake up early in the morning and work all day. You know, it's not something I do, but I understand it. And so I did Farm Aid every year for many years. And one year I remember I was in Kentucky or one of these states and I was sitting with a local politician on the stage being interviewed like this. And I just looked at the guy and I said, 'By the way, how come the number-one cash crop of this state is still illegal?' And I think that was the last time I played Farm Aid. They didn't invite me back. Now it wasn't Willie by the way, but I think some of the people that put these things on don't need some smart-ass, wise-cracking, big-mouth folksinger to be putting them in jeopardy or something. I would do it again, frankly, which is probably why they haven't invited me back. Sometimes, you know, you just have to say what's on your mind and you have to point out the obvious, and I was being funny, but at the same time there's a lot of people sitting in jail right now who cannot afford to be as humorous about some of these things as I can. And I just think it's wrong. I just think the world has got too many important things to be doing besides worrying about what farmers are growing for money. And especially when it's just natural things out there. I'm not somebody who's advocating anything. I quit doing everything so many years ago now that I can't remember the last time I had any fun. But the world is a big place. And people who are not harming each other ought to be left alone."

"It's too bad we have to keep on doing it," says Neil, "but the problem is so much bigger than anybody ever imagined it being when we started taking it on. But now we're getting a focus. We're getting a good focus on family farms and organic farming and sustainable agriculture. Now we have something to hang our hat on about the family farmers. Corporate America has given us something to fight, by having all these huge farms that use chemicals and give us food that causes all these diseases that we get. The government and the corporations, working together to make life more beautiful."

Beautiful for their bank accounts, maybe. Agribusiness does not have your best interests at heart. Agribusiness wants to make money. And they will take every shortcut, and do everything the cheesiest way, and use the most powerful pesticides and herbicides on earth, and lie, cheat, and steal and buy politicians to make it happen. Agribusiness is *bad.* That's why so many of us are in favor of organic farming—which *only* the little guy can do. It's labor-intensive and it requires too much love. That's why we love organic farmers, because they're the exact antithesis of agribusiness.

"It seems to be that in order to turn something around and to go through the legal channels," muses Willie, "you have to get the attention of some intelligence somewhere. So you sort of cry out in the wilderness for that intelligence. And when you don't see it and you don't hear it, it's frustrating. But every time we've had a Farm Aid, there's always been more hands go up than we have slots. And that shows you that they know and they care and they want to help. That's why it's so easy to put these on. The fact that there are enough people out there who care and can bring people together and talk about an issue is the good news. The fact that we have to do it is what's wrong."

"To be truthful," admits Neil, "the idea of a benefit, of doing a benefit, was not something that really turned me on very much. I really wasn't into the benefits. And I really . . . especially at the beginning . . . disliked the benefits. All these people, all doing benefits all the time. To me, I was more interested in . . . I guess it was just the music. I was really focused on just the music. Wasn't interested in doing benefits. But life is so long that things can change, you know? So by the time I got to be whatever age I was, forty or something, the Farm Aid benefit and the Bridge School benefit had become a part of my life. Both of them were things that appealed to me so much as something that I can have a part in, some way that I can help and where I can make it better. So Farm Aid was the first one, and then the Bridge School was the second one."

"Neil Young gathers everybody around because one of his kids goes to that school," says Robin Williams. "It's called the Bridge School up in San Francisco, and it's for learning-disabled kids; it encompasses a lot of different categories."

Neil has two kids that are affected by cerebral palsy, one much more severely than the other. In a 1988 interview with *Rolling Stone*, Neil talked about his son, Ben: "He's learning how to communicate and play games and solve problems using a computer. And he is handicapped inasmuch as he has severe cerebral palsy, and he is a quadriplegic, and he's a non-oral child. So he has a lot of handicaps. Cerebral palsy is a condition of life, not a disease. It's the way he is, the condition he's in. He was brought into the world in this form, and this is the way he is. A lot of the things that we take for granted, that we can do, he can't do. But his soul is there, and I'm sure that he has an outlook on the world that we don't have because of the disabilities."

According to the doctors, Ben wasn't supposed to live more than about eight years—and he's twenty now. Neil and Pegi just refused to accept what the doctors told them. And they were right. He's stayed alive almost entirely because of their love for him. That's why I think they are two of the most courageous people I've ever known.

Along with another parent, Pegi Young founded the Bridge School in 1986 for severely speech-impaired children in the San Francisco Bay area, because she knew from her own experience that these children were not being given the kind of care and instruction they needed. The Bridge School started with only four kids, but over the years has worked successfully with hundreds more. Even better, the Bridge School has become a model for other programs around the country, and even around the world.

Jim "Soni" Sonefeld is the drummer for Hootie & the Blowfish (or "Bloatie & the Whofish" as I like to call them—it's a term of affection; they're great guys). He says: "Part of the whole benefit thing is realizing what you're there for. And the Bridge School . . . just slapped me right in the face, what it's for. You're sitting in front of about fifteen kids in wheelchairs and, at that moment, you know exactly why you're there and you become very humble and it's a good feeling."

Says Robin, "The extraordinary thing is it's an acoustic benefit—the only rules are you can't bring an amp."

Neil puts a lot of time into planning the Bridge School shows, and the acoustic format is something he's thought through very carefully: "There's a level playing field, because except in some rare instances, we have managed to contain people to just acoustic music. And as more time goes by, the more insistent we become. It's like you're naked, okay? When everybody has to strip down and jump in the pool, we're all the same, okay? So the acoustic thing kind of does that, too. Because if somebody . . . even if they're not used to playing acoustic, just the fact that they're playing acoustic makes them so vulnerable that you'll see another side of them that you would never see, and it's a really pure thing you're seeing, something that's usually hidden. So everybody has this in common. Some people are new to it and have never done it before. Others are expert at it and it's what they do all the time. But they're all even. They're all on the same plane for this one night. That's what I like about it. That's why we can get different kinds of people, because they're all disarmed."

Dean Felder, bassist for Hootie, says: "I think the format thing is one of the reasons why the Bridge School benefits work so well. . . . [The] musicians look forward to having that avenue, to be able to go there and just do something different and change everything up and have it not be a ton of pressure, either. I mean, it's not like a media event."

Because of the nature of the benefit and because people love and respect him, Neil's been able to get everybody—I mean *everybody*—to come and play at the Bridge School shows.

Bob Barsotti of Bill Graham Presents has been involved in producing the annual Bridge School benefit concerts since Neil and

Pegi did the first one in 1986. He says: "Over the years, we've been involved in a lot of different causes and the ones that are the most effective are the ones where there's an artist who feels the same thing. Neil has taken the Bridge School and it's his inspiration because of his children and what he's wanted to do for them. And by having that personal inspiration he's been able to carry it through . . . the shows keep getting better and better, because it's not just a person from the Bridge School calling, it's Neil Young calling up Eddie Vedder, it's Neil Young calling up Lou Reed. And the response is very few people turn Neil Young down."

I kidded Eddie Vedder about how I found it hard to imagine that Pearl Jam could even *play* acoustic: "Well, *Metallica's* done it," he said laughing. "We have both sides of the fish going . . . the soft underbelly and the hard stuff on the back." As for playing music with (and for) Neil, Vedder said something really wonderful: "He's learned more than me at this point, so I can learn from him, and it's been a blessing to have that. And I think he's enabled me to see what dignity looks like."

The Bridge School concerts put new musicians on the same stage with people who have been performing for thirty years. And they create these amazing combinations that you won't see anywhere else: Simon & Garfunkel singing "The Sounds of Silence" with *Eddie Van Halen* on guitar; Neil, Eddie Vedder, James Taylor, Sammy Hagar, and Shawn Colvin backing up Elton John on his "Love Song"; Bruce Springsteen, Steven Tyler, Chrissie Hynde, and Hootie & the Blowfish all "Rockin' in the Free World" with Neil; the Smashing Pumpkins and Marilyn Manson . . . *acoustic*; Neil, David Bowie, and Patti Smith all doing "Helpless" together. You have to see it to believe it. (In fact, sometimes even when you *do* see it, you still don't quite believe it.)

Hootie's lead singer, Darius Rucker, remembers a specific musical experience from their Bridge performance: "I'll never forget. It was the first time we'd ever played 'Be the One' live. That's one of my favorite songs we've ever written. We played it just on a whim. We weren't even planning to play it. And it just moved me to no end.

I just thought it was one of the best performances we ever had, and it was wonderful."

Right after I got out of a Texas prison in 1986, Neil asked if we would come together and do a Crosby, Stills, Nash & Young thing at that first Bridge School benefit. (Before I went in, Neil told me that if I got straight and stayed straight for a year, he'd make a record with me. He kept that promise. I knew that I was going to stay straight, so I knew that I would wind up playing with him again.)

Even without CSNY, Neil had already assembled an impressive lineup for that inaugural Bridge show: Bruce Springsteen, Don Henley, Tom Petty, and my pal Robin Williams. The concert was at the Shoreline Amphitheatre, south of San Francisco. The backstage area is kind of a quadrangle, with the dressing rooms on the square. By the time I arrived, everybody else was already there. As I came up the ramp and walked in, Robin spotted me from across the way. Everybody was bunched up in a group on the far side of the square, and he jumped up and yelled very loudly, "Free at last! Free at last! Good God almighty, I'm free at last!" It put us all completely on the floor. We were all laughing so hard we couldn't talk. Everybody knew that I'd just gotten out of prison, so it was a damn funny thing to say. You can't help laughing with Robin anyway because he's got a great take on the entire world. And he certainly had a great take on that moment. It felt really good to be free.

Says Robin, "And that was the first time I saw you—the first time after you'd gotten out of the big house. I saw you and yelled out *Free at last!* That falls into the category of benefits that are very personal, but quite extraordinary and really wonderful. Along with doing these things, sometimes you catch extraordinary moments, you know, like you playing the first time out of prison. Nice. Without the shackles, it makes it a lot easier: *'We're going to have to undo these now, David. We're just going to take them off for a while so you can play chords . . . '*"

(If I were to tell you that Robin Williams is one of the most compassionate, giving human beings in the entire world, you'd be right to question my bias. I love him and his wife, Marsha, very much. So instead, here's a story Carlos Santana told me about Robin, entirely without prompting: "Bill Graham called me the day before . . . actually it was the *day* he died, and he said, 'Carlos, I want to tell you something.' I said, 'Yes, Bill?' And he said, 'Do you know how great it feels for somebody to call *me* and offer their services? Because I've been doing this all my life. I always have to call people and beg them to do [benefit] concerts.' He said, 'I never begged you, you were always there. But I want to tell you—Robin Williams called me on the phone and said, "I'm calling you because I know you want to do something for the people who lost everything in Oakland with that fire, so I'm there—you can count on me."' Bill was almost crying."

On October 13, 1986, Pegi Young stepped out on the Shoreline stage. She thanked everyone for being there and supporting their dream, and then she introduced her husband. Neil opened the first Bridge School show with "Comes a Time" and "Heart of Gold," before inviting ". . . my friend Bruce to do one with me. And Nils, bring that accordion." Belying the song's title, Bruce Springsteen and Nils Lofgren came out and joined Neil for "Helpless."

After doing another solo tune, "I Am a Child," Neil brought out Stephen, introducing him as his "old friend from Buffalo Springfield." Then, as if it were an afterthought, Neil added that "he's brought along a couple of his friends too."

When I walked out that first time, there was a big upwelling of applause and feeling. In that place, at that moment, with everything that had happened to me—it was an unbelievably thrilling sensation just to be standing up there. When you somehow manage to pull yourself out of the gutter, people actually do root for you. It's very moving and very humbling. And I could really feel how much the audience was behind me. Even in that kind of din, you hear things . . . phrases, maybe a sentence. "We love you, Dave!" "Welcome back!" "I'm glad you're alive!" "What happened to your hair?" (It hadn't grown back yet from prison so, needless to say, I did *not* sing "Almost Cut My Hair.")

We led off with one of the last songs we'd played together—disastrously—at Live Aid the year before. This time, though, the harmonies on "Only Love Can Break Your Heart" were as good—maybe better—than they'd ever been. "Change Partners" was next, a song of Stephen's that's always served as a perfect metaphor for the four of us. Neil and Stephen swapped guitar solos on "Daylight Again," and we finished our four-song set with "Ohio," which had the audience on its feet singing the chorus back at us. My voice was strong and my energy that night was the best it had been in years. It was a blessed moment for me, one I could almost taste. At that instant, I really understood how lucky I'd been—and how lucky I was. When you're up there and you're playing, it's as good as life ever gets.

Nils Lofgren followed us, and he did a great set, including "Keith Don't Go," "Wonderland," "Man at the Top," and a song dedicated to Neil's son, Ben.

Don Henley was next, squelching the preshow rumors of an Eagles reunion when he came out with his own band, J. D. Souther, Danny Kortchmar, and Jai Winding. (One Eagle, Timmy Schmit, was there too.) Don told the crowd that playing unplugged was like "standing here in a jockstrap and a pair of socks." Despite his heightened sense of vulnerability, Don did great acoustic versions of his own "Boys of Summer" and the Eagles' "Best of My Love," "New Kid in Town," and "Desperado." Then, he and the others completely floored us with an unbelievably beautiful four-part version of the Beatles' "Yes It Is," before finishing up with "You Don't Miss the Water 'til the Well Runs Dry."

After a short break, Tom Petty came out and did "American Girl," "The Waiting," "It'll All Work Out," "Blue Moon of Kentucky," and "Twist and Shout." Robin then did ten minutes of stand-up, including a hysterical version of "Proud Mary" as performed by Elmer Fudd: *"Wollin'. Wollin'. Wollin' on duh Wiver."*

Despite the fact that he'd done a killer set, as Robin left the stage he still heard the inevitable chants of *Brooce! Brooce!* They didn't have long to wait. Neil introduced Springsteen, who started off with an a cappella rendition of "You Can Look but You Better Not Touch," followed by a blues-tinged version of "Born in the USA." With the help of Nils and Danny Federci, the Boss did seven more songs, "Seeds,"

"Darlington County," "Mansion on the Hill," "Fire," "Dancin' in the Dark," "Glory Days," and Elvis's "Follow That Dream," which he dedicated to "Neil and Pegi, and to you folks for your support and kindness." Watching from the wings, I had an epiphany. I finally realized how good Bruce Springsteen really is. I liked him before, but when he bared America's soul in "Seeds," I really *got* it.

Then, turning to the wings and smiling right at us, he asked, "Where are those *old-timers?*" All four of us returned to support him on "Hungry Heart."

At the end, everybody came back onstage and formed a long line for the finale, which Graham told the crowd was for "my friend Ben." Ben and many of the future students of the Bridge School were watching from right near the stage in wonderment and delight while we all did (what else?) "Teach Your Children," with Robin "singing" along in frenzied sign language, as if he were interpreting for deaf people on speed. It was the perfect conclusion to a magical event. After doing so many shows for so many years, after a while some of them begin to blur together. Not that first Bridge show. It's one I'll remember in absolutely perfect detail for the rest of my life. There are some shows you just never forget.

Farm Aid and the Bridge School concerts weren't the only benefit series spawned in the burst of activism that followed Live Aid. Nor were musicians the only artists inspired by its success.

Comedian Bob Zmuda was Andy Kaufman's best friend before the talented comic actor's sudden death from lung cancer in 1984 at the age of thirty-five. "When Andy died, I went off the deep end. I never had a friend close to me die before, let alone my best friend. And it hit me pretty hard. So for about a year I didn't do much. I kind of just sat at home, and the one-year anniversary of his death was coming up. And a little voice in me said, *Bob, quit crying in your soup. You got to do something.* So I put on a benefit in his name at the Comedy Store in Los Angeles with twenty major comedians."

The Kaufman tribute was a success, but after he saw Live Aid, Zmuda started to think on a much bigger scale. "I was watching Live Aid and it hit me like a ton of bricks. And I'm from Hollywood, so I figure, 'What a great idea to steal.' The whole town was abuzz about Live Aid, because Live Aid turned around the image of what musicians were. Before that, they're pretty much guys taking a lot of drugs, busting up hotel rooms . . . the groupies and the whole thing. Live Aid really changed the awareness that people had of what musicians could do, of the good they could do for the world. And so with that I went to HBO and said, 'How would HBO like to do the Live Aid of comedy?' And that was it—that was the pitch."

"There's a guy who used to work with Andy Kaufman named Bob Zmuda," says Robin. "Sometimes if you see Andy's old specials, you'll see Bob. And Andy would play off him—abuse the shit out of him and then Bob would leave. He came up with an idea . . . to raise money for the homeless and use comics, because he'd seen musicians doing it. And then he said, Why don't we get together a group of comedians? I think he talked to a couple of people and found out that HBO would be willing to do it if he could get all the comics together. And then he came to Billy and Whoopi and myself and said, Let's do this. We said, It sounds wonderful."

"I brought Whoopi Goldberg and Billy Crystal to the mix," recalls Zmuda, "and with those three, they became the cornerstones and, to this day, the hosts of Comic Relief. And because of them we were then able to call up all the other comedians."

Whoopi Goldberg told me that one day she got a phone call about the idea. "Somebody said, 'We're doing this thing.' And you know, being benefit prone, I said, 'Sure!' 'And you're gonna do it with Billy Crystal and Robin Williams.' I said, 'Oh, I'm the *Vanna White*. I'm the chick in the middle.'"

Continues Whoopi, "There are performers who do Comic Relief because their family was immediately affected by the issue of homelessness. Louie Anderson—a great comedian—in point of fact, did the show because he had a brother who was homeless whom he could not find for ten years. And he thought by doing Comic Relief that he would find his brother, and he talked about this on the Comic Relief telethon. He asked his brother if he's out there to please get in contact with the family—which did happen."

Jim Carrey used to tell a joke in his stand-up routine: "My father lost his job and we actually became homeless for a long time. Of course I grew up in Canada, so I thought we'd just gone *camping.* . . ." Zmuda says it's a true story: "His dad lost his job and took the whole family out camping. And after about eight weeks of camping, Jim turned to his dad and said, 'We're not camping, we're homeless— aren't we?' And the dad confessed. He was embarrassed, ashamed to let the family know. So there are some performers who were out there themselves, who really understand this issue."

Continues Zmuda: "I think everybody does feel the issue of homelessness because it really can happen to anyone and does. The greatest percentage of the homeless population is not the guys coming up to you on the street—give me a buck here or there—it's really families. And many times it's employed families. It's fami- lies where both adults could be working . . . you know he could be working as a security guard, she could be working over at McDonald's, and they have four kids and they're living out of their car! They're contributing to the society. It's tough. We all see how much things are costing nowadays. First month's rent, last month's rent, security. It's tough for people to move into a place. And so this is something that everybody sees, and there's kind of a fear that if it could happen to those people, it could easily happen to us. You know, Willie Nelson and I are buddies, and one day we might do an event together—we always talked about it—bringing Farm Aid and Comic Relief together and maybe calling it Funny Farm. I think that Willie came up with that title—Funny Farm. As he says, when the farmers lose their farms they're homeless. So we're all connected to each other with this issue, and it *can* happen to everyone."

Whoopi Goldberg is a perfect example of someone who viscerally understands this issue. "I have my last Medi-Cal card from the state of California on my mantel," Whoopi acknowledges, "just in case, you know . . . 'cause this movie stuff might not work out. You know, I want to make sure I got some health benefits somewhere. You know, 'cause it could disappear in a minute."

Then she turns serious: "No, I kept it for my own conversation. Because I thought people should know that yes, *I* did this. I grew up in Manhattan and I didn't know I was poor. Because who was I poor in comparison to? There was a lot of people doing a lot worse than we were. So, I didn't know . . . kids, they don't know. They don't know about money, they don't know they don't have any money. So, I had no idea, but I do know that my mother taught me that I had to respect everybody I met, or try. And that if you had . . . one crust of bread, you cut and you share it with another person and then you have two crusts of bread. And I always pictured this thing in my head, and I thought, Why would anybody eat a crust of bread? Why not just a whole slice of bread? But she was being philosophical. So she said a crust of bread. And I came to understand that regardless of where I sat in the society, that if there was someone who wasn't doing as well as I was, that my job was to make sure that whatever I had I could hand over some of. It didn't mean you had to give it *all* up. But that there was no one who wasn't entitled to help. And it's a very hard thing to do in this country, to ask for help, because you are ashamed. You are shamed into believing that there is something wrong with you because you say, I'm unable to handle this situation by myself."

What struck me when I interviewed Robin and Whoopi is that both of them, separately, told me the exact same thing. They said the strongest part of the whole Comic Relief experience for them wasn't the performance; it was when they went to a homeless shelter and saw clothes and food and medical supplies and personnel and knew that they'd affected something, that all of this work had actually made somebody's life a little bit better.

"Doing Comic Relief," says Robin, "you raise the money, then . . . you take the money to these different shelters and you see people—a woman who has come from living on the street and now has a job or who has got her family and has moved out and is now . . . back in life again. I mean, it's extraordinary. I don't know what the numbers are, but if you get anybody out of that, it's worth doing."

Zmuda says it was a painful experience for them to see the conditions firsthand. "The first project site we ever went to was in L.A., and we went down to one of the missions where it's just a terrible, terrible situation. It was hard-core homelessness. This was as bad as it gets. And I remember we brought Robin Williams there. And Robin, who's usually bouncing off the walls—you never saw a guy just . . . God, he was in shock by what he saw. Afterwards people came up to him from the project site and said, 'Robin, why weren't you funny?' He was in such shock from what he was seeing these people go through that he closed up. Now, after all the different homeless project sites that he's gone to, he doesn't close up anymore. He understands he should be himself, he should be funny. You know, they are fans too. Just 'cause you're homeless doesn't mean you're not a fan."

Robin and Whoopi and Billy assigned themselves to America's homeless. And they've done show after show after show—all of them brilliant—containing some of the funniest, wildest, craziest stuff you've ever seen in your life. Since 1986, they've done eight all-star Comic Relief events, raising almost $50 million for Healthcare for the Homeless projects in twenty-three U.S. cities.

"We kind of thought," says Whoopi, "and this is again naive hippies with too much money, okay? We thought, 'Oh, we'll raise the money in one night. And we'll wipe it out.' Never occurred to us we'd be doing this shit for ten years. Never occurred to us. We thought, 'What do you *mean* there's still homeless people? We just raised a couple of million dollars.' And thinking that the government—and this was me being an asshole—thinking that the government was gonna match what we raised. They didn't, *they didn't* . . . "

In 1989, Phil Collins wrote a song that's become identified with the whole issue of homelessness, even though he never intended it that way: "Another Day in Paradise" was not written as an anthem for the homeless; it was just an accident that kind of happened one evening. Says Phil, "It came out . . . it came out of me. I suppose that's how the good songs do come—like that. But I had very specific photographs in my mind of things that I've seen, as we all see in our travels. We see it probably better than other people that live there. We see things, we don't get used to them. Like you haven't seen a child for a month, you notice how much it's grown. If you're living with a child every day, then you don't necessarily see that quite as much. And if you live in the city, you don't notice the piles of rubbish. You don't notice the graffiti, you don't know the people, families living on street corners in New York. And when I was in Rio in the late seventies with Genesis, I'll never forget this hill that separated the hotel we were staying at from Copacabana Beach, where some of the wealthiest people in the world live. But to get there you pass by this mountain, this hill of shacks with no running water, no electricity, nothing. And I've never forgotten that picture in my mind.

"And also in Washington," continues Phil, "I remember arriving in Washington once at night and it was snowing. And there were all these people sleeping on the streets in cardboard boxes. And I didn't know they were sleeping, you know? I didn't know that's where they lived. I thought there was some kind of demonstration. People just queuing up to demonstrate in the morning for something, as it was Washington. And the driver said, 'Oh no, these people *live* here. This is where they live.' That seemed to me completely at odds with Washington, you know, the hub of the most powerful country in the world . . . you could have thrown a stone and hit the White House. So those two pictures specifically were in my mind. I just started to write . . . this is one song actually that I was trying to write all day and nothing happened. And I had a break, came back, and—before I turned the gear off to call it a day—I just started mucking around and that first verse and chorus all happened there and then. There was no writing it down. It just came out."

She calls out to the man on the street
"Sir, can you help me?
It's cold and I've nowhere to sleep,
Is there somewhere you can tell me?"
He walks on, doesn't look back
He pretends he can't hear her
Starts to whistle as he crosses the street

Seems embarrassed to be there
Oh think twice, it's another day for
You and me in paradise
Oh think twice, it's just another day for you,
You and me in paradise
She calls out to the man on the street
He can see she's been crying
She's got blisters on the soles of her feet
Can't walk but she's trying
Oh think twice, it's another day for
You and me in paradise
Oh think twice, it's just another day for you,
You and me in paradise
Oh lord, is there nothing more anybody can do
Oh lord, there must be something you can say
You can tell from the lines on her face
You can see that she's been there
Probably been moved on from every place
'Cause she didn't fit in there
Oh think twice, it's another day for
You and me in paradise
Oh think twice, it's just another day for you,
You and me in paradise

I was honored when Phil asked me to sing harmony on "Another Day in Paradise." It's a very intelligent, very emotional song. And, as chance would have it, it also became a huge hit. Because of that, I've had several opportunities to perform it live with Phil, including at the Grammys. It was the beginning of a long and really good friendship with him that continues to this day.

Sadly, some of the most powerful artistic benefits of the last fif-teen years have stemmed from the tragedy of the AIDS epidemic. Most of us in the arts community were affected early on by this deadly scourge. All of us know someone who has died. Many of us have lost close friends, even family. "The AIDS benefits are very close to me," says Melissa Etheridge. "I have lost way too many friends and acquaintances and businesspeople to AIDS. I just lost my best friend from high school—the guy that took me to the prom."

In 1985, when many Americans had not even heard the word *AIDS*, Elizabeth Taylor brought the issue to the forefront of national awareness. After the very public death of Taylor's close friend Rock Hudson, she became a tireless crusader for AIDS research and treatment. It was her idea to create an award honoring others who had the courage to engage in what was then still a very difficult and unpopular fight. The first recipient of AIDS Project Los Angeles's Commitment to Life Award was former first lady Betty Ford.

That first event was held in a downtown Los Angeles hotel and included performances by Madonna and Rod Stewart. Over the next ten years, the AIDS Project Los Angeles annual gala evolved into a high-powered entertainment extravaganza, drawing on the support of top stars from both the film and the music industries. Subsequent recipients of the Commitment to Life Award would include Hillary Rodham Clinton, Barbra Streisand, and David Geffen. David used the occasion to publicly "come out" by saying, "As a gay man, I've come a long way to be here tonight." (David and I have had our ups and downs over the years, but I really admired him for how he handled himself that night. I was proud of him and proud to know him. I called him up the next day and said, 'David, I've always been ready to criticize the hell out of you when I thought you were wrong, but on the other hand, I felt when you did something this right I should call you up and tell you.')

Commitment to Life VIII was held at the Universal Amphitheatre on January 19, 1995. The honorees were Tom Hanks, agent (and future president of Universal Pictures) Ron Meyer, and Elton John. And the gala's entertainment was produced by Elton's longtime lyricist Bernie Taupin. Six thousand people paid a total of *$3.5 million* for their seats, so they had every reason to expect one hell of a show.

They wouldn't be disappointed. Titled "Under the Influence: Words Inspired by Image, Images Inspired by Words," the gala event was hosted by Whoopi, who instantly endeared herself to the crowd by revealing that she had to decide between hosting this event or hosting the Oscars. "And I had my choice. So I chose *this*."

After brief speeches from AIDS Project's executive director, James Loyce, and chairman of the board, Dana Miller, the program took a poignant turn. In his first public appearance since the recent death of his wife, AIDS activist Elizabeth Glaser, actor Paul Michael Glaser reaffirmed the message of hope offered by the example of her courageous life: "Always to persevere, never to give up."

Actor Michael Douglas gave the evening's first Commitment to Life Award to Ron Meyer, his longtime friend and agent. Meyer accepted it by aptly quoting the philosopher Edmund Burke as saying, "The only thing necessary for evil to win is for the good to do nothing."

The musical part of the program then began with Ru Paul doing (what else?) Aerosmith's "Dude Looks Like a Lady," followed by short performances from Julie Andrews, Sandra Bernhard, and Marianne Faithfull. AIDS Project's Dana Miller recalls that "Marianne Faithfull flew from England to sing 'I Will Survive' to the slowest tempo in the world. And she walked offstage and she was so moved and so blown away by it." Nona Hendryxs then did a futuristic version of "Bennie and the Jets," followed by Terence Trent D'Arby, who covered Bowie's "Rebel, Rebel."

Next was the presentation, by actress Mary Steenburgen, of the second Commitment to Life Award. The recipient was her costar from *Philadelphia*, two-time Oscar winner Tom Hanks. Clearly moved by the enormity of his reception (the audience leaped to its feet as soon as he was introduced), Hanks seemed close to tears during much of his eloquent acceptance speech. Addressing the twin issues of AIDS discrimination and homophobia, which were the central elements of the *Philadelphia* story, Hanks was forthright: "I have been raised to believe that the diversity of my country is the strength of my country."

Tom Hanks is a hard act to follow . . . unless you're Whoopi Goldberg. Mugging to the crowd on every word, she introduced the next artist by saying, "Lot's of people *do* rock 'n' roll. But very few . . . *very few . . . VERY FEW! . . .* people can claim to *be* rock 'n' roll. In a world of ever-shifting values, it's good to know that the Beauty is still on Duty. And now, ladies and gentlemen, the one, the only, Little Richard!"

Little Richard, who at sixty-two years of age (as he was quick to remind everyone) could still blister the keyboards, opened with a rollicking rendition of "Good Golly, Miss Molly," which got a very good response from the crowd. The problem for Richard is never when he's singing. It's when he's *not* singing and the microphone is still on that Richard gets himself into trouble. After "Molly," Richard launched into a rambling rap (managing to work in the fact that he didn't have a record deal at the moment) that left some in the audience squirming. Fortunately, before a hook was required, Richard did his last song, "Keep a Knockin'," and got off.

You've got to love this next segue. Little Richard was followed by . . . Garth Brooks. Garth brought along a singer-songwriter named Jenny Yates, who accompanied him on acoustic guitar. They did a gentle, beautiful duet on a song that Garth told the audience had never been performed in public before that night. There was great significance to Garth's willingness even to *appear* at an AIDS fund-raiser, particularly one with a predominantly gay audience. As AIDS Project's Miller observes, "I've always been amazed by music stars who really . . . put their careers on the line to do an AIDS benefit. And specifically, I think of Clint Black and Garth Brooks. Homophobia in country music, believe it or not, still exists, but back then it was much more prevalent. I think you could say, they didn't *care*. They showed up and did it for all the right reasons."

Sheryl Crow came out and did a fine version of Van Morrison's "Domino," before being joined onstage by Don Henley, for whom she used to do work as a studio backup singer. They sat side by side for a duet of "Love Is Everything," with Don remaining onstage for a solo of "Sit Down, You're Rockin' the Boat."

When it was first built, the Universal Amphitheater was an open-air venue. By the time of this event, it had long since been enclosed.

That night, Melissa's performance of "Maggie May" came as close as anything could to blowing that roof back off. She charged onstage, the energy almost exploding out of her guitar. The throaty rumble of her voice made it obvious to anyone listening that she was truly passionate about singing *this* song. By the time Melissa was finished, the audience appeared physically spent. It didn't matter. They staggered to their feet and gave her a prolonged and emotional standing ovation.

Pity the unfortunate soul who had to go on after that, but Clint Black gave it his best shot. The stage had been converted into a gaudy Las Vegas set for Clint to do a high-spirited version of Elvis Presley's "Viva Las Vegas." Then the late, great Tammy Wynette won the hearts of the hip Hollywood crowd with the simple truthfulness of her signature song, "Stand By Your Man." The tone got a lot racier when Salt 'N' Pepa did their hip-hop hit "Let's Talk About Sex," its refrain changed to "Let's Talk About *AIDS*."

Sex was still the topic when Joni Mitchell walked out, armed only with an acoustic guitar—which is all she ever needs. Joni's genius for telling the tale is evident in every song she's ever written. I've said it many times—a hundred years from now, people will look back and say, Who was the greatest singer-songwriter of this time? And in my ever so *un*humble opinion, it'll be Joni. It's just my opinion, but I think she's as good a poet as Dylan (although radically different) and a *way* better musician. The stark refrain of the song she chose to perform that night, *"Sex sells everything / And sex kills,"* was a brutally honest reminder of the real reason that everyone was there.

The gala was coming to a close, with only two performers still left to appear. The first was George Michael, who was in the middle of "Don't Let the Sun Go Down on Me" when a surprise vocalist—Elton John—joined him for a duet on the song's last verses. A few minutes later Elton was back out onstage to receive the third and final Commitment to Life Award, fittingly presented to him by his friend and lifelong collaborator, and the evening's brilliant producer, Bernie Taupin.

Elton's opening remark drew cheers from the audience: "I stand here tonight as your official *gay* recipient!" When the applause finally died down, he continued: "I'm an Englishman, as you might well know, and I've had a lot of love and acceptance in this country. This has been my second home for many, many years. This is where I came out, in this country. I've *slept* with half of it. And boy was it good . . . "

The laughter turned to rapt attention when he added, "I said I've slept with half of America . . . and I've come out of it HIV *negative*. I'm a lucky, lucky person. It's my job to repay that debt. As long as I live I will help fight [for] this cause, and I will do anything I can to help the people—my friends, my ex-lover, and people I haven't even met—that die from this disease. You know we must never forget. I've been to Auschwitz, I've been to the Vietnam Memorial, and I've cried at both places. I've seen the [AIDS] quilt and I cried. And those people who died for those causes unnecessarily—we must never forget them. We must never, *never* forget the dignity and courage they showed. I want to honor their courage and dignity by making a commitment to myself that I will always, always try to do the best I can for people with HIV and AIDS."

Elton's moving speech ended as it began, with a standing ovation. The audience also continued cheering for another reason. As soon as he'd finished his speech, Elton turned to a roadie and announced, "I *need* to see my piano. Get the piano *out!*"

"Believe," Bernie Taupin's ode to the healing power of love, was one of Elton's two choices to close out the show. The other was a song that had become Elton's personal anthem, a defiant but positive declaration of survival, "I'm Still Standing." For the finale, the show's entire cast came back out to sing it with him.

"When the history of the war on AIDS is written," says Dana Miller, "they're going to look back and say, 'It was musicians and celebrities who were brave enough at the beginning to take this thing on. And they did it at a time when no one was going to help.' The government wasn't responding. Eight years and AIDS wasn't even mentioned. The musicians, through compassion and heroism, were the ones who said, We've got to use what God gave us, our talent, and our celebrity, and pull together and help these people, help these men, women, and children that are dying. They're not living with AIDS, they're dying. And we've got to use what we can. It's not one or two celebrities who were hooked on a cause; it's everything from country to opera stars, to Broadway stars, to rock 'n' roll to heavy metal stars, that have come forward and said, We're going to lend our name and our talent to fight and help people living with AIDS. It's pretty awesome."

AIDS is an issue that's not hard for people to figure out. No one needs to be persuaded that it's a huge problem, which is a major reason why so many artists are willing to get involved with AIDS charities. It's a no-brainer.

Not all problems are as clear-cut as AIDS. Some require a lot of persuasion before an artist will agree that it's worth his or her time to get involved. And that's what my friend Wavy Gravy can do better than any other human being on the planet. Persuade. He also cajoles, pesters, wheedles, and begs—anything necessary to get who he wants. And he almost always succeeds.

Wavy is one of a kind. When God made Wavy, he didn't use a mold. He must have known right from the start that this was a creation that couldn't be duplicated, not even by Him. It would have been too expensive—Wavy's heart is made from pure gold.

For more than thirty years now, Wavy has been the catalyst in getting musicians to support all sorts of good causes, some of which—like the issue of preventable blindness in Nepal—you wouldn't ever have thought about if it hadn't been for Wavy.

"I think I first met him at the Watts Acid Test," recalls the Grateful Dead's Phil Lesh, "which was held in what I remember as an almost burned-out old garage in Compton, the hub city. Wavy Gravy was Hugh Romney back then. And I remember him being there. I don't really remember much about him at the Acid Test itself, but afterwards we all went back to his house and hung out on the lawn while he did his religion inside, which was kind of strange—it consisted of him sitting in a lotus position and howling.

So that's how I first remember Wavy. And later, of course, he became quite a figure in the area of doing things for good causes and a leader in that. And he's also been an inspiration to all of us."

Another member of the Dead, Bob Weir, says of Wavy, "I really think the guy's a saint. I really, honestly believe the guy's a saint—a living, walking saint. Living, breathing, walking around."

"Wavy Gravy is a saint savant, if you know what I mean," agrees Paul Kantner, adding sardonically: "Why and how he does it, to the extent and extreme he does it, is beyond me. I would not have the energy to be Wavy Gravy. I would not *want* to have the energy to be Wavy Gravy. It would just be too complicated in my life. My head would explode."

Whoopi says she met Wavy at one of the first benefits she ever did. "I just remember thinking, *Look at Wavy. There's a benefit* mother-fucker. *Okay? Wavy* does some benefits. *Okay? He can raise money out of the* dead. I don't know what he does . . . he just says, 'Come, people. Come.' And it's great. *Kids* come to his benefits. That's the great thing. You look out, there's like *kids* at the benefit . . . "

I asked Wavy how he persuaded the Grateful Dead to support a cause that's very close to his heart, the Seva Foundation (which, among its other good works, helps prevent blindness in Nepal): "I was on this aircraft coming back from Detroit, we had come together—me and Ram Dass and Larry Brilliant, folks who worked on the smallpox erad-ication, which was the first disease in the history of the world to be eradicated . . . and we're on the aircraft, and I had already talked to Weir, and the Grateful Dead were all on the aircraft—they couldn't go anywhere; they were sitting ducks—I just walked up to each one of them and nailed 'em for the [first Seva] show. And it came out Bill Graham didn't know it was a benefit. 'Why am I the last to learn these things?' And he came up to me during the show and slipped me a piece of paper—I thought it was some kinda note to get out of town, and instead it was a check for ten thousand dollars. I said, 'Bill, why are you doing this?' He says, 'Because you did not hit on me.'"

"In fact," says Lesh, "those [the Seva shows] were some of the first really big benefits that we did. And I guess that started back in the seventies—I'm not really sure. That was something that sounded like 'Why hasn't somebody thought of doing this before?' I mean the problem of cataracts in the Nepalese people. The number of them was so great, and then suddenly there was this one foundation that was doing something for them. And Bobby—our rhythm guitarist Bob Weir—had a connection with that foundation . . . and he suggested that we do a benefit for them. We went along with that because we felt that they were really doing something unique and sorely needed."

Having joined the band as a teenager, Bob Weir has spent his entire adult life as a member of the Grateful Dead. You might think he would have become a burnout by now, in keeping with the superficial media stereotype of the Dead's fans. You'd be wrong. He is soft-spoken, but incredibly articulate. Very introspective, very philosophical. We started off talking about Seva, but he had a lot more on his mind: "In the rest of the world, blindness is not like it is here. Here, if you're blind you get a Seeing Eye dog. I mean in the developing world if you're blind, you get a little kid who'll lead you around with a stick until he gets old enough to go work in the fields or whatever and then you get nothing. And the community can't afford to have you around anymore. The suffering involved in being blind in the developing world is a lot more intense than it is here. It's a real hideous affliction. And the people in the Seva Foundation have been in the developing world and seeing a lot of the real deep causes of suffering. And that's what they're after. They're after those really deep wells of human suffering. And so you come to one of these events and you see the people coming in and you know the money is going to the alleviation of that suffering—it feels good. There's something about it that feels good. You don't have to be real sensitive or real idealistic or spiritual to perceive this. It's palpable. I think it's a natural sense maybe. I'm wondering about this a lot. But I'm thinking maybe it's a natural sense. Maybe there is something that we are endowed with by the Creator that gives us an opportunity to naturally figure out how to make this a better place."

Tom Campbell has produced a number of Seva shows, including one he specifically remembers doing with Jackson Browne: "Wavy Gravy used to say, 'Give me three dollars and someone can see.' This benefit concert that we were doing in Pasadena was particularly for the cataract operations that they would do in third-world countries, and Jackson Browne said poignantly, 'You are in the audience, you hear the sound of the music that I am making, and somewhere, someone halfway around the world gets to see.' It was one of those moments where you just knew it had been called exactly like it was."

Lesh says the Grateful Dead's involvement with Seva "turned out to be a very, very fruitful relationship because when we started our foundation they were very helpful."

"The Grateful Dead have always put themselves out there for their community and communities around the world," says Bob Barsotti of Bill Graham Presents. "It's in their blood. It's something that's just a part of them. And I was so honored to be able to be a part of that over the years and to help with all the concerts, the benefits. At one point they realized that so much of the money they were making was being taxed that [they said], Why don't we start a foundation? And they started the Rex Foundation, where they could give all the money away. And I was involved in all but one of the Rex benefits over the years. We raised a lot of money for a lot of good causes, and the way they would give it away was just amazing—they just would get together and say, Okay, here's the list of people; and everyone would make suggestions and *boom*—these ten-thousand-dollar checks would go out to people, and it was quite inspiring to be able to see that."

"There's so much that needs to be done and so much help that's needed out there in the world," explains Lesh, "that just doing benefits for each little cause that came along didn't seem to us to be a very efficient way of helping out. So back in '84 we created a foundation, the Rex Foundation. We guaranteed *x* number of shows per year that [the Grateful Dead] would play for this foundation. And then the board of directors (which consisted of three band members and other people that we brought on board that weren't all connected with the Grateful Dead) would decide where the money went. Over the eleven years or so that the foundation was functional, it funded the whole spectrum of causes from homeless to environment, to the arts, to schools, to training videos—just the whole spectrum of available causes."

Says Weir: "The Rex Foundation is the Grateful Dead's philanthropic wing. I guess we all developed individually and also collectively a notion that life has been pretty damn good to us. We get to do what we love to do and would do any old way. In our spare time, if we weren't doing it for a living, we'd be making music. And it just sort of feels right to give a little back, one way or another. It also makes good sense. If you can make the world a better place, then you live in a better place. It's entirely self-serving, enlightened self-service, I guess, is what they call it.

"So given that we all pretty much felt that way, it seemed like a pretty natural thing to do—to sort of focus our efforts a little bit. And so we put together the Rex Foundation and, you know, you get a bunch of maniacs in a room and then try to get stuff straight, it took a little bit of work. But it was worth it. The Rex Foundation, though it has no specific area of concern like a lot of foundations do—a lot of foundations pretty strictly benefit things like medical research, or public health issues, or homeless issues—the Rex Foundation has got a really broad, sort of a shotgun approach to how it benefits things. But there is one sort of specific area of concern and that's the kind of stuff that might fall through the cracks with regard to other beneficial agencies or outfits. Sort of off-the-wall charities or people or issues that would have difficulty getting funding, by virtue of their oddness or their meekness. We kind of look for stuff that appeals to one or another of the individuals on the Rex board and then we kick it around for a while. And if everybody feels strongly enough about kicking some support their way, then that's what we do."

In 1992, Jerry Garcia told an interviewer that "the people who come to ask their local rock 'n' roll band for help are the forgotten people, believe me. I mean if you have to call the *Grateful Dead* for assistance, you're definitely falling between the cracks of all major charity."

"It's kind of nice to be a part of an organization that exists solely for the purpose of making this world a better place," concludes Weir, thoughtfully. "And not through the aegis of any sort of religion or philosophical or political rhetoric, but just by going on a feel basis—what *feels* right. And sort of arriving at what feels right by consensus. And it really seems right—though, you know, it occurs to me that that is also how lynch mobs get started. And I really can't definitively tell you what the difference is between the Rex Foundation and your standard lynch mob, but there is one."

Not all benefits work. The idea of "lending a hand," as this chapter is titled, is based on two principles: the first is that the recipient needs and wants a hand; the second is that he deserves one.

In 1990, Crosby, Stills, Nash & Young's former drummer Dallas Taylor was given the terrifying news that he required a liver transplant. Hepatitis C had caused his liver to deteriorate to such an extent that if he didn't receive a transplant quickly, he'd surely die. Ironically, this was the exact same prognosis I would be given four years later. (They're thinking now that there may be as many as 170 *million* cases of hepatitis C in the world, and almost *none* of those infected know they have it, since only a few developed countries can test for it. There are probably 4 million cases in the United States alone. As bad as AIDS is in the third world, hepatitis C could well be worse. And virtually no one is even aware of it.)

Apparently Dallas's insurance covered the expense of a transplant operation but wouldn't extend to the costly (and lifesaving) antirejection medicine he would need for the rest of his life. So while he waited for word of a matching liver donor, Crosby, Stills & Nash agreed to do a benefit concert for him, as well as for the cause of organ donor awareness itself. I called Neil, who said to count him in, as did both Don Henley and Chris Hillman (who came with the Desert Rose Band). The concert was held at the three-thousand-seat Santa Monica Civic Auditorium and, as this was the first CSNY performance in southern California in nineteen years, the tickets sold out in six minutes. (With that kind of lineup, it was no surprise that someone would ask us to do a second show. That someone was Jane Fonda, whom I've never been able to turn down. She was lead-ing a campaign for an environmental initiative on the California state ballot that all of us supported, so it was an easy call. We added a show the following night and it, too, sold out immediately.)

Musically, the Dallas Taylor benefit was a great experience. The Desert Rose and Henley sets were terrific, as was Neil's solo perfor-mance, which opened the second half of the show. Crosby, Stills & Nash did the last set, with Neil joining us toward the end. Dallas was still well enough to sit in on drums for the last two songs, "Wooden Ships" and "Teach Your Children." It was a good feeling, knowing that we were helping our friend when he needed us the most.

A short time later Dallas underwent a transplant operation, and we were all relieved to learn that the doctors expected him to make a full recovery, which he did. I'd like to tell you that the story ended there, but unfortunately I can't.

Dallas, who after the operation had gone back to work as a sub-stance abuse counselor, seemed to be angry that he wasn't able to parlay his brief return to the limelight into a new career in the music industry. (What I haven't mentioned up to now is that CSNY *fired* Dallas in the early seventies, because he was so loaded that he couldn't cut it as our drummer. And if you were too loaded to play with *us*, you were in pretty bad shape.)

Then Dallas wrote a book about his life that included some unkind things about Nash, which, given what we'd done for him, struck me as being pretty ungrateful. At that point, I still didn't realize that gratitude was not part of Dallas's character.

We remained friends until 1996, when I was served with a notice that Dallas was suing me (along with Neil, Graham, and Stephen) for moneys he claimed we'd owed him since he was fired. It was just his way of trying to hang on, to stay connected to the fame he thought he deserved. In my opinion, Dallas was the most overpaid mediocre drummer in history who'd already made millions of dol-lars off us and wanted more. Besides that, for him to sue us after we'd stood up for him and helped him was just an unbelievably obnoxious and ungrateful thing to do.

We settled the suit to make him go away, but the whole experience was a very bitter pill. You find out about some people being shits less expensively, and sometimes it costs you. But when you find out, you've found out, and then you can move on.

This brings me back to the whole question of doing benefits to give someone a hand. Neil and I talked about it, and I think his take on the lesson of Dallas Taylor is the best one to have: "When I look at the different benefits that I've done, most of them have turned into good, positive things. I've only done one benefit for an individual, that I can remember. [It] was one I did for a personal friend who later sued me. It turned out to be good inasmuch as the benefit was successful and we saved the guy's ass and he got a new liver . . . and that was good. Life is good. That was a success. But you never know what you're gonna get into. Since we're talking about benefits, the safest benefit I think you can play is one that is not for an individual."

Neil's right on both counts. I'm glad we did the benefit for Dallas, because we came to it from the right place. And Neil's also correct in saying that it's better to work on behalf of a group or organization that you can hold accountable. It's once again the same reason that's always made me reluctant to support individual politicians: People are flawed. We all are. That's why in the Twelve-Step programs they tell you not to believe in any one person. Because if you do, you're going to say, I'm only making it because I believe in this person who's got more years sober than me. If he goes out, then where are you?

Happily, most benefits are deeply rewarding experiences where the only disappointment comes from feeling that you should have done even more. That's especially true in the wake of some kind of natural disaster. There's so much devastation, you feel like no matter what you do it won't be enough. At those times, I always try to remember what Harry Belafonte said when he was trying to get his fellow artists to do something—*anything*—about the famine in

Africa: "Don't sit there and be overwhelmed by the enormity of the problem. Just pick out that portion which is yours, and kick butt. Go out there and make a difference. Change it. Change it. *Change it.*"

Some of the greatest benefit concerts have come about in response to the human crises resulting from natural catastrophes such as earthquakes, hurricanes, and typhoons. Times when Nature has shrugged her shoulders and put a whole lot of people at risk and put them out of their homes.

The Concerts for Bangladesh and the Stones' Nicaraguan earthquake benefit are two such events that were already mentioned in an earlier chapter. There have been a lot more. For example, after a major flood inundated Wyoming in 1985, Neil was flown in to do a special benefit performance for the victims. "When the National Guard flies *me* into Wyoming for a benefit," said Neil dryly, "we've come a long way."

The Royal Albert Hall was once again the site of a major benefit event in 1986, when Annie Lennox, Chrissie Hynde, Pete Townshend, and David Gilmour participated in what was billed as a "Colombian Volcano Appeal Concert." Two years later, when Hurricane Gilbert pounded Jamaica, Ziggy Marley flew to England and rallied support from fellow artists like U2 and Keith Richards (whose home was among those damaged in the storm) at a "Smile Jamaica Concert" in London's Dominion Theatre.

Following the devastating San Francisco earthquake of 1989, Crosby, Stills & Nash participated in a Bill Graham–produced telethon from the Cow Palace, along with the Steve Miller Band, Santana, the Chambers Brothers, and Neil (who did a solo set). The telethon, together with simultaneous events in Oakland and Watsonville, raised more than a million dollars in emergency relief. But the amazing thing was when Bill—and this is something that'll give you an idea of what kind of guy Bill Graham really was—*matched* what we raised with a check for a million dollars out of his own pocket.

In 1990, 200,000 people gathered in Berlin's Potzdamer Platz for one of the most spectacular concert events ever held, benefit or otherwise. Within sight of the infamous Berlin Wall, Roger Waters staged an extraordinary (and politically appropriate) production of Pink Floyd's "The Wall." The international cast included Bryan Adams, James Galway, the Hooters, Cyndi Lauper, Joni Mitchell, Van Morrison, Sinead O'Connor, the Scorpions, and Marianne Faithfull. The television broadcast, beamed live around the world, raised funds for international disaster relief.

When Hurricane Andrew cut a deadly swath across south Florida in 1992, it took Gloria Estefan and Comic Relief only three weeks to pull together an all-star benefit concert at Miami's Joe Robbie Stadium, with performances by Estefan, Whoopi Goldberg, Paul Simon, the Bee Gees, Jimmy Buffett, and Crosby, Stills & Nash. For me, the best performance was the amazing Latin band of Tito Puente, with Ruben Blades and Andy Garcia sitting in. Hurricane Relief raised $2.5 million for the more than ten thousand people left homeless by Andrew.

Just a few months after Hurricane Andrew hit Florida, Hurricane Iniki nearly decimated the Hawaiian island of Kauai. Along with Bonnie Raitt, Jackson Browne, and Jimmy Buffett, we flew over there to perform two benefit concerts on Oahu (where the money is). One of my favorite memories of any benefit experience came the day after those two shows, when we went over to Kauai and did a free concert on the high school football field. The purpose of that event wasn't to raise money; it was to raise spirits. And it really worked . . . it was one of the most joyous afternoons you could ask for. They loved it because somebody cared enough to show up and sing for them. They loved it because somebody gave a damn.

I've always been completely baffled by the fact that some people are able to witness a disaster, to see the pain in a child's face, and then simply look away. I don't get it. I never will. I just don't understand how anyone can do that.

CHAPTER 8

Human Rights:
"Keep On Rockin' in the Free World"

What I wanted to do was somehow fuse human

rights and nonviolence . . . the right to live being the

first human right of all of us.

Joan Baez

A few years ago I attended a Free Tibet rally on the steps of the Capitol in Washington, D.C. I didn't have any part in organizing the rally. I was there because I believed in the cause, as well as to interview people for this book and the companion documentary film.

While I was listening to one of the speeches, a reporter approached me and said, "Excuse me, Mr. Crosby, can I ask you a question?"

Now, I'll generally talk to anybody who's reasonably polite, so I said, "Sure, what's your question?" And in this very patronizing tone of voice she said, "You don't really think that you can get China out of Tibet, do you? I mean, *really?*" I stared at her for a second and then all I said was "No."

I was hoping that would be the end of it, but she wouldn't give up. "Well then, none of this is going to do any good, right? So what are you even doing here?" She was obviously trying to bait me at this point, so I did what I usually do when a reporter gets obnoxious—I asked her, "Is this your first time? Because you're really not very good at this." Then I gave her the real answer, which was "I am not so constructed as to be able to sit idly by." She looked at me as if I were a fish and disappeared into the crowd, no doubt in a frantic search for somebody else to harangue.

Although it was just a minor irritation—the whole exchange didn't last more than a minute—it stuck with me. I started thinking about what else I could have said to her. Even though her purpose was to get me to say something controversial or just stupid (always a possibility), which she then would have used to sell more newspapers, it struck me that her question had more merit than I wanted to admit. If I truly didn't believe China was going to stop oppressing Tibet—certainly not because of some rally in the United States—then what *was* I doing there?

I talked about it with Eddie Vedder, who got asked the same question when Pearl Jam played at the Tibetan Freedom concert the day before the rally. He used an analogy to explain why he'd chosen to be there: "It would be like driving down this road in a line of cars that's moving very slowly, and on the side of the road you're seeing two people get the shit pummeled out of them by eight bullies. Now you're going slow enough that you can actually jump out and help, or do you just stay in the car and keep going and drive past? I just feel like I have to get out of the car. Even if the guys are bigger than me."

That's why Eddie Vedder plays at the Tibetan Freedom concerts. And it's why I was at the rally. You do what you're able to do. I know I *personally* don't have the power to go over to Tibet and force the Chinese to leave, but I do have the power to say it's wrong. Sometimes you can't see down the road any farther than that. Almost nobody believed that Martin Luther King could effect significant change on civil rights in this country, especially without using violence as part of his strategy. And nobody *ever* believed that a little man named Gandhi wrapped in a bedsheet would be able to stop the entire British empire in India. Stop it in its tracks, cold.

Jackson Browne sees "a real thread that runs from Thoreau, to Gandhi, to Martin Luther King . . . civil disobedience began in the United States with Thoreau . . . the idea that by being arrested for something, and showing his neighbors and his friends that he is willing to go to jail for an ideal, that it would be a very influential thing."

Don Henley was profoundly influenced by Thoreau's ideas when he was growing up in Texas. They were so important to him that when he heard a news story about a plan to develop part of Walden Woods, where Thoreau did much of his writing, into *condominiums*, he organized a series of benefit concerts and raised the money needed to protect that land, which was the real birthplace of the American environmental movement.

Continues Jackson, "That idea [civil disobedience] was taken up by Gandhi, and he used it very, very well in India, and the entire liberation in that country was done nonviolently. And, of course, Gandhi was a great influence on Martin Luther King, so it comes back to us. I think that's really a very powerful global idea. I think it illustrates how far an idea like that can travel and how you can really put a value on an idea."

No matter how good an idea is, it won't have any power unless there's a way for people to hear about it. One part of our job as artists is to entertain, but another part is also to be the messenger, to spread the word. It's an important tradition that goes back over many centuries.

For as long as I can remember, going back to the earliest days of the civil rights movement in the fifties, no one has done more to honor that tradition than Harry Belafonte. As an activist, he's made the entire world his stage, taking with him a repertoire of ideas and stories that nobody can match. What other artist can say he's walked with both Martin Luther King and Nelson Mandela? If you go to Africa you'll hear his name mentioned in the same breath with theirs—and with the same respect.

Because he worked so closely with Dr. King, I'd always just assumed that Belafonte also shared King's strong belief in the power of nonviolence. It wasn't until our interview that I learned he'd actually seriously doubted that nonviolence would ever work. "When Dr. King walked in, my earliest commitment to him was really quite tenuous. I was deeply committed to him as a person. I trusted him, but I wasn't quite sure about how this nonviolent, moral thing was going to work. But, what the hell, we tried everything else, so why not that? And as I got more into it and watched what it did and how it galvanized people and how it forced this nation to a wake-up call that it never dreamed it would have to answer . . . what a remarkable experience. And the more I understood what it did, the more I was encouraged to put my voice wherever I could that would make a difference. Because I knew that I had at my disposal probably the most formidable weapon mankind had ever come up with in order to do battle against injustice."

In the eighties, Belafonte took that weapon into the battle against apartheid in South Africa, easily one of the most unjust ideas ever conceived. Apartheid was a pathetic attempt to put a legitimate face on something truly evil—South Africa's policy of keeping its black-majority population separate from the white-minority ruling class. The practical effect of apartheid was to subjugate an entire race of people. Most blacks were forced to live in conditions of mind-numbing poverty and were denied the basic privileges of citizenship, including the right to vote.

Under increasing pressure from the world community, the United Nations passed a resolution in December 1980 calling for a complete cultural boycott of South Africa until apartheid was eliminated. To help enforce it, the UN started publishing an annual list of "Entertainers, Actors, and Others Who Have Performed in Apartheid South Africa." Belafonte and his friend, the late tennis star Arthur Ashe, formed a group called Athletes and Artists Against Apartheid whose purpose was to inform their peers of the boycott and enlist support for it.

I was already out of the Byrds when they went to South Africa in 1968, and they got a lot of flack for doing it. Crosby, Stills & Nash would never agree to play in front of a segregated audience, so for us the boycott wasn't an issue; it was something we'd already been doing for a long time without having to be asked. Some people, like Queen and Rod Stewart, continued to play in South Africa, and their names made it onto the UN list.

In 1985 Stevie Wonder recorded "It's Wrong," a song condemning apartheid, and was arrested for performing it outside the South African embassy in Washington, D.C. Stevie was more amused than angry, "They said I was disturbing the peace, but I was just singing." (That same combination of ironic humor and absolute determination sustained Stevie throughout his long and ultimately successful campaign to create a national holiday in honor of Martin Luther King.)

Peter Gabriel has followed the apartheid issue closely for more than twenty years. In 1977 he heard about Steven Biko, a prominent black activist who had been summarily arrested and severely beaten by the South African police. Then, naked and almost unconscious, Biko was transported seven hundred miles to prison, where he eventually died from his injuries. Steven Biko's savage murder so affected Gabriel that it moved him to write the first overtly political song of his career. It's an achingly beautiful song with a haunting refrain.

September '77
Port Elizabeth weather fine
It was business as usual
In police room 619
Oh Biko, Biko, because Biko
Oh Biko, Biko, because Biko
Yihla Moja, Yihla Moja
—The man is dead
When I try to sleep at night
I can only dream in red
The outside world is black and white
With only one colour dead
Oh Biko, Biko, because Biko

Oh Biko, Biko, because Biko
Yihla Moja, Yihla Moja
—The man is dead
You can blow out a candle
But you can't blow out a fire
Once the flames begin to catch
The wind will blow it higher
Oh Biko, Biko, because Biko
Yihla Moja, Yihla Moja
—The man is dead
And the eyes of the world are
watching now
watching now

"'Biko' really originated from the coverage that he was getting in the press and the television to some extent," recalls Gabriel. "And many of us that were interested in the antiapartheid movement were quite convinced that . . . there was enough publicity to ensure nothing would happen to him. So I think there was a real sense of shock when we learned of his death . . . it became sort of an emotional high point in concerts."

I've said this before, but it's worth repeating: when you write a song and send it out into the world, on radio and television, you have absolutely no idea who it will reach or what effect it will have. As it turned out, "Biko" would become an anthem in the antiapartheid movement, making many more people aware of the issue, including other artists. One of them—"Little" Steven Van Zandt, lead guitarist in Bruce Springsteen's E Street Band—would become as inspired by "Biko" the song as Peter Gabriel had been by Steven Biko himself.

Says Gabriel, "Little Steven told me around the time of 'Sun City' that ['Biko'] had been his introduction to apartheid issues."

Van Zandt became so interested in South Africa, he went there to check out the situation for himself. On that trip he met with activists, as well as other musicians, and they all told him about a

place called Sun City. Sun City was an entertainment and gam-
bling resort built in Bophuthatswana, a supposedly separate country within South Africa. Van Zandt learned that Bophuthatswana
existed solely as a means to get around the cultural boycott.
Nobody but the South African government recognized it as an
independent state. Against their will, blacks were forced to relo-
cate to this "homeland" so that the charade of independence
would be maintained. All of this was really about attracting more
tourists to the Sun City resort, and, of course, big-name performers were recruited to help increase its drawing power. Musicians
were offered huge fees—in the millions of dollars—just to play
Sun City.

"I was down there for a month and I met quite a lot of people,"
says Little Steven. "You know, they had certain things they agreed
on with each other and certain things they didn't. One thing that
they all said was, 'Please go back and tell the musical community to
please *not* play Sun City.'"

One of the people who heard the message was Bruce Springsteen:
"Steven has been my best friend since we were about sixteen years
old and had gotten very involved in what was going on down there.
He came back and talked to me about it from time to time, and what
he was seeing. And I don't think you can sit and see—watch it on TV
every night and see some of the pain and injustice that's going on
down there, without wanting to do something, in some fashion,
about it."

"Years ago," said Darryl Hall in a 1985 interview, "before [Hall &
Oats] really had achieved the commercial status that we have now,
they asked us to play there and offered us a ridiculous sum of
money, like two million dollars to play there, and we could have
used the money then, but at least we were smart enough to know
what was going on. And I think that anybody that has played there—
I don't want to . . . actually, I *will* mention names . . . Rod Stewart
and Queen and people like that have played there are jerks for doing
it. They were more than aware of what they were doing and I think
they should be called out for it."

When he came back from South Africa, Little Steven wrote "Sun City," a song designed to spread the word about what he'd learned during his time there. In the summer of 1985 he recruited musicians from all different styles of music—rock, reggae, salsa, rap, jazz, and R&B—to sing on parts of it. Of course, Bruce Springsteen was one of the first to agree—as did an amazing group of others, more than fifty in all. Among them were Miles Davis, Ruben Blades, George Clinton, Jackson Browne, Gil Scott-Heron, Lou Reed, Bonnie Raitt, Bobby Womack, Run-DMC, Bono, Bob Dylan, Jimmy Cliff, Pete Townshend, and, still heady from Live Aid, Bob Geldof. Ringo Starr (who first became aware of apartheid in 1965, when the Beatles declined an invitation to play in South Africa) and his son Zak played drums together for the first time on the "Sun City" record.

Van Zandt also wanted a four-man black South African vocal group called Malopoets to sing on "Sun City." But he was worried about their participation because some of them still lived there. He says he told them, "'It could be dangerous to be on this record. Who knows what reprisals may happen?' And they just felt . . . they told me, 'We *have* to be on this record. We don't care about reprisals, even if it means our death.' When somebody tells you they're ready to *die* to be on a record, you know . . . that's commitment."

There's a great moment captured by a documentary crew during the recording of "Sun City." Miles Davis has just laid down a horn track and Bonnie Raitt is introduced to him for the first time. Bonnie says, "Hi, nice to meet you. You sounded great." And Miles says, "That's my *thang*." Miles told the interviewer, "South Africa makes me ill. Sick all over. When I think about it I can't do nothin', can't even play."

Although proceeds from "Sun City" would go to benefit the families of South African political prisoners, Van Zandt didn't write it as a fund-raising vehicle. Unlike "We Are the World," which avoided political statements in order to attract the broadest possible audience, "Sun City" didn't pull any punches. It openly ridiculed Ronald Reagan's so-called constructive engagement approach to dealing with South Africa, a policy based on the idea that we would have

more influence on apartheid if we remained their friends and continued to do business with them. Yeah, right.

Interspersed among repeated shouts of "I ain't gonna play Sun
City" are lines that directly attack apartheid:

Relocation to phony homelands
Separation of families I can't understand
Twenty-three million can't vote because they're black

"The idea is not to offend people, but to raise some consciousness," Little Steven told a reporter at the time. "It's just to start the
discussion about an issue that needs attention. There's a lot that
America does and is responsible for beyond its borders that people
should be informed about."

It worked. Even though a few radio stations in the South stopped
playing the single after receiving threats from the Ku Klux Klan, it
still did very well. Sun City became a place people knew they *didn't*
want to visit, and everyone became aware that musicians were
proactively taking a stand against apartheid. Even Rod Stewart and
Queen agreed to support the boycott, and their names were
removed from the UN list.

The cultural boycott gave us an opportunity to do something tan-
gible. It allowed us to say, "Hey, we bring an economic benefit wherever we go; we can withhold it as well." It had an impact. When those
cash registers and slot machines in Sun City stopped making a
noise, it had an impact.

In a speech he gave at the United Nations for the premiere of the
"Sun City" video, Little Steven said, "Although the money made from
the sales of this record will go to help wherever it is needed, this is not
a benefit record. Because though the black South African needs are
great, they do not ask us for our charity. And though the black South
African suffering is horrifying, they do not ask us for our pity. All they
ask us is that we look at them and see them. Because by seeing them,
we see ourselves. Their struggle is our struggle. Because their struggle
is not against men—this is a temporary condition. Their struggle is
against a disease, a disease called racism and bigotry."

Following "Sun City," the antiapartheid campaign picked up momentum. International pressure on the South African government to change its policies was getting stronger and louder every day. Through their music and public statements, artists continued to play a major role in keeping the issue on the front burner.

By 1988, the principal focus of the antiapartheid movement had become the freedom of just one man. Nelson Mandela, the living symbol of resistance to white-minority rule in South Africa, had spent twenty-six years in a Johannesburg prison. The government didn't dare kill him, as they had Steven Biko. But they were terrified of the political upheaval that might result from releasing him. So they'd kept him locked up for more than a quarter-century, hoping that old age would do the job for them.

Mandela's supporters were equally aware of his advancing age. They decided to use his seventieth birthday as an opportunity to stage a musical tribute that would serve as an international call for Mandela's release. On June 11, 1988, at that great benefit fixture, London's Wembley Stadium, some of the world's biggest artists gathered for Freedomfest, an eleven-hour concert event seen by more than one billion people in sixty countries, easily making it the largest antiapartheid rally in history.

The political significance of Freedomfest was obvious from the beginning when Harry Belafonte, his hair a little grayer but his manner still as dignified and elegant as it was when he marched with Dr. King, strode to the microphone and welcomed the Wembley crowd to this extraordinary event. Speaking directly to Mandela, one of the few people in the world who couldn't hear him, Belafonte said, "The message is quite simple. We salute you, and we want to see you and your fellow prisoners free."

For those in the Wembley crowd who'd been there three years earlier for Live Aid, it must have seemed a little like . . . deja vu. Sting, George Michael, Phil Collins, and Dire Straits were all back. So were some of those who'd played in Philadelphia, like Eric Clapton and Simple Minds.

But there were also some important differences between the two shows. The first was in the music itself. Live Aid was a nonpolitical event, and so was the music. At Freedomfest, the opposite was true. From Peter Gabriel's rousing, emotional "Biko" to a jubilant all-star performance of "Sun City" by Gabriel, Little Steven, Jackson Browne, and Simple Minds' Jim Kerr, the political message of the day was unmistakable. Sting said it best with the song he chose to finish his set: "If You Love Somebody Set Them Free."

The other major difference between this event and Live Aid was the presence at Freedomfest of many black artists, including Tracy Chapman, Al Green, Roberta Flack, Natalie Cole, Hugh Masekela, and Miriam Makeba. But the real coup was when Stevie Wonder and Whitney Houston both agreed to perform. Jim Kerr, one of the artists involved in organizing the concert, told a reporter he was particularly surprised by Houston's decision to play. "A hugely popular black artist really made it credible. I'd never have thought she'd take a political stance."

Although her renditions of "Didn't We Almost Have It All" and "The Greatest Love of All" (in a duet with her mother) drew ovations from the Wembley audience, Houston wasn't going to win any popularity contests among her fellow artists at Freedomfest. Her bodyguards are reported to have shoved Whoopi Goldberg out of the way, and when Stevie Wonder's set was delayed because some of his equipment had been stolen, she wouldn't shorten her own forty-five-minute set to accommodate him. When he finally went on, Stevie had only seven minutes. He did "Dark 'n' Lovely" and "I Just Called to Say I Love You" (changing the lyric to "I just called to say Happy Birthday, Nelson Mandela"), and got the most prolonged applause of anyone at Freedomfest, including Whitney Houston.

Then, just as Harry Belafonte had done almost eleven hours before, Stevie spoke directly to Nelson Mandela: "Until you are free, no man, woman, or child, whatever color, is really free." The concert ended with a spectacular fireworks display over London as the great opera singer Jessye Norman gave a stirring a cappella performance of "Amazing Grace."

Peter Gabriel describes it as "a very emotional day, and it somehow accumulated this momentum, which was sort of snowballing.

Although Mandela was clearly well known . . . he became an international icon in a different way after that event, I think."

Two years after Freedomfest, Nelson Mandela was finally permitted to leave prison. Four years later, in 1994, he became president of South Africa. Bonnie Raitt says, "The situation in South Africa is so moving and people are so united in their joy that Nelson Mandela was released." For Tracy Chapman, who participated in antiapartheid rallies while she was in college, "It seemed like a miracle, really, to see him finally free. People were able to see in the past that the protests for the civil rights movement actually made a change. People are able to see Nelson Mandela free from prison. They were able to see him become president of South Africa."

Just as Nelson Mandela was jailed for his opposition to South Africa's minority government, it's no secret that other governments have also routinely imprisoned their political dissenters, depriving them of their rights as well. Since 1961, Amnesty International has worked to expose these abuses and gain the release of what they call "prisoners of conscience."

Sting says the first time anyone asked him to do a benefit was in 1979. "I was asked by Amnesty International to perform at something called The Secret Policeman's Other Ball, which they held at Drury Lane Theatre in London. It was with the Monty Python comedy team and various singers. It was myself, Eric Clapton, Jeff Beck, Bob Geldof. They didn't want me to bring the band. I was with the Police at the time. They said, 'Well, we don't want the band, we just want you to come and sing on your own with your guitar.' I said, 'Well, I don't [usually] do that.' They said, 'Come anyway.' So I came and I sang 'Roxanne' and 'Message in a Bottle,' just with the Fender guitar. And I had a great time doing it, and met Monty Python, who had been my heroes. I met Eric Clapton and played with Jeff Beck. I was like a kid in a candy store."

I remember seeing the film of The Secret Policeman's Other Ball. It was the first time I ever saw Sting and I was stunned. I thought, "How could he stand up there with a Fender guitar, just by himself, and *do* that?"

"As a result," continues Sting, "I got to find out about Amnesty International. I'd heard of them, vaguely, but didn't really know what they did. I found out about their work through performing for them. I was told that they organize the writing of letters to nations who don't treat prisoners well. I learned about the prisoners of conscience, and how many there are in the world. I became a member and started to write letters. How do you change the world? You can go outside of an embassy and throw paint, scream and shout, and have a placard. Or you can write letters. And letters are very powerful. You know, the pen is mightier than the sword. It's a cliché that actually works. I consider them to be one of the most civilized and civilizing organizations in the world."

To coincide with Amnesty International's twenty-fifth anniversary in 1986, a major concert tour of the United States was organized by Amnesty's American chapter. Bill Graham was the only logical choice to produce a concert tour on the scale Amnesty was hoping to achieve. Before it started, someone showed Bill a video clip of the great film director John Huston describing Amnesty International as "a conspiracy of hope." In his book, Bill wrote, "That hit me. The name of the tour became 'A Conspiracy of Hope,' with the logo being a candle with barbed wire around it."

"I was asked by the American branch of Amnesty to join a tour," recalls Sting. "And what they wanted to do was recruit more letter writers, more members, and advertise what we do. So we toured through the States with U2 and Peter Gabriel."

Bryan Adams, Lou Reed, the Neville Brothers, and Joan Baez were also on the six-city tour, which began in San Francisco, with stops in Los Angeles, Denver, Atlanta, and Chicago. A Conspiracy of Hope wound up at Giants Stadium in New Jersey for an all-day event culminating in the surprise reunion of the Police.

Sting says: "The Police had broken up two years before. There was a lot of pressure, desire for us to get back together, but what a wonderful way to do it. Not for the big sellout stadium tour, but to do it for a really good cause, to find our friendship again that way. It was very good."

Jackson Browne, who played at that Giants Stadium show, says, "You have events like the Amnesty events where they say, 'Well, we're not trying to make a lot of money. No amount of money will actually take care of this problem, but we want to get twenty thousand more people to join and to write letters. We want to increase our numbers. We are going to increase awareness.' And those are kinds of obtainable goals. What's more, with groups like Amnesty, you actually come into contact with people who were in prisons for political reasons, and who are now out because people, everyday people, became aware of the situation and did something positive . . . that's a very moving thing. I think just about everything that's done in this way contains seeds of a first-class political education."

Joan Baez believes the Conspiracy of Hope tour was very effective in raising awareness. "I think it was very important. I think that young people . . . really did get a concept of 'human rights.' What did that mean? And what did it mean in other places in the world? And I think the important thing is, I've seen a lot of people who have continued working . . . "

In 1988, energized by the results of the U.S. tour, Amnesty mounted an even more ambitious effort. The Human Rights Now! campaign went around the world, playing in some countries where rock 'n' roll was essentially unknown. Sting recalls: "We raised the Amnesty numbers in America very successfully—so successfully that they then asked us a few years later to do a similar tour around the world to raise consciousness about human rights, and also to raise the numbers. So Bruce Springsteen, Peter Gabriel, and myself went around the world on behalf of Amnesty. We went to South America, we went to Asia, we went to Europe doing this thing and playing in countries that weren't that far removed from the countries we were targeting. We played in Zimbabwe, which is right next to South Africa, before the regime changed. We played in Argentina, right next to Pinochet's Chile. We would attract audiences from those regimes, supportive audiences, and to give them support, we'd say that the world *is* watching what's happening in your country."

"One illustration," says Neil, "of something that *did* work, that I thought worked, was the one that Springsteen and Peter Gabriel and Tracy Chapman did . . . the Amnesty tour. Now *that* was an interesting thing. There's something about that that had depth. That had more focus than on one individual's problem. [They] were focusing on a problem that really runs through all the countries and through all the world."

When I interviewed Elton John, the subject of Amnesty International came up, since he'd just joined its board of directors. Neither of us was a part of the Amnesty tours. As it turns out, we had similar reasons. Says Elton, "When they did that tour with Peter Gabriel and Tracy Chapman and Bruce Springsteen and people like that, I was very envious because I would have liked to have been on that tour . . . it was a cause I really believed [in] passionately. But I wasn't in a fit state to be. I was watching it from a bedroom going, 'Oh, I wish I was on that tour.' And you can't really be on it unless you're a hundred percent alert. When you take drugs, your whole life centers around taking drugs. I mean, you can say one thing but . . . being an activist is actually getting off your backside and doing something about it. And I don't think you can become an activist unless the thing that you're really passionate about is a hands-on thing. And I never was in this fit state to be hands-on with anything, except where's the next gram of coke coming from."

I went through the same thing Elton did when he went into treatment: having that feeling that I'd been given a second chance. And I also felt that I wanted to give something back because of that. That first Amnesty tour, the U.S. tour in 1986, happened while I was in a Texas prison. At the time I remember feeling ashamed of myself because I was so fucked up that I had wound up in prison and was unable to be there for something that I wished with all my heart I could have contributed to. It was a very bad moment. But it became one of a series of things that were good incentives for me; positive things that would only be possible if I stayed clean.

The Human Rights Now! tour wasn't permitted into Chile in 1988. Two years later, after General Pinochet was gone, a special

Amnesty concert took place in Chile to celebrate the restoration of human rights.

"In Chile," explains Sting, "young people were just taken from their homes and murdered because of their views, not because they had committed any crime. Their mothers wanted to know where the bodies of their children and husbands were. They wanted the government to answer questions. The government refused to.

"And their form of protest was that they would dance outside of government buildings, a traditional dance normally done with a man and a woman. They would dance on their own, with an invisible partner, with pictures of their loved ones pinned to their arms. This story moved me greatly, because whether or not you understand the politics of South America, you could understand that symbol anywhere, the feeling of loss and the demand for justice was so powerful in that image. So I wrote this song called 'They Dance Alone' and tried to explain the situation as I saw it. I ended the song in a hopeful key. It went to a major chord, and actually ended up in a samba, a dance for the future."

I've seen the pictures of those women. It's an incredible thing that they thought to do this dance by themselves and express it that eloquently. If you are simply pure of heart and have something really truthful to say, it can be immensely powerful. And Sting does that brilliantly in "They Dance Alone." I told him I wished I'd written it. I confess I love Sting's music, but this song stands out. It's one of my favorites of all the songs I know.

> Why are these women here dancing on their own?
> Why is there this sadness in their eyes?
> Why are the soldiers here
> Their faces fixed like stone?
> I can't see what it is they despise
> They're dancing with the missing
> They're dancing with the dead
> They dance with the invisible ones
> Their anguish is unsaid

They're dancing with their fathers
They're dancing with their sons
They're dancing with their husbands
They dance alone
They dance alone
One day we'll dance on their graves
One day we'll sing our freedom
One day we'll laugh in our joy
And we'll dance
One day we'll dance on their graves
One day we'll sing our freedom
One day we'll laugh in our joy
And we'll dance

"I think there [are some] great examples of . . . amazing songs," says Jackson Browne. "One that really comes to mind is Sting's song 'They Dance Alone,' in which he appropriated the imagery of something that was happening in Chile and wrote an amazing song that communicated the reality. These women were dancing without their husbands in a dance that is traditionally done with a man and a woman. It was the only way they had of communicating that their husbands and sons had been disappeared by the military regime. A very talented and clever musician took that image and made it into a song and communicated it to millions and millions of people who would not otherwise have given it that much attention had they read about it—*if* they could read about it—in *Newsweek*. Maybe it'd be covered there and maybe not. But the point is that music has the power to communicate feelings and ideas."

"A lot of the family members were present in Chile," remembers Peter Gabriel. "We were in stadiums that had been used as sort of large, open prisons. Some of the families would come up to us afterwards and [said they] felt that it was like a sort of exorcism that somehow purified the place that had stayed as a sort of symbol of pain and oppression in their minds. It was a very humbling experience. You see people in tears and reliving memories, and it's impossible not to be very moved."

For Sting, the experience was almost overwhelming: "I performed that song in Chile with the mothers onstage with me, in the very stadium [in which] a lot of their children and husbands were murdered. They brought thousands of them into this football stadium, tortured them, and murdered them downstairs. We performed onstage right there. I danced the samba at the end of the song with each one of these women and I'll never forget it, that feeling. It was probably the greatest, most powerful moment of my career."

Sting also returned from Latin America with a new cause. He'd traveled into the Brazilian jungles, home of the Kayapo Indians, and learned that massive deforestation was robbing them of their lands. Not only were the human rights of the Kayapos threatened, but the Brazilian rain forests, vital to the ecological balance of the planet, were in danger of extinction. To help fight this, Sting created the Rainforest Foundation, which he's funded with a series of annual benefit concerts at Carnegie Hall organized by his wife, Trudie Styler. Their work has provided the Kayapos with the resources necessary to help defend their lands, which in turn serves to protect the benefits of the rain forest for the rest of the world.

That 1990 Amnesty show in Chile was held in the same stadium in which Victor Jara was murdered. In twenty years' time, there have been some tremendous changes in the world, particularly around human rights issues. And a new generation of artist activists has come forward to help guarantee that those changes continue.

"I got involved in human rights because of the Amnesty International concerts and Live Aid," says Erin Potts who, with Adam Yauch of the Beastie Boys, cofounded the Milarepa Fund in 1994 to promote "compassion and nonviolence." She adds, "I loved U2 when I was younger and they played at those concerts and that's what got me involved in it."

Adam Yauch is a really decent young guy. Somewhere along the line he got turned on to Tibetan Buddhism. And then he realized that the mother lode of Tibetan Buddhism was being destroyed. By destroyed, I mean they take artillery pieces and shell the monasteries. And if the priests won't leave they just bomb the priests; they just blow them up. So every year since 1994 Yauch and the Milarepa Fund have sponsored Free Tibet concerts as a way to raise awareness about the situation in Tibet.

"Adam Yauch called us," says Bob Barsotti of Bill Graham Presents, "and said that he was interested in doing a big benefit concert and could we help him. I had just gotten back from Tibet—I had been in Tibet for a couple of weeks and experienced the devastation of the monasteries and the devastation of the people firsthand, so I was very interested in getting into this."

The first Free Tibet concert was in Golden Gate Park in San Francisco. Recalls Barsotti: "Now Adam really went the full nine yards and we had all the monks there . . . he was very serious about getting the word out. So instead of just doing a concert where he brought all his friends together and we raised a lot of money for a cause, he took the whole cause and infused it into the whole event. Starting off in the morning with the big press conference, having all the artists come in and say what they had to say about it, bringing the monks up onstage in between the acts to speak to the audience, and having a lot of the artists themselves give their impressions of what was going on. And I have to hand it to Adam. By the end of the day people knew more about what was going on in Tibet than could possibly be imagined by doing anything else. You couldn't have written a book or given them anything else that would have given them more information. Because it came along with their favorite music, their spirits were open and ready to receive and what they got was way more than just the music."

"He's gone from being one of the Beastie Boys fighting for his right to party," says Milarepa's Erin Potts, "to being one of the most committed activists I've ever met. [Adam] is really inspirational as well to a lot of other young people out there. When we're walking around, people always come up to him and want his autograph, but a lot of people also come up to him and say thank-you to him for getting them involved in activism."

"It was Adam Yauch who asked my friend if he could give me a call," says Eddie Vedder. "I think the first one we didn't do. I felt like I had to do my research. I had to read up on it, and it was happening in a month. . . . I said, 'Well, send me stuff.' So I started reading and thinking, reading more, seeking out people who had been there, people who lived there, [trying to get] as much information as I could to really understand the issue. Because these are big issues. I can't imagine jumping on a stage, you know, yelling *Free Tibet!*, because it's just much more . . . it's like an adolescent just saying *Fuck the police . . .* "

"What's so unique about the Tibet Freedom concert," says Sean Lennon, "is that it's so sincere and that the artists involved are highly educated and that the audience is highly educated about the issues, whereas a lot of benefit concerts kind of tend to almost miss the point because the audience doesn't get educated, the artists aren't educated, and so it's kind of superficial."

Just as Nelson Mandela became the symbol of the antiapartheid movement, the Dalai Lama has become a powerful inspiration to people all over the world, including many of the younger artists who are working to free Tibet from Chinese domination. My wife, Jan, is a Buddhist who once had the privilege of meeting His Holiness. The experience touched her profoundly. She believes him to be a truly enlightened human being.

"The Dalai Lama gives me a lot of hope," says Sean Lennon, "because I feel like he's an example of a very influential figure in our society who . . . has compassion for his enemy and has a nonviolent perspective. He's like the modern Gandhi, and it's really beautiful that we still have someone like that on the planet. Because when Martin Luther King was assassinated, when Gandhi was assassinated, Malcolm X was assassinated, when my dad was assassinated, those people were never replaced. And the world has a huge void because of it. I feel like the Dalai Lama is one person that can kind of fill that void for us."

Sean was only five years old when John Lennon was murdered. He's obviously been inspired by his father's legacy. I see the same brilliance in Sean that I saw in his dad. He's articulate and informed, and he does his homework. If I'd been that together when I was his age, I would have conquered the world.

I see these young guys—Yauch, Stipe, Vedder, Lennon—and what makes me proud is that they didn't need an instruction booklet. They have a strong sense of who they are and what they want to achieve. They didn't need any push from us. Robin Williams says, "There was a time when people were very worried that this generation was not going to kick in . . . [but today] people are doing as much work, if not more so, and real personal stuff."

The Tibetan Freedom concert in Washington, D.C., was a two-day event at RFK Stadium in the summer of 1998, featuring performances by Pearl Jam, the Beastie Boys, Red Hot Chili Peppers, REM, Dave Matthews Band, Sean Lennon, and a dozen other major acts. By coincidence, it was happening less than ten days before Bill Clinton's historic trip to China. Adam Yauch and the other organizers hoped the concert (and a rally at the Capitol the next day) would influence Clinton to put the issue of Tibet high up on his agenda with China.

The following day, under a hot summer sun, fifteen thousand people gathered on the steps of the Capitol at the rally for a free Tibet—the same rally at which I was asked what good any of this would ever do.

Adam Yauch spoke with quiet clarity: "In working for Tibetan freedom I think we're all really working towards world peace, because the values that are within Tibetan culture and Tibetan religion, of compassion for all beings and nonviolence, these are the basic principles that are going to help humanity take that next step into really becoming what we are meant to be. And so in a sense I feel really inspired to be here today and see all these people here, but it's also a little bit scary because there's still a long way to go, there's still a lot of work that needs to be done. And I want to be sure that none of us start to rest on our laurels and think 'Oh, these were some exciting concerts' or 'We had a big demonstration here,' and think that we really accomplished anything. Because there's a long way to go on this to actually get Tibet free." (Two weeks later, Clinton did press the Chinese president to open direct negotiations with the Dalai Lama about Tibet. At least it was a start.)

I was surprised when one of the organizers suddenly asked me if I would sing. Thom Yorke of Radiohead let me borrow his guitar, and only a few minutes later I found myself up on the stage before a crowd that stretched out toward the Washington Monument. I did "Long Time Gone," and it was a real kick to have Sean Lennon playing guitar with me—he'd come up to help me out.

When we finished I was stunned by the reaction. The crowd, who I'd assumed were mainly Beastie Boys or REM fans, was clapping and cheering enthusiastically. I wasn't going to do another song, but I felt I had to say something.

"Thanks. I'm here for the same reason you are. Just to stand up and be counted for what I believe . . . "

Which is all anyone can do. Nobody kids themselves into believing that they can solve the world's problems. We're just trying to make a difference, to change things for the better wherever we can. And if it takes a long push, then we're in it for the long haul. A lot of times this isn't about the genius of the moment. It's about *persistence.* It's about being in there and *staying* in there.

I know that we helped create a climate where those changes can happen. There's no question in my mind that music affected things, because we really did make it clear that there was another way. We made it clear that you could believe in life instead of death. In peace and freedom, instead of war and hatred. And we told that story every way you could tell it. We sang it with a thousand voices.

CONCLUSION

Okay, so what have we learned? I hope it's clear that by drawing on the examples of men like King and Gandhi, people have proved time and again that one man or one woman can make a difference. Emerson wrote that "If a single man plant himself firmly on his conviction and there abide, the huge world will come 'round to him." We—all of us who do this—believe that.

What do I hope you'll take away from reading this book? Only this: that the power of standing up for what one believes is not reserved only to people in the spotlight. It is a power anyone can use. Anytime, anywhere. You can start in your own backyard. You can walk down any street in the country, in the world, with your eyes wide open and you will not get far before you see something that you can make better.

My real heroes are the people who work every day trying to alleviate suffering, trying to fight injustice, trying to make the world a better place, often without any recognition at all. They do it without thinking about it, without needing to be told. To them, it's as natural as breathing.

As a matter of fact, they're puzzled by people who don't do it. I love this about human beings. When we put other people's interests ahead of our own, when we work for the common good, we get very shiny. This is us at our best, I think.

INDEX

abortion, 113–17
"Act of Love," 116
Adam Ant, 158
Adams, Bryan, 149, 165, 181, 211, 224
Africa, 214; apartheid, 215–23. *See also* African famine relief
African Americans, 50; African famine relief and, 150, 159–60; civil rights movement, 1–24; folk music, 1–24; Freedomfest (1988), 222; Hurricane Carter cause, 88–96; in Vietnam War, 50–51
African famine relief, 209–10; Band Aid (1984), 145–50, 156; Live Aid (1985), 157–77; "We Are the World," 149–56
After Dark, 82
Agnew, Spiro, 44, 65
agribusiness, 183
AIDS benefits, 196–202
AIDS Project Los Angeles, 197–201
"Ain't Gonna Let Nobody Turn Me Around," 22
Alabama, 9, 30; bus boycott (1955), 4–5, 6, 14; Selma-Montgomery march (1965), 18–22, 25
Alabama (band), 181
Ali, Muhammad, 93, 136
"Alice's Restaurant," 77
Allende, Salvador, 73–78
Allende show (1974), 73–78, 88
Allman, Gregg, 109–10
Allman Brothers, 109–10, 181
American Indians, 89, 139
American Music Awards, 152, 153
Amnesty International, 70, 223–29; Chile concert (1990), 226–29; Conspiracy of Hope tour (1986), 224–25; Human Rights Now! tour (1988), 225–27

Anderson, Louie, 191
Anderson, Marian, 16
Andrews, Julie, 198
Animals, 88
"Another Day in Paradise," 194–96
antiapartheid movement, 215–23; Freedomfest (1988), 221–23; "Sun City" recording, 217–22
antinuclear movement, 118–40; No Nukes (1979), 122, 123, 127–33, 135, 137–39; Peace Sunday (1982), 133–39
antiwar movement, 25–47, 50–53, 68–69, 87–89, 98, 118, 119, 121, 133; CAFF concert (1966), 34–36; Chicago Eight, 41–43; Kent State killings, 46–47; Moratorium Day rallies (1969), 44–45; Shea Stadium Peace Festival (1970), 51–53; War Is Over rallies, 87–89; Winter Peace Festival (1970), 50–51
apartheid, 215–23
Argentina, 225
Armstrong, Louis, 2
Artis, John, 89–90, 94–95
Ashe, Arthur, 215
Ashford & Simpson, 160, 168
Attica prison riots, 66
Axton, Hoyt, 144

Badfinger, 56
Baez, Joan, 6–10, 26, 74, 79, 85, 86, 125, 133, 212, 224, 225; *And a Voice to Sing With*, 165; antiwar movement, 29–30, 36, 37, 40, 41, 45, 88, 89, 121; civil rights movement, 6–10, 15–22; global activism, 141, 144, 162–63; Live Aid (1985), 162–63, 165, 175; Peace Sunday (1982), 135–36; Rolling Thunder Revue, 91, 92, 94

Baker, Josephine, 15
Baldwin, James, 20
Banarama, 147
Band, 86
Band Aid (1984), 145–50, 156
"Bangladesh," 58
Bangladesh concerts (1971), 53–60, 72, 74,
 122, 123, 143, 176, 210
Barsotti, Bob, 80–82, 185–86, 205, 230
Beach Boys, 78, 144, 181
Beastie Boys, 132, 229, 230, 232, 233
Beatles, 26–28, 45, 54, 55, 56, 58, 59, 61, 62,
 79, 97, 108, 142–43, 163, 189, 219
Beatty, Warren, 104, 105
Beck, 181
Beck, Jeff, 223
Bee Gees, 211
Belafonte, Harry, 1, 2, 50, 88, 89, 145, 149,
 214–15; African famine relief, 149–52,
 156, 160, 209–10; antiapartheid cause,
 215–16, 221–22; civil rights work, 1–7,
 14, 19–23
Belafonte, Shari, 3
Bello, Alfred, 90
Benatar, Pat, 175
Bender, David, 39, 104, 107
benefits, 34–36; administrative issues,
 59–60, 72, 122, 123, 176, 180; for AIDS,
 196–202; for Allende (1974), 73–78;
 Amnesty International, 223–29;
 antiapartheid, 215–23; antinuclear,
 122–40; antiwar, 50–53, 68–69, 87–88;
 for Bangladesh (1971), 53–60; birth of,
 48–96; Bridge School, 184–90; Comic
 Relief, 190–94, 211; Farm Aid, 178–84;
 Four for McGovern (1972), 104–8; global
 activism, 141–77; for Hurricane Carter,
 91–96; Kampuchean concerts, 141–45;
 lending a hand, 178–211; Live Aid (1985),
 157–77; for natural disasters, 209–11; for
 Nicaragua (1972), 69–73; No Nukes
 (1979), 122, 123, 127–33, 135, 137–39;
 Peace Sunday (1982), 133–39; political,
 97–117; Rex benefits, 205–7; Seva shows,
 203–5; Sinclair event (1971), 61–67;
 SNACK concert (1975), 81–86; Taylor
 (Dallas) benefit, 207–9; Tibetan
 Freedom concerts, 132, 212–13, 229–33;
 see also specific concerts, causes,
 performers, and venues
Bennett, Tony, 19
Berlin Wall concert (1990), 210–11
Bernhard, Sandra, 198
Bernstein, Leonard, 19

Betts, Dickie, 109–10
Bibb, Leon, 19, 22
Big Brother and the Holding Company, 35
"Biko," 216–17, 222
Biko, Steven, 216–17, 221
Black, Clint, 199, 200
Black Panthers, 42, 62, 63
Black Sabbath, 157, 163
Blades, Ruben, 211, 219
Blakely, Ronee, 93
Blood, Sweat & Tears, 50
"Blowin' in the Wind," 10, 16, 21, 57, 135,
 159, 175
Bonham, John, 143
Bono, 147, 148, 165, 170, 219
Boomtown Rats, 145–46, 147, 160
Bowie, David, 93, 97, 157, 166, 170, 176, 186
Boy George, 147, 148
Bradley, Arthur, 90
Brando, Marlon, 14, 84–86
Brazil, 229
Bridge School benefits, 184–90; of 1986,
 187–90
Brooks, Garth, 181, 199
Brower, John, 60–61
Brown, Jerry, 110–11
Brown, Oscar, 19, 22
Browne, Jackson, 28, 49, 79–81, 118, 140,
 205, 211; antinuclear movement, 122,
 123, 125–31, 135–40; human rights
 causes, 214, 219, 222, 225, 228
Brubeck, Dave, 50
Buckingham, Lindsey, 151
Buffalo Springfield, 32, 34–35, 188
Buffett, Jimmy, 29, 99, 211
Bush, George, 120, 140
Butterfield Blues Band, 52
Byrds, 7, 10, 25–27, 34, 53, 54, 78, 215; CAFF
 concert (1966), 34–36

CAFF concert (1966), 34–36
Calley, Lt. William, 68
Camil, Scott, 68–69
campaign finance reform, 117
Campbell, Tom, 113–15, 123, 128, 205
Canada, 149, 192
cancer, 120, 127, 190
Carnes, Kim, 151, 155
Carpenter, Mary-Chapin, 114, 181
Carrey, Jim, 192
Cars, 166, 170
Carter, Jimmy, 108–10, 144
Carter, Rubin "Hurricane," 89–96; The
 Sixteenth Round, 90

Central Intelligence Agency (CIA), 73, 78, 120

cerebral palsy, 184–90

Chad Mitchell Trio, 19

Chambers Brothers, 210

Chapin, Harry, 151–53

Chapman, Tracy, 181, 222, 223, 226

Charles, Ray, 156

Cheech & Chong, 70, 71, 73

Cher, 175

"Chicago," 42–43

Chicago Eight, 41–43, 60, 62

Chile, 73–78, 225; Amnesty concert (1990), 226–29

China, oppression of Tibet by, 132, 212–13, 229–32

China Syndrome, The (movie), 126, 127

civil rights movement, 1–24, 118, 119, 121; Alabama bus boycott (1955), 4–5, 6, 14; Evers murder, 10–11; March on Washington (1963), 13–18; Selma-Montgomery march (1965), 18–22, 25

Clapton, Eric, 56, 57, 143, 157, 161, 170, 221, 223

Clark, Gene, 25

Clash, 142

Clayton, Adam, 147

Clearwater, 132

Clemente, Roberto, 69–70

Cliff, Jimmy, 219

Clinton, Bill, 100, 101, 103, 232

Clinton, George, 219

Clinton, Hillary Rodham, 197

Clooney, Rosemary, 39

Cobain, Kurt, 115–16

Cohn, Nick, 94

Cold War, 133

Cole, Nat King, 1–2

Cole, Paula, 178

Collins, Judy, 7, 50

Collins, Phil, 147, 149, 157, 221; Live Aid (1985), 161–64, 170, 171, 175; work for the homeless, 194–96

Colombian Volcano Appeal Concert (1986), 210

Colvin, Shawn, 186

Comic Relief, 190–94, 211

Commander Cody & His Lost Planet Airmen, 62

Commitment to Life VIII (1995), 197–201

communism, 28, 51, 73, 99, 133, 144

Concerts for the People of Kampuchea, 141–45

Congress, 102, 103, 137

Conspiracy of Hope tour (1986), 224–25

corporate money, 97–98; farming and, 183; rock 'n' roll and, 48–49, 97–99, 138

Costello, Elvis, 142, 143, 163

Cranston, Alan, 111

Credence Clearwater Revival, 51, 52

Cronkite, Walter, 4

Crosby, Bing, 88

Crosby, David: birth of his daughter, 82; childhood of, 2–4, 98; drug problems and recovery, 130–32, 171, 187, 226; in prison, 187, 226

Crosby, Donovan, 82

Crosby, Jan, 231

Crosby, Stills, Nash & Young, 27, 35–36, 40, 42, 45, 71–72, 79, 122, 146, 207, 208; antiwar movement, 40–47; Bridge School benefit (1986), 187–90; Live Aid (1985), 157, 158, 162, 164, 171–72, 188

Crosby, Stills & Nash, 36, 40, 110, 124, 158, 181, 210, 211, 215–16; No Nukes concert, 130–32; Taylor (Dallas) benefit, 207–9

Crosby and Nash, 68–69; Winter Soldier benefit (1971), 68–69

Crow, Sheryl, 113, 199

Crystal, Billy, 191–94

Cuba, 103

Culture Club, 147

Dalai Lama, 231, 232

Daltrey, Roger, 167

Danko, Rick, 86

D'Arby, Terence Trent, 198

Davis, Miles, 80, 81, 219

Davis, Ossie, 14

Davis, Sammy, Jr., 14, 19, 20, 21

"Daylight Again/Find the Cost of Freedom," 172

Days of Rage, 41

Dee, Ruby, 14

Delsener, Ron, 74, 78, 79

Democratic National Convention (1968), 41

Denver, John, 44, 181

"Deportees," 78

Desert Rose Band, 207, 208

De Wilde, Brandon, 32

Dickson, Jim, 34, 35

DiFranco, Ani, 115

Dire Straits, 157, 165, 221

Doobie Brothers, 82, 83, 127, 131

Doors, 32; CAFF concert (1966), 34–36

"Do They Know It's Christmas (Feed the World)," 145–50, 156, 170, 175

Douglas, Michael, 126, 198

drugs, 26, 27, 34, 56, 61, 67, 72, 95–96, 109, 131, 226; Sinclair event (1971), 61–67
Drummond, Tim, 86
Duran Duran, 147, 157, 161, 172–73
Dury, Ian, 142
Dylan, Bob, 8, 10–12, 16, 26, 27, 36, 37, 41, 61, 86, 125, 155, 200, 219; Allende show (1974), 74–78; Bangladesh concert (1971), 55, 57–58, 74; Farm Aid, 174–75, 178–79, 180; "goes electric," 27; Hurricane Carter and, 90–96; Live Aid (1985), 157, 159, 162, 174–75, 178–79; The Night of the Hurricane (1975), 92–94; Ochs and, 37, 74–79; Peace Sunday (1982), 135–36; Rolling Thunder Revue, 79, 91–94; SNACK concert (1975), 86

Eagles, 110–11, 189
Eckstine, Billy, 19
Elliot, Cass, 12, 105
Elliott, Ramblin' Jack, 94
Ellsberg, Daniel, 78
Emerson, Ralph Waldo, 234
England, 54, 62, 124, 210; Band Aid (1984), 145–50, 156; Freedomfest (1988), 221–23; Kampuchean concerts, 141–45; Live Aid (1985), 157–76; Secret Policeman's Other Ball (1979), 223–24
environmental movement, 214; Rainforest benefits, 229
Ertegun, Ahmet, 47
Estefan, Gloria, 211
Etheridge, Melissa, 36, 100, 114, 197, 200
Evening with Salvador Allende, An (1974), 73–78, 88
Evers, Medgar, 10–11

Faithfull, Marianne, 198, 211
Farina, Mimi, 82
Farm Aid, 101–2, 178–84, 192; of 1985, 180–81
FBI, 19, 62, 64, 66
Felder, Dean, 185
Flack, Roberta, 91–92, 94, 222
Flanagan, Bill, Written in My Soul, 90
Flippo, Chet, 92
Florida, 7–8; Miami benefit concert (1992), 211
Fogelberg, Dan, 43, 139
Fogerty, John, 52, 180–81
folk music, 26–27, 37, 60; black, 1–24; civil rights movement and, 1–24
Fonda, Jane, 68, 132, 133, 136, 208

Fong-Torres, Ben, 71
Ford, Betty, 197
"For Everyman," 49
"Fortunate Son," 52
"For What It's Worth," 32–33
Four for McGovern benefit (1972), 104–8
Four Tops, 160, 163
Fowler, Wyche, 112
Frand, Deni, 78
Frankie Goes to Hollywood, 147
Franklin, Len, 22
Freedomfest (1988), 221–23
Frey, Glenn, 111

Gabriel, Peter, 73–74; human rights causes, 216–17, 222–26, 228
Galway, James, 211
Gandhi, Mahatma, 6, 13, 213, 214, 231, 234
Garcia, Jerry, 83, 145, 206–7
Garner, James, 14
Geffen, David, 197
Geldof, Bob, 145, 150, 219, 223; Band Aid (1984), 145–50, 156; Live Aid (1985), 157–77; "We Are the World" recording, 151–54
Georgia Straight, 146
Germano, Lisa, 115
Germany: Nazi, 80; "The Wall" concert (1990), 210–11
Gill, Vincent, 181
Gilmour, David, 143, 210
Gingrich, Newt, 102
Ginsberg, Allen, 62–63, 87
Give Peace a Chance festival, aborted, 61
Glaser, Elizabeth, 198
global activism, 141–77; Band Aid (1984), 145–50, 156; Kampuchean concerts, 141–45; Live Aid (1985), 157–77; "We Are the World" recording (1985), 149–56
Goldberg, Whoopi, 3–5, 101, 198–99, 211, 222; Comic Relief, 191–94
Goldsmith, Harvey, 142
Goldwater, Barry, 125
Graham, Bill, 70, 71–72, 79–87, 124, 142, 144, 178, 188, 205, 210, 224, 230; death of, 87; Live Aid (1985), 158–64, 172, 175; SNACK concert (1975), 81–86
Graham Central Station, 82
Grammy Awards, 196
Grateful Dead, 28, 79, 80, 82, 83, 144–45, 181, 202, 203; Rex benefits, 205–7; Seva shows, 203–5
Gravy, Wavy, 42, 202–3
Green, Al, 222

Greenwood rally (1963), 10–11
Gregory, Dick, 15, 20–21
Groppi, Father James, 63
Guthrie, Arlo, 74, 75–78, 182
Guthrie, Woody, 5, 10, 27, 77, 121

Hackman, Gene, 105
Hagar, Sammy, 186
Hair, 44, 50
Haley, Bill, 2
Hall, Darryl, 155, 218
Hall, John, 122, 123
Hall & Oates, 173, 175, 218
Hanks, Tom, 197, 198
"A Hard Rain's Gonna Fall," 57
Harrison, George, 46, 54, 61, 69, 89, 143;
    Bangladesh concerts (1971), 53–60, 176
Havens, Ritchie, 50
Hawaii, 211
Hawn, Goldie, 105
HBO, 191
Healthcare for the Homeless, 194
Heaven 17, 147
Helm, Levon, 86
Hendrix, Jimi, 35; death of, 51; Winter Peace
    Festival concert, 50–51
Hendryxs, Nona, 198
Henley, Don, 47, 98, 181, 187, 189, 199, 207,
    208; political activism, 98, 10, 102, 104,
    111; Walden Woods benefits, 214
Hentoff, Nat, 11
hepatitis C, 207
"Here Comes the Sun," 57, 108
"Here's to the State of Richard Nixon," 64
Heston, Charlton, 14
"He Was a Friend of Mine," 13, 78
Hiburn, Robert, 116, 174
Highwaymen, 181
Hillman, Chris, 25, 35, 207, 208
Hiroshima, 120
Hoffman, Abbie, 41
Hollywood Women's Political Committee,
    108
homelessness, 191–96, 206; "Another Day
    in Paradise" recording, 194–96; Comic
    Relief, 191–94, 211
homosexuality, 100, 101; AIDS and, 197–201
Hooters, 163, 211
Hootie & the Blowfish, 113, 181, 184, 185, 186
Hoover, J. Edgar, 99
Hopper, Dennis, 78
Horne, Lena, 14
Hornsby, Bruce, 181
Houston, Whitney, 222

Hudson, Garth, 86
Hudson, Rock, 197
Humanitas International Human Rights
    Committee, 144–45
human rights, 7, 212–33; Amnesty
    International, 223–29; antiapartheid
    movement, 215–23; Freedomfest (1988),
    221–23; Free Tibet concerts, 132, 212–13,
    229–33; "Sun City" recording, 217–22
Human Rights Now! tour (1988), 225–27
"Hurricane," 90–91, 92, 94
Hurricane Relief concerts (1992), 211
Hurricane Trust Fund, 91, 94
Huston, John, 224
Hynde, Chrissie, 166, 175, 186, 210

"I Feel Like I'm Fixin' to Die Rag," 30–31
"If I Had a Hammer," 132
Indigo Girls, 114
Ingram, James, 154
Internal Revenue Service, 59, 69, 122
Iran-Contra, 140
"It's Alright, Ma (I'm Only Bleeding)," 93–94

Jackson, Jesse, 14, 136
Jackson, Jimmy Lee, 18–19
Jackson, Mahalia, 16–17, 23
Jackson, Michael, 151, 155, 156, 159, 176
Jagger, Bianca, 69–73
Jagger, Mick, 55, 56, 157; Live Aid (1985),
    164, 173, 175; Nicaraguan earthquake
    benefit (1972), 69–73, 210
Jamaica, 210
Japan, 72, 120
Jara, Victor, 73–78, 229
Jarreau, Al, 155
Jefferson Airplane, 32, 35
Jefferson Starship, 82, 83–84, 144
Jewel, 113
Joel, Billy, 154, 159, 180
John, Elton, 157, 168, 170, 181, 186, 226;
    AIDS cause, 197, 200–201
Johnson, Lyndon B., 19, 29, 30, 87, 125–26
Jones, James Earl, 105
Jones, John Paul, 143, 170
Jones, Kenney, 143
Jones, Quincy, 104, 106, 107, 151, 153
Joplin, Janis, 35, 52–53, 93; death of, 53
Judaism, 50

Kampuchean benefit concerts, 141–45
Kantner, Paul, 41, 49, 102–3, 145, 203
Kauai benefit concert, 211
Kaufman, Andy, 190, 191

Kaufman tribute, 190
Keith, Ben, 86
Keltner, Jim, 56
Kennedy, John F., assassination of, 11–13,
    18, 29, 39, 125
Kennedy, Robert, 37–39; assassination of,
    38–40
Kennedy, Ted, 100
Kent State killings (1970), 46–47, 118
Kerr, Jim, 166, 222
Kershaw, Nik, 163
Khan, Chaka, 127, 128–29
King, Alan, 19
King, B. B., 180
King, Carole, 104–5, 107
King, Coretta, 44
King, Martin Luther, Jr., 4–7, 10, 13–24, 213,
    214–15, 216, 231, 234; antinuclear
    movement, 36; assassination of, 17, 39;
    March on Washington, 13–18; Selma
    march, 18–22
Kirk, Roland, 81
Klein, Allen, 55–56
"Knockin' on Heaven's Door," 86, 94
Kool and the Gang, 147
Kortchmar, Danny, 189
Kragen, Ken, 149–53

LaBelle, Patti, 160, 173, 175
labor movement, 5
Lancaster, Burt, 14, 105
Landau, Jon, 128
Lane, Ronnie, 143
Larson, Nicolette, 144
Lauper, Cyndi, 153, 155, 211
Law, Lisa, 135
"Lean on Me," 131
learning-disabled children, Bridge School
    benefits for, 184–90
LeBon, Simon, 148, 172–73
Led Zeppelin, 143, 157, 161, 170–71, 172
lending a hand, 178–211; AIDS benefits,
    196–202; Bridge School benefits,
    184–90; Comic Relief, 190–94, 211;
    Farm Aid, 178–84; homelessness,
    194–96, 211; natural disasters, 209–11;
    Rex benefits, 205–7; Seva shows, 203–5;
    Taylor (Dallas) benefit, 207–9
Lennon, John, 27–28, 45, 55, 87, 137, 143,
    231; peace activism, 45–46, 59–67;
    Sinclair event (1971), 61–67
Lennon, Sean, 231–33
Lennox, Annie, 147, 210
Lesh, Paul, 28, 83, 202–4

"Let it Be," 169
Levy, Jacques, 90
Lewis, Huey, 87, 155, 160
Lewis, John, 18
Life magazine, 46
Lindsay, John, 52
Little Richard, 199
Live Aid (1985), 70, 157–77, 221; benefits
    inspired by, 178–79, 190–91; funds
    raised, 176
LL Cool J, 113
Lofgren, Nils, 188, 189
Loggins, Kenny, 155, 175
"Long Time Gone," 38–40, 233
Los Angeles, 72; Commitment to Life VIII
    (1995), 197–201; Four for McGovern
    benefit (1972), 104–8; Nicaraguan
    earthquake benefit (1972), 70–73; Peace
    Sunday (1982), 133–39; Sunset Strip riot
    (1966), 32–34; Taylor
    (Dallas) benefit, 207–8
Los Angeles Times, 116, 174
Love, Michael, 78
Lovett, Lyle, 181
L7, 115
"Luck of the Irish," 66
Lynn, Loretta, 180

Madison Square Garden, New York, 51, 62;
    Allende show (1974), 73–78; Bangladesh
    concerts (1971), 53–60; The Night of the
    Hurricane (1975), 91, 92–94; No Nukes
    concerts (1979), 122, 123, 127–33, 135,
    137–39; Winter Peace Festival (1970),
    50–51
Madonna, 168–69, 197
Makeba, Miriam, 222
Malcolm X, 231
Malopoets, 219
Mamas & the Papas, 35
Managua earthquake (1972), 69–73
Mandela, Nelson, 214, 221–23, 231
Manson, Marilyn, 186
Manzarek, Ray, 34, 35
March on Washington (1963), 13–18
Marley, Ziggy, 210
Masekela, Hugh, 222
Matthews (Dave) Band, 181, 232
May, Elaine, 19
McBride, Martina, 181
McCarthyism, 37, 121
McCartney, Paul, 26, 28, 55–56; global
    activism, 141–44, 157, 169–70, 176
McDonald, Country Joe, 30–32, 36, 40

MC5, 62
McGovern, George, 104–8
McGuinn, Roger, 13, 25–27, 35, 79, 94
Melanie, 74
Mellencamp, John, 101–2, 158–59, 180;
    Farm Aid, 179–80
Melody Maker, 82
Merchant, Natalie, 115, 168–69
Mercury, Freddie, 166, 170
Merrill, Gary, 19
Metheny, Pat, 167, 168
Meyer, Ron, 197, 198
Michael, George, 147, 148, 157, 168, 170,
    200
Midler, Bette, 136, 138, 173
migrant workers, 121
Milarepa Fund, 229–30
Miller, Dana, 198, 199, 201
Miller, Henry, 12
Miller, Steve, 210
Mississippi, 9, 10, 30
Mitchell, Joni, 79, 91, 149, 200, 211; Rolling
    Thunder Revue, 91–93
Mobilization Committee Against the War, 36
Mondale, Walter, 112
Monterey International Pop Festival, 35–36
Monty Python, 223
Moratorium Day rallies (1969), 44–45, 50
Morgan, Lorrie, 181
Morrison, Jim, 35
Morrison, Van, 211
Moss, Jon, 147
motor voter bill, 113
MTV, 165, 167
Musicians United for Safe Energy (MUSE),
    123–32, 134, 137
My Lai massacre, 68, 118

NAACP, 8
Nader, Ralph, 132
Nash, Graham, 42–43, 46–47, 56, 113, 152,
    158, 188–89, 190, 208; antinuclear
    movement, 123–24, 126, 130–39; Peace
    Sunday (1982), 133–39; Winter Soldier
    benefit, 68–69
National Guard, 46, 210
natural disasters, 209–11; Nicaraguan
    earthquake benefit (1972), 69–73
Nelson, Willie, 102, 152, 153, 155, 159, 192;
    Farm Aid, 178–84
Nepal, blindness in, 203–5
Neuwirth, Bobby, 93, 94
Nevada, 139
Neville Brothers, 224

New Jersey Correctional Institute for
    Women, Rolling Thunder Revue at,
    91–92
New Mexico, 139
Newport Folk Festival (1965), 27
New York, 9, 60; Allende show (1974),
    73–78; Bangladesh concerts (1971),
    53–60; The Night of the Hurricane
    (1975), 91–94; No Nukes concerts
    (1979), 122, 123, 127–33, 135, 137–39;
    Shea Stadium Peace Festival (1970),
    51–53; War Is Over rally (1975), 87–89
New Yorker, 11
New York magazine, 94
New York Times, 4, 18, 44, 172
Nicaragua: contras in, 140; earthquake
    benefit (1972), 69–73
Nichols, Mike, 19
Nicholson, Jack, 105, 174
Nicks, Stevie, 136
Night of the Hurricane, The (1975), 92–94
Nixon, Richard M., 46–47, 62, 63, 64, 65,
    68, 104
No Nukes (movie), 137
No Nukes concerts (1979), 122, 123, 127–33,
    135, 137–39
nonviolence, 6, 13, 18, 214–15
Norman, Jessye, 222
Northern Lights, 149
nuclear waste disposal, 139
nuclear weapons. *See* antinuclear movement

Ocean, Billy, 163
Ochs, Michael, 73, 87–89
Ochs, Phil, 36–38, 45, 68, 87–89, 91;
    Allende show (1974), 73–78, 88; death of,
    89; Bob Dylan and, 37, 74–79; Sinclair
    event, 62–64; War Is Over rallies, 87–89
O'Connor, Sinead, 211
Odetta, 10, 15, 16, 19, 26, 88
"Oh Freedom," 15
Ohio, Kent State killings in, 46–47
"Ohio," 46–47, 165, 171, 189
"Only a Pawn in Their Game," 10–11, 16
Ono, Yoko, 45–46, 55, 60–67, 87
Orbison, Roy, 180
Osbourne, Ozzie, 163
Oswald, Lee Harvey, 11, 12

Page, Jimmy, 161, 170–71, 173
Pakistan refugees, 53–59
Palmieri, Eddie, 83
Pariser, Alan, 35
Parks, Rosa, 4, 5, 118

Peace Sunday (1982), 133–39
Pearl Jam, 113, 115–16, 132, 186, 213, 232
Pendergrass, Teddy, 160, 168
Perkins, Anthony, 19
Perry, Steve, 155
Peter, Paul & Mary, 8–10, 16, 19–22, 26,
      34–35, 50, 159, 175
Petty, Tom, 127, 136, 157, 170, 180, 187, 189
Philadelphia, 51, 52; Live Aid (1985), 157–76
Philadelphia (movie), 198
Phish, 115, 181
Pink Floyd, 143, 211
Plant, Robert, 143, 161, 170–71
Police, 223, 224
political activism, 97–117; Four for
      McGovern benefit (1972), 104–8; human
      rights causes, 212–33; Rock the Vote,
      112–13; Voters for Choice, 113–17; *see
      also specific concerts, performers,
      politicians, and venues*
Pot, Pol, 141
Potts, Erin, 229, 230
Power Station, 157, 161, 170
Presley, Elvis, 61
Preston, Billy, 56
Pretenders, 142, 157, 166
Prince, 159
Public Enemy, 113
Puente, Tito, 211

Quakers, 124–25
Queen, 142, 157, 166, 216, 218, 220
Queen Latifah, 113

racism, 2–24, 89–96, 119, 215–20. *See also*
      apartheid; civil rights movement
Radiohead, 233
Rag Baby, 30
Rainforest Foundation, 229
Raitt, Bonnie, 48, 103, 116–17, 181, 211, 219,
      223; antinuclear movement, 122, 123,
      124–25, 131, 136–40
Rascals, 50
Ray, Amy, 114
Reagan, Ronald, 111–12, 133, 137, 140,
      219–20
Reagon, Bernice, 15
Red Hot Chili Peppers, 232
Reed, Lou, 165, 186, 219, 224
REM, 100, 112, 113, 132, 232, 233
Republican National Convention (1972), 62
"Revolution," 97
Rex Foundation, 205–7
Rich, Buddy, 81

Richards, Keith, 174, 175, 210
Ritchie, Lionel, 150–54, 156, 175
Rizzo, Frank, 52
Robertson, Robbie, 79
Robeson, Paul, 14
Robinson, Jackie, 6
Rockestra, 143
rock 'n' roll music, 26–27, 35; antinuclear
      movement, 118–40; antiwar movement,
      26–47, 50–53, 68–69; birth of benefit
      concert, 48–96; corporate money and,
      48–49, 97–98, 138; global activism,
      141–77; for human rights, 212–33;
      lending a hand, 178–211; political
      activism, 97–117. *See also specific
      musicians and songs*
Rockpile, 143
Rock the Vote, 112–13
Rogers, Kenny, 150, 151, 154
Rolling Stone, 52, 55, 71, 84, 92, 127, 141,
      158, 168, 171, 173, 184
Rolling Stones, 26, 79, 143, 165; Nicaraguan
      benefit (1972), 70–73, 210
Rolling Thunder Revue, 79, 91–94; The
      Night of the Hurricane (1975), 91–94
Ronson, Mick, 93
Ronstadt, Linda, 110–11, 136, 144
Rose Bowl, Los Angeles, Peace Sunday
      (1982) at, 133–39
Ross, Diana, 153, 155
"Roulette," 129
Rubin, Jerry, 42, 60, 61–63, 65, 67
Rubin, Miles, 105–8
Rucker, Darius, 186–87
Run-DMC, 163, 219
Ru Paul, 198
Russell, Leon, 55, 56, 57, 181

Sade, 163
Sainte-Marie, Buffy, 74
Saliers, Emily, 114
Salt 'N' Pepa, 200
San Francisco, 80–87; Bridge School
      benefits, 184–90; earthquake telethon,
      (1989), 210; Free Tibet concert, 230–31;
      Kampuchean benefit concert, 144–45;
      SNACK concert (1975), 81–86
Santana, 70–71, 73, 81, 82, 83, 144, 162, 210
Santana, Carlos, 59, 70–73, 80–81, 85, 87,
      103, 167–68, 188
Schmit, Timmy, 189
Schocked, Michelle, 181
Scorpions, 211
Scott-Heron, Gil, 121, 127, 219

Scruggs, Earl, 44
Seale, Bobby, 42, 62, 63
Sears, Pete, 84
Sebastian, John, 52
Secret Policeman's Other Ball (1979), 223–24
"Seeds," 189, 190
Seeger, Pete, 4–5, 8, 14, 19, 22, 26, 27, 31, 36, 37, 44, 74, 77, 88, 121, 125, 132
Seger, Bob, 61, 62, 63
segregation, 4, 5, 7–8, 13–24, 215–20. *See also* apartheid; civil rights movement
Selma-Montgomery march (1965), 18–22, 25
Seva Foundation, 203–5
Sexton, Tim, 134
Shankar, Ravi, 53–55, 56, 58, 59, 69
Shea Stadium Peace Festival (1970), 51–53
Silkwood, Karen, 122, 125, 127
Simon, Carly, 6–7, 101, 105; antinuclear movement, 122, 127, 128, 131
Simon, Paul, 51, 88, 89, 128, 154, 156, 159, 181, 211
Simon & Garfunkel, 186
Simone, Nina, 19
Simple Minds, 157, 166, 221, 222
Sinatra, Frank, 74
Sinclair, John, 61–67, 94
Sinclair event (1971), 61–67, 69, 94
Slick, Grace, 84
Smashing Pumpkins, 132, 186
Smile Jamaica Concert (1988), 210
Smith, Patti, 186
SNACK concert (1975), 81–86
SNCC, 15, 18
SNCC Freedom Singers, 15–16, 22
Somoza, Anastasio, 72
Sonefeld, Jim "Soni," 184–85
South Africa, 225; apartheid in, 215–23; cultural boycott of, 215–22; Sun City, 217–22
Souther, J. D., 144, 189
Southern Christian Leadership Conference, 8
Soviet Union, 133, 137
Spandau Ballet, 147, 157
Specials, 142
Springfield, Rick, 158, 163
Springsteen, Bruce, 111–12, 159, 217; Bridge School benefit (1986), 186–90; human rights causes, 218, 219, 225, 226; No Nukes concerts, 127–31, 134; "We Are the World," 152–56
"Stairway to Heaven," 171

Starr, Ringo, 55, 56, 57, 61, 143, 181, 219
Starr, Zak, 219
Status Quo, 147, 157, 160, 162
Steenburgen, Mary, 198
Steinem, Gloria, 113, 115
Steppenwolf, 52
Stewart, John, 19
Stewart, Rod, 197, 216, 218, 220
Stills, Stephen, 7, 32–33, 35, 42, 47, 49, 68, 131, 141, 158, 188–89, 208; political activism, 108–10
Sting, 97, 99, 101; African famine relief, 146, 147, 157, 161, 163; human rights causes, 221, 223–29
Stipe, Michael, 100–101, 113, 232
"Stoney End," 107
Streisand, Barbra, 104, 197; "One Voice" concert, 108; political activism, 106–8
Styler, Trudie, 229
"Sun City," 217–22
"Sunday Bloody Sunday," 165
Sunset Strip riot (1966), 32–34
Supreme Court, 112
Sweet Honey in the Rock, 15

"Tambourine Man," 10, 25–26, 27, 57
Taupin, Bernie, 197, 200, 201
Taylor, Dallas, 207; benefit concert for, 207–9
Taylor, Elizabeth, 197
Taylor, James, 104–5, 122, 127, 128, 131, 144, 186
"Teach Your Children," 47, 164, 171, 190, 208
"Tears Are Not Enough," 149
television, 3–4, 16, 102, 116, 117, 137, 138, 150, 191, 217; Live Aid broadcast, 158–76
"There but for Fortune," 88
"They Dance Alone," 227–29
"This Land Is Your Land," 94
Thomas, Clarence, 112
Thompson Twins, 157, 162, 170
Thoreau, Henry David, 214
Thorogood, George, 166
Three Mile Island accident, 121, 126–27, 129
Tibetan Freedom concerts, 132, 212–13, 229–33; in Washington, D.C. (1998), 232–33
"The Times They Are a Changin'," 10, 94
Tolces, Todd, 82
Toronto Star, 95
Tower of Power, 82, 83
Townshend, Pete, 41, 142, 143, 167, 169, 170, 210, 219

Travers, Mary, 9–10, 19, 159
troubadour tradition, 214
"Turn, Turn, Turn," 27
Turner, Tina, 153, 154, 160, 173, 175
Twelve-Step programs, 209
Tyler, Steven, 186

Ultravox, 145, 147, 157
UNICEF, 46, 59
United Nations, 133, 141, 215; "Entertainers,
    Actors, and Others Who Have Performed
    in Apartheid South Africa," 215, 216, 220
Uplinger, Hal, 160, 162
Ure, Midge, 145
USA for Africa, 156
U2, 147, 157, 165, 210, 224, 229

Van Halen, Eddie, 186
Van Ronk, Dave, 78
Van Zandt, "Little" Steven, 217;
    antiapartheid cause, 217–22
Vaughn, Stevie Ray, 181
Vedder, Eddie, 115, 186, 213, 230–31, 232
Vietnam boat people, 144
Vietnam Moratorium Committee, 44, 50, 51
Vietnam veterans, 31, 68–69
Vietnam Veterans Against the War, 68–69
Vietnam War, 25–47, 50–53, 63, 68–69,
    87–89, 98, 105–6, 113, 118, 119, 126. See
    also antiwar movement
Voight, Jon, 105
"Volunteers," 84
Voorman, Klaus, 56
Voters for Choice, 112, 113–17

Walden, Phil, 109–10
Walden Woods benefit, 214
Waldheim, Kurt, 141
Wallace, George, 21–22, 99
"The Wall" concert (1990), 210–11
War Is Over rallies, 87–89
Warwick, Dionne, 155
"Wasted on the Way," 158
Watley, Jody, 147
"We Almost Lost Detroit," 121
"We Are the World," 149–56, 176, 219
Weathermen, 41
Weavers, 2
Weir, Bob, 83, 203–7
Weiss, Cora, 88

Weller, Paul, 147
"We Shall Overcome," 15, 18
White, Josh, 2, 5, 16
Who, 41, 142, 143, 157; Live Aid (1985), 162,
    167
Williams, Hank, 93
Williams, Robin, 184, 185, 187–88, 232;
    Bridge School benefit, 185, 187–90;
    Comic Relief, 191–94
Wilson, Dennis, 78
Winding, Jai, 189
Winter Peace Festival concert (1970), 50–51
Winters, Shelley, 19
Winter Soldier benefit (1971), 68–69
Womack, Bobby, 219
Wonder, Stevie, 14, 61, 62, 64–65, 67, 154,
    159, 216, 222; Peace Sunday (1982),
    134–37
Wood, Ron, 174, 175
"Wooden Ships," 49, 208
Woodstock (1969), 31, 40–41, 44, 48, 61,
    162, 163
world beat, 54
World Hunger Year, 151
World War II, 5, 80, 124, 133
Wyman, Bill, 72
Wynette, Tammy, 200
Wyoming flood benefit (1985), 210

Yarrow, Peter, 9, 16, 18–22, 25, 27, 29, 36,
    40, 44–45, 159; early benefit concerts,
    49–53
Yauch, Adam, 132, 229; Free Tibet concerts,
    229–32
Yippies, 41, 60
Yoakam, Dwight, 181
Yorke, Thom, 233
Young, Ben, 184, 189, 190
Young, Neil, 35, 42, 68, 71, 119, 149, 170,
    171–72, 210, 226; antiwar movement,
    46–47; Bridge School benefits, 184–90;
    Farm Aid, 179–84; political activism, 112,
    115–16; SNACK concert (1975), 82, 85,
    86; Taylor (Dallas) benefit, 207–9
Young, Paul, 147, 148, 149, 157, 165
Young, Pegi, 184–90
"You've Got a Friend," 105

Zimbabwe, 225
Zmuda, Bob, 190–94